✓12/06

DATE DUE   JUN 0 6

11/24			
12/15			
GAYLORD			PRINTED IN U.S.A.

INDEFENSIBLE

INDEFENSIBLE

ONE LAWYER'S JOURNEY

INTO THE INFERNO OF

AMERICAN JUSTICE

DAVID FEIGE

LITTLE, BROWN AND COMPANY
New York   Boston

Little, Brown and Company
Hachette Book Group USA
1271 Avenue of the Americas
New York, NY 10020
Visit our Web site at www.HachetteBookGroupUSA.com

First Edition: June 2006

Library of Congress Cataloging-in-Publication Data

Feige, David.
    Indefensible : one lawyer's journey into the inferno of American
        justice / David Feige.
            p.   cm.
    ISBN-10: 0-316-15623-X (hardcover)
    ISBN-13: 978-0-316-15623-3 (hardcover)
    1. Feige, David.   2. Public defenders — New York State — Bronx
        County.   3. Criminal justice, administration of — New York
        (State) — New York.   4. Bronx (New York, N.Y.) — Social
        conditions.   I. Title.
    KF373.F37A3   2006
    345.747'27501 — dc22   2006001283

10 9 8 7 6 5 4 3 2 1

Q-MART

Printed in the United States of America

*FOR PUBLIC DEFENDERS EVERYWHERE
AND, AS EVERYTHING IS,
FOR MY FATHER*

AUTHOR'S NOTE

THIS BOOK IS A WORK OF NONFICTION. All of the characters in it are real, and most of them still work in and around the Bronx Criminal Courthouse. Although I have changed many client names and details to ensure privacy and privilege, most everyone else, including judges, prosecutors, and defense lawyers, is identified by his or her real name throughout the book.

The book begins in the morning and ends at night—compassing a single day in my life. The day was real, and though I have taken some license with the chronology and in a number of instances brought together incidents that happened on different occasions, there is no character compositing.

Finally, because I didn't take notes on every utterance in every court appearance (I was up there doing much of the uttering, after all) or obtain transcripts, much of the in-court dialogue is closely approximate rather than verbatim.

INDEFENSIBLE

INTRODUCTION

I TOOK MY FIRST HOMICIDE on a Saturday night. It was 1994, at the tail end of a year of almost incomprehensible criminality. In the preceding year, 1,927 people had been gunned down, stabbed up, or beaten to death in the streets, slums, and parks of New York City. More than 430,000 — a number exceeding the population of Atlanta, Georgia — were victims of a serious crime.

Of the five boroughs of the city of New York, Brooklyn contributed nearly 40 percent of the murders: 724 in one year — an average of two every single day. People were being shot at in Brownsville, bludgeoned in Bed-Stuy, flattened in Flatlands. There were certain stoplights in East New York that were reputed to be so likely to produce a gunpoint robbery or carjacking that the common practice was to blow right through them. Crook-fear racked the city, and judges, prosecutors, and the *New York Post* made careers out of tough-on-crime posturing.

The day I reached for that case, I had been a public defender for fewer than three years. Legal aid lawyers weren't actually supposed to touch homicides; murder cases were generally reserved for fancier appointed lawyers from what was known as the "homicide panel." But with the glut of bodies, no one was paying too much attention. Besides, there were always several murder cases kicking around the office, handled by grizzled veterans, confirmed in their seniority by the fact that they had homicides.

I still remember seeing the thin sheaf of white paper in the wire basket. Gillian Sands. First arrest. Murder in the second degree.

Glancing around, besotted by my own ambition, I picked it up. Typed on the onionskin page in the blotted script of the computer printer was the single sentence that implied a potential life sentence: "The deponent is informed by the defendant's own statements that, at the above time and place, the defendant did stab Rodney Sands repeatedly about the body with a knife, causing Rodney Sands's death."

That was it. One sentence. Knowing then what I know now, I'd never have touched it.

➳──❧

Gillian couldn't stop crying. She was guilty. She told me so right off the bat, insisted on it really.

"I could just plead guilty now," she told me. "It's okay. Whatever happens, I deserve it." Gillian had a big bruise on her cheek, her eyes were red and swollen, and she had a look of utter defeat on her face. "I killed him. . . . I loved him, and I killed him. It was all my fault," she said, sobbing. "I couldn't help it — I'm so sorry. He was beating me — it's all my fault."

"Umm, Ms. Sands." I'd hardly uttered a word before her confession. "You can't actually plead guilty now anyway. This proceeding is just to determine whether you stay in jail or get to go home. And besides, no matter how bad you feel right now, I'm not clear that pleading guilty is the right decision — especially if you were being beaten up."

"It doesn't matter," she told me flatly. "I already told the police I did it. It's all there on the videotape."

Things had been good at first, Gillian told me, at least until she got married. Then the hitting started. She'd go to work each day, washing and braiding hair, doing nails in the painstaking French style favored by women in the Marcy projects where she and Rodney lived, and come home, happy to see her man, happy to hand him the clump of cash she'd made that day in tips. "Hmm," Rodney would say, looking at the money. They'd have dinner, and then, as predictable as rain, his fist would slam down on the table or his booted foot would smash into her shin or he would smack her face, her ear, the side of her head — hard. It got worse fast; within months of her wedding, Gillian, who still didn't understand how the fights and violence escalated so quickly, began to arrive at work with bruises, welts, and, at least once, a fracture or two.

On the night Gillian stabbed him, Rodney had chased her into the kitchen. He was drunk and swinging; Gillian saw a knife on the counter, picked it up, and poked him with it. Then she stabbed him again, nicking an artery and killing him.

As guilty as Gillian thought she was, and as much as she was ready to be punished for what she'd done, the more I listened to her, the more convinced I became that under the law of self-defense she might actually be innocent.

By the time I emerged from the interview booth over an hour later, excitedly flipping through a sheaf of notes, I was convinced. It was by far the most comprehensive interview I'd ever done with a client. And as I wandered back into the garishly lit court-room, tiptoeing around the crowded bench, sitting down to compose my thoughts, in those moments of distilling the complicated narrative of Gillian's life into a persuasive argument for her release, I'd never felt as alive, as terrified, or as righteous.

"Is it true you took a murder?" one of my colleagues asked suspiciously. Short and pretty, with a wide, expressive face, Lisa was a great lawyer but a huge rule follower. I just nodded quietly, concentrating on doing the best bail argument I'd ever done.

"Eddie is gonna fucking kill you," she said.

"It's just for arraignments — and Liz was busy anyhow," I explained rather unconvincingly.

"I'm just saying. You're fucked. Eddie already thinks you sneak cases."

"Eddie *knows* I sneak cases, Lisa. Eddie respects me *because* I sneak cases. Eddie doesn't want pussies — he wants people who yearn, people who long to fight. He'll get over it."

"Whatever. I just don't wanna be you come Monday," Lisa said, shrugging. She was trying to protect me. Lisa did that a lot.

Like several other people in the office, Lisa always wanted to save me from myself — often with good reason.

"People versus Gillian Sands," chimed a court officer, handing a small stack of paper to Judge Marty Karopkin. "Charged with murder in the second degree."

"David Feige, F-E-I-G-E, of the Legal Aid Society appearing on behalf of Ms. Sands," I declared boldly.

The prosecutor twisted his head around to glance at me. His face was quizzical: *Feige's doing a murder?*

"Dino Lombardi on behalf of the people," the prosecutor said, proceeding to serve the formal notices required at every arraignment.

Lombardi was a good man. Big and round and oozing a kind of Brooklyn smooth, Dino was the kind of thoughtful, laid-back prosecutor it was a joy to have a case with. Unlike most of the people in his office, Dino seemed to viscerally understand that the line between victim and perpetrator was always fine and not always clear. Dino didn't get exercised about much and was respected as a guy who'd do what he thought was right, not just what his boss told him to do.

"Your Honor," Dino said slowly, "the defendant admitted stabbing the victim, causing his death. This being a homicide, I'm required by my office to ask for remand." To remand a defendant means to hold him or her without bail — no amount of money will get them out.

Bail applications are usually short and sometimes nonexistent in murder cases. No judge in his right mind is ever going to let someone charged with murder out, and it is not uncommon for lawyers facing a particularly nasty judge to reserve a bail application all together, preferring to make the argument once additional investigation is done and there is a different, more reasonable judge. That's why I figured there'd be little harm in my doing the arraignment in the first place — everyone gets held without bail, so even if I screwed up, the results would be indistinguishable from having done everything right. And who knew? Maybe I'd get lucky.

"Anything else, Mr. Lombardi?" Judge Karopkin asked.

"No, Judge," Dino said firmly.

"Mr. Feige?"

This was my moment, and glancing down at the outline I'd prepared, I launched into one of the most exhaustive and extensive bail arguments I've ever made. I described Gillian's work history and her ties to the community, laying out in detail her family, her friends, and her connection to the city. There was no way that Gillian Sands was going to jump bail. And then I turned to Rodney — to their relationship, their love, and the crushing tragedy of an intimate life turned violent. I talked about the witnesses to prior instances of violence, of her fear of Rodney, of his criminal record and his history of violence, and I talked about Gillian, about her remorse, her pain, and her guilt; about how Rodney said he'd kill her this time, how she'd fled before his rage; about how desperate she was to make him stop hitting her; and about how she had no choice but to stab him. As I did, Gillian wept silently next to me — tears of pain and remorse and self-loathing.

I ended with a simple plea: "I beg you, Your Honor," I said, my voice quavering from the potent mixture of stress and passion, "I beg you to please just release this woman."

I had spoken for nearly fifteen minutes. The judge turned back to Dino Lombardi.

"Mr. Lombardi," he said, "Mr. Feige has raised some significant issues concerning the strength of this case and the claim of self-defense. Would you like to respond?"

And there and then, Dino Lombardi did the most decent thing I've ever seen a prosecutor do: looking straight at Karopkin, his voice low and steady, he said, "I have seen the videotape, Your Honor." And then, shaking his head slowly and emphatically back and forth, his chin nearly touching each shoulder in sequence, he said, "And I am *required by my office* to ask for remand."

There was silence in the courtroom. Karopkin looked hard at Dino, as if to reassure himself of what he was seeing, and Dino Lombardi held his gaze, his jaw set in a look of determination. And then he did it again: slowly and deliberately, he gave Karopkin the head shake. *I don't believe in what I'm saying,* he telegraphed silently so that the court reporter (who only notes words) couldn't take it down. If a supervisor ever reviewed the transcript of the proceeding, Dino would be totally clean — a bored ADA who was just following procedure late on a Saturday night. But there in the courtroom, before the silent gaze of Marty Karopkin and the astonished looks of the assembled legal aid lawyers waiting for me to go down in flames in my first murder case, Dino was silently saying something else entirely.

"Though unusual given the charges," Karopkin declared a moment later, "given the history of abuse Mr. Feige has brought to my attention and the defendant's ties to the community, as well as the fact that this is her first arrest and that the entire case seems to rest on a confession that may itself make out a defense, I am going to release Ms. Sands on her own recognizance."

There was an audible gasp in the courtroom. Dino nodded slightly, pursing his lips in an approving look. Gillian stood stock-still.

"Step out!" declared the court officer behind us as the courtroom breathed a collective sigh of relief.

"C'mon," I said to Gillian, gently guiding her out of the well of the courtroom, "let's get out of here."

Thanks to Dino Lombardi, I'd gotten my first murder client released without bail. It would be more than a decade before I was able to do it again.

As I would spend that decade discovering, most of the 300,000 people criminally prosecuted in New York City every year don't get a thoughtful judge or a compassionate prosecutor. Most are hounded by assistant district attorneys who lack either the heart or the courage needed to defy the institutional imperative to convict *no matter what.* Many are just plain shuffled through the system so damn fast that no one has time to think about much beyond the docket number stamped on the case files at arraignment. They are paraded before judges who have seen it all a thousand times and couldn't care less about the factors that make each case unique and each defendant human. But they did that night.

⇒•⇐

Arriving home at 2:30 A.M., I barely slept. My small Manhattan apartment was almost completely bare. Besides a small table and a used mattress lying in a corner on the floor, I had a lamp, a computer, a TV, and a stack of books perpetually waiting for shelves. All night long I thought about Gillian, about Dino, about how not only was I going to keep the case, I was going to win it.

And seven hours later, at 9:30 on Sunday morning, I had a plan. Jumping up to pull on a pair of jeans, I decided to do what every good homicide cop or investigator learns to do early — go to the scene of the crime.

The G train is the only one of New York's two dozen or so subway lines that never kisses Manhattan. I'd never even ridden it before, and as the train rumbled to a stop, and as I emerged, blinking into the summer sunlight, picking my way down the trash-strewn streets past vacant lots toward the house where Gillian had spent the night, I thought a lot about how different Gillian's day would have been without Dino Lombardi and Marty Karopkin.

Gillian was still shaken, and her darting eyes and skittish-ness made talking to her difficult. I tried to be soothing, but the trauma of what she'd been through was just too fresh. Traces of Rodney's blood were still visible on the sidewalk in front of her building. I got pictures of her injuries and at least part of the crime scene. I interviewed neighbors, talked to Gillian's friends, and compiled a list of the names and addresses of everyone who'd witnessed or heard that she was being beaten. I began to put together a timeline of who saw what and where everyone was, and just as important, I tried as best I could to get Gillian to understand that what she'd done wasn't necessarily a crime. And toward the end of day, as the sun cast shadows across the weedy lots and shimmered off the broken bottles and shards of auto glass that littered the streets, for a brief, memorable moment, I felt like a real lawyer.

I'd done everything I could think of to do. I was ready to face Eddie.

⇒⟫‹⇐

I couldn't beat Eddie Mayr into the office. No one could. By 6:45 A.M., the supervisor of our group of lawyers had already clipped and digested the *New York Law Journal*, Xeroxed summaries of the day's most important cases, placed those copies in his famous legal files, distributed them to the mailboxes of every lawyer in his complex, and done whatever other crazy stuff he did during those ungodly hours. As far as I knew, no one had ever seen Eddie walk through the door in the morning, and the actual time of his arrival was a matter of whispered reverential speculation.

Because I couldn't beat him in, I spent the entire ride to Brooklyn figuring the sight lines of the office and wondering whether I could slip past Eddie's door unnoticed. Maybe, I thought, he'd be psyched, and he'd do the case with me. He'd done homicides in the past, I reminded myself. Or maybe he hadn't looked too carefully at what each lawyer had done in arraignments Saturday night.

Wrong.

"What the fuck?"

It was him.

I'd been dashing around the corner where Eddie's office was, hoping to have a moment to compose myself before he took my head off. No chance.

"Get in here!" Eddie's voice was so menacing my whole body twitched. I was busted.

"You took a homicide?" Eddie was shaking his head at me. "You took a fucking *homicide?*" I couldn't tell if he was furious or disbelieving; he had this smirk on his face that I just couldn't read.

Taking a big breath, I fixed Eddie with a determined look.

"Don't even fucking talk to me," he barked. "Just go see Marvin."

Marvin Schechter was the head of the Criminal Defense Division for all of Brooklyn. Marvin was Eddie's boss.

"But . . ."

"Just go see Marvin."

"Now?"

"Now. Go!"

"He knows?"

Eddie just stared at me as if I'd disappointed him with the stupidity of my question, as if I should've figured he couldn't protect me from a fuck-up of this magnitude. I opened my mouth to say something, but Eddie's eyes were wide and volcanic. He shook his head slowly and pointed his index finger diagonally upward toward Marvin's office. *Go take this like a man* I could almost hear him say to me.

Being called up to Marvin's office was bad. It's not that Schechter was scary or mean, it was just that if Marvin was involved, you'd already gone beyond the bounds of anticipated misbehavior — like a principal's office, just being sent there was reproof enough. But Marvin Schechter was actually far less terrifying than Eddie. Eddie was a different species from me, and his tyrannical blend of manly disapproval, maniacal intensity, and aloofness was a potent combination I never quite knew how to deal with. Marvin, by contrast, was easy. Marvin was a little, smart, wisecracking Jewish guy who, unlike Eddie, liked to be liked. Eddie just liked to be feared.

"Hi, David — he's expecting you," Dianne, Marvin's almost inhumanly lithe secretary, chirped as I appeared at the door to his office. "Go right in."

Marvin was sitting behind his long desk. There was a carpet on the floor — it was perhaps the only place in the whole building where the linoleum wasn't bare.

"So I heard you took a homicide," Marvin said, looking up and casually motioning me toward a tall chair facing the desk. His voice was noncommittal, the same tone he used for both commendation and condemnation.

"I did, Marvin. And I want to keep it," I said, giving him my most serious stare. "So before you say anything, please just hear me out. I believe I can do this, and I'd really like it if you gave me a chance."

I saw him take a breath, and in that millisecond, I knew he was going to interrupt me and shut me down. So I charged ahead: "I got her out, Marvin!" I said. "I spent all day yesterday at the crime scene. I have photos, got them developed last night." I held out the packet of photos I'd taken. "I got witnesses — names, addresses, everything — I've already talked to them. I've done tons of investigation — I've met my client's family and talked to the neighbors. I've got a great self-defense claim, and I want her to testify before the grand jury. I know I shouldn't have taken the case. I know it, and you can yell at me all you want, but, Marvin" — I scrunched up my face to be sure he understood just how serious I was — "I want to keep this case. I can do it. I'll abide by whatever conditions you put on me — I'll work with Eddie on it if you want, or anyone else, but I believe in the case, I've done the work, and I'm ready. Really. I'm ready."

Marvin's eyes had narrowed slightly. "You said you got her out?"

"Karopkin cut her loose — ROR." I nodded for emphasis. "I met with her yesterday."

"And you understand why this is an issue?"

"Yes, Marvin. It was in the basket — I know I probably shouldn't have done it. I understand."

"And you'll work with Eddie on it? It'll be his officially."

"That's fine."

"If that's okay with Eddie, it's okay with me," Marvin said. "You'll keep me posted on what's happening with it?"

"I promise. I will."

"Okay. Go talk to Eddie about it." Marvin was smiling slightly. "And good work. I know you really want this."

I was stunned; I never really thought he'd give it to me.

"I'll do good, Marvin, really I will."

"Don't fuck up."

"I won't. I promise."

"You better not," Marvin said, his gaze shifting down to whatever he was doing before I walked in. The tips of his fingers made the slightest brushing motion, as if I was an errant fly who'd landed on the wrong slice of pie.

"Thanks, Marvin," I said. "Thanks a lot. I really appreciate it."

He didn't look up.

Sometimes a little rule breaking goes a long way.

⇒≫⊰⇐

Downstairs, Eddie was waiting.

"He said *what?*" Eddie was disbelieving. "If you're breaking my balls about this," Eddie said in his special way, "I'll *rip your fucking lungs out* — you understand me?"

"Yes, Eddie. I swear, Marvin said I could do it as long as you worked on it with me."

"Don't make me regret this," Eddie said, glowering.

"I won't, Eddie. I promise."

Eddie nodded with his chin toward the brown Naugahyde swivel chair next to his desk and composed his face.

"Okay," he said soberly. "What'ya got?"

I told him, and for the next few exhilarating hours, I got my first tutorial on how to think about a homicide.

⇒≫⊰⇐

Controlled completely by prosecutors, a grand jury is a venue unusually hostile to defendants and defense lawyers. Unlike a trial, grand jury proceedings are secret — in most cases defense lawyers don't even know what happened inside until the eve of a trial, and even then they're only partially informed. Only the prosecutors know who was called to testify, or what they had to say, and though a defendant has the right to testify before a grand jury, it is a right that is exercised sparingly: testifying subjects a client to an almost unlimited cross-examination, with no opportunity for rebuttal. Prosecutors make the rules in the grand jury, and they do so with minimal judicial oversight.

Still, if the grand jury believes that someone has not committed a crime, they can refuse to hand up an indictment by voting what is known as a "no true bill." In effect, a no true bill ends the prosecution.

Thus, testifying before the grand jury is a high-risk, high-reward strategy. But with Gillian having explained everything on videotape, it wasn't as if our defense was going to be a surprise. Besides, now was a good time to have her tell her side of the story — it was still fresh in her mind and emotionally resonant, and who knew how she'd come off if we waited two years for a trial?

The criminal justice system is grounded in the idea that truth is a slippery thing. In the vast majority of cases there is no high-angle, omniscient camera recording the events precisely as they unfold. As a result, the attorneys, juries, and judges are left to cobble together, from questionable perceptions, shifting recollections, and forensic evidence, some vague facsimile of truth. Because our system is based on the procedural mechanism of proof rather than on some ontological notion of truth, knowing what the prosecutors have is often as critical as knowing what they don't have. Since most (certainly more than half) of my clients are actually guilty, figuring out how easily the prosecution can prove the case is often invaluable in deciding what a good plea deal is. Paradoxically, sometimes even the most damning evidence winds up being the best for a client — because it allows him to see that fighting the case is fruitless and persuades him to take a deal early, before the price goes up.

I worked with Gillian twice a week for more than two months to prepare her testimony. First we agreed on a structure — who she was, the story of meeting and courting her husband, and finally, what happened the night she stabbed him. And when she was finally ready, after the prosecutor called to let us know that they were actually proceeding against her (I'd hoped against hope that they might just dismiss the case), on the day that she walked nervously into the grand jury room and took her seat before the risers containing the twenty-three citizens that would decide whether or not to indict her, that afternoon, when she put it all together for the first time, explaining her hardscrabble life, her deep love for Rodney, and how their marriage had disintegrated when he started to beat her, I knew we had a shot.

"He was so good to me," Gillian choked out before dissolving into tears, "so gentle and funny, strong and handsome. I loved Rodney so much. And I killed him." She took a deep breath, steadying herself. "It was getting worse and worse. He kept hitting me harder, longer. I knew I should have just covered up and taken it." There was a hiccup as Gillian struggled for air, for control over her voice. "I should have let him do it . . . I know. I know."

"Take your time, Gillian," said the prosecutor.

"He was hitting me so hard," Gillian continued in a whisper. "We were in the kitchen, and the knife was there."

She was almost hyperventilating now.

"And I just did it. I grabbed the knife and I poked him and he was still hitting me and yelling and beating me and I just . . . I just . . . killed him. I loved him, and I killed him."

Gillian broke down completely, racked with the kind of heart-wrenching, remorseful sobbing that takes your breath away with its piercing intensity. And as I tried to contain myself, looking down at the floor so that the jurors wouldn't see my own tears, I noticed the assistant DA in the back of the room looking as though she was going to cry too.

There wasn't much cross-examination.

The ADA had said she intended to vote the case right away. Apparently, after Gillian's emotional testimony, she changed her mind. She may have been on the verge of tears, but she still wanted that indictment. Two days went by, and I began calling the ADA. "When are you going to vote the case?" I'd ask. "Oh, I'm not done with my presentation yet," she'd reply unconvincingly. It was clear to me what was going on — she was icing us, waiting so as to diminish the impact of Gillian's testimony, hoping that as time wore on, the grand jurors would forget everything except that she admitted to stabbing Rodney, and would therefore charge her with murder. The longer the ADA waited, the more Gillian's testimony would recede in their minds — and the more likely it was that they'd indict. There was nothing to do but wait.

For three weeks I called the ADA daily, with no results. As bad as I was about waiting, Eddie was a lot worse. As another week edged into past tense, we met in his office. Eddie's blue eyes were blazing. He'd been drinking for about an hour, and on his desk, lined up neatly like obedient soldiers, were five empty cans of Budweiser.

"Listen to me, you little fuck." Eddie's speech was slow and menacing. *"You think you're good."* Eddie was staring. The other people in the room looked on nervously as he leaned in, his cold eyes locked on mine. "You think you're *so fucking good.*"

"No," I said slowly. "I don't think that at all."

"Yes, you do . . . , you fuck." Eddie was wagging his finger now, his Vietnam-vet eyes furious and brutal. "You know what? Somebody's gotta put you in your *fucking place.*" I wasn't sure where he was heading with this. The other lawyers watched me the way rubberneckers watch a car accident. Eddie staggered to his feet.

"Let me tell you something," he declared, his words slurring together just a little. "If they indict that woman for murder, I'm putting you on a fucking bus back to Wisconsin. You hear me?" Eddie leaned forward, his powerful square chin thrust toward me.

"They're not gonna indict her, Eddie," I said slowly, looking him straight in the face. "And if they do" — I paused for just a second before deciding to give Eddie exactly what he wanted — "you don't have to worry about it. I'll take myself back to Wisconsin."

It was 5:45 P.M. when I finally got the call: no true bill.

I'd won my first murder case.

In the dozen years since I took that case, I've represented murderers, rapists, prostitutes, and drug dealers. I've seen cops lie and maim and subvert the rules of orderly society, watched as heartless, exhausted judges herded people through their court-rooms and into jail, barely glancing up to see who they were sentencing. And yet, after all these years, I can still see what was so plain about the woman who grabbed the kitchen knife and stuck it to her husband: it's often not as obvious as it was in her sad case — battered mad at the hands of a violent husband — but always, if you look hard enough, there is a story, a human drama that casts in a different light the horrific specter of criminality.

This book is about those stories. It is about justice for the haves and the have-nots, about what it is like to be a lawyer in the big city — not a lawyer at a firm in a tall building, defending clients in expensive suits. No, this is about law without the cuff links, about law as it's really practiced — in the drab and common precincts, where man's inhumanity to man is writ large in every tragic detail of otherwise invisible cases. It is about a single day in my life as a public defender in the South Bronx. And it is, in the end, about everyday life in a thousand city courtrooms across America, in the grimy brick buildings and corroding concrete warehouses where American injustice is dispensed bathed in flickering, fluorescent light.

One

WOKE UP DREAMING. OF ANGELO TONA.
Judge Tona made me cry.
King of the calendar, dean of dispositions, Tona could do a
hundred cases in a single night without breaking a sweat. He
rarely listened to lawyers and barely glanced at the people he
processed like so much Spam. "Three days' community service,"
he'd bark without looking up. Clients had about ten seconds to
decide. "Fifteen days' jail. You want it, yes or no?" he'd bellow.
There wasn't much bargaining room.

Tona was an equal-opportunity bully: if he didn't like a prosecutor's offer, he'd release the defendant; if he thought defense
counsel greedy, he'd jail the client. But this wasn't about balance
or equity. Tona's courtroom was about power, *his* power, pure
and simple.

This was a lesson I learned the hard way. I had been a public
defender for less than a year.

It was late at night, and the dingy seventh-floor courtroom
was packed with anxious faces, watching as their loved ones were
paraded before Judge Tona. I don't remember the client's name
anymore, nor do I remember what possessed me to argue with
Tona. In retrospect, I'm sure I thought my client was getting
screwed. After all, most people got a raw deal in Tona's court.
The charges were certainly minor, the defendant likely half decent, at least.

Maybe it was the hour — it had to be 11:00 P.M. or so.
Because of the huge number of cases, night court routinely ran
into the wee hours of the morning. "Legal Aid Society, by David
Feige," I announced as I had a dozen times already that night.
Then, in the standard formula used in every arraignment to get
things moving along, I said, "Waive the reading but not the
rights." This meant we were fine with skipping the recitation of
the charges, but that didn't mean we were giving up any other
procedural or substantive rights the client might have.

"No offer here, Judge," the assistant DA replied.

"Okay," said Tona. "Bail is set in the amount of five hundred
dollars, cash or bond."

"Huh?" I exclaimed. The way the process worked was that
the prosecutor made his request and the defense got a chance to
respond. I hadn't yet opened my mouth to make a bail argument,
and Tona was moving on.

"Next case, please," Tona said matter-of-factly.

"B-but, Judge!" I stammered. "I didn't get to . . . uhhh . . .
I'm asking you to release my client on his own recognizance."

From the bench: "Be. Quiet. Mr. Feige."

"Your Honor! My client is a high school graduate, he's working full-time, and —"

"I said, next case please." Tona couldn't have been cooler.

"His *mother* is here, in court." I was getting frantic. As far as
I was concerned, this was clearly a kid who shouldn't be going to
jail — a place of violence and depredation, a place where even a
single night in a cell risked robbery, mayhem, or even prison rape.

"One more word from you, Mr. Feige, and bail is going *up*.
One hundred dollars a word."

"Your Honor!" I cried.

"Seven hundred dollars!" he said.

"You can't do that!"

"Eleven hundred!"

My mind was racing; I didn't know what to do. My client
looked stunned. A uniformed court officer handcuffed him and
led him toward the back of the courtroom, through the door that
led to the largest penal colony in the world — Rikers Island.

I was panicking.

"Judge, I'm begging you. Please . . . my client deserves to be released. He's a college-bound kid. He'll come back to court. He's never been arrested before, and he has family here . . . please . . . , Judge!"

Tona looked down at me with bovine placidity. "Bail is twenty-five hundred dollars, cash or bond. Anything else, Mr. Feige?"

I was trembling. I couldn't believe it. By pushing the bail amount beyond anything my poor client could hope to post, I had effectively argued him *into* jail. I felt my forehead start to flush; tears welled up in my eyes. The bridge officer called the next case. I turned to the back of the courtroom and, spying the doors, ran.

It's no wonder that Tona haunts my dreams — his bulbous, scowling face cast as the personification of my powerlessness — and no wonder it's him I'm chasing, swimming to the surface of consciousness on a cold morning ten years later when, despite my passion for criminal defense work, I would relish a little extra time in bed.

⇢⤙

I like the cold — for personal and professional reasons. On cold nights, people stay off the street corners; less corner traffic means fewer arrests, and fewer arrests mean a lighter arraignment load. A light night in arraignments means a little dip in a public defender's caseload — a moment of respite in a churning sea of relentless criminality. All year long, I sleep with the window open, hoping the air drifting in might signal a frost.

The radio mumbles about Iraq as I finally shake off sleep. The news of the moment: two guys stabbed and a little girl caught in a cross-fire shooting. My ears perk up, but both turn out to be in Brooklyn. No news at all from the Bronx. The sky is overcast, a portent of the snow forecast for later in the week. That would be nice.

My own law-breaking this morning involves having drilled out the water regulator in my showerhead — a crime for which I feel no remorse whatsoever. Every day I can look forward to about six minutes of illegal, superheated bliss. In the shower, I map out the day's schedule, trying to imagine which clients will show up on time, which judges I have already pissed off during the week, which courtrooms are going to be glacially slow. When on trial, I visualize my cross-examination, whittling down my important questions to their spare, eviscerating essence. Some of my best summations have been devised or delivered amid the steam and scald. Mickey Richards, Omar Chavez, Juan Torres, and Steven Smith: all owe their freedom in some small measure to my shower inspiration. And it's always been like that: even back when I couldn't wait to get to work, couldn't stand being away from the office and the action, I never passed up my contemplative shower moments. Indeed, they were the only moments of luxury back when I got into all this.

⇒•⇐

Oddly, for someone who is, or on occasion has been called, a big, self-righteous blowhard, I did not get my start in the public-defender business for righteous reasons. Really it was an accident.

It was in the spring of 1985. I was a sophomore in college. And while most of my classmates had summer plans long since settled, I had been too preoccupied eating barbecued beef and trying hard to seduce the woman who won the University of Chicago's prize for best BA paper in English to bother planning my summer. Of course, the longer I waited, the more likely it seemed that somehow the decision would be made for me rather than by me.

Waiting out an April shower, an overstuffed sandwich safely in my stomach, I ducked one afternoon into the damp stone building that housed the university's career and placement office. Justice couldn't have been further from my mind, but as I flipped through the postings "Criminal Defense Investigator Wanted" caught my eye. I scanned down the page . . . *investigating criminal cases . . . finding witnesses, serving subpoenas . . . visiting crime scenes.* It all sounded cool to me. And rather than high-toned rhetoric about grade point average, self-motivation, and all the rest of the corporate nonsense, this ad sought people who were adventurous and had good communication skills. The Washington, DC, Public Defender Service, as it turned out, was looking not for brilliant students, but for people who could talk, drive, and take chances, and were willing to work for free. It had my name written all over it. I promptly lined up a public-interest summer grant and fired off an application.

The DC PDS investigator internship was exactly as advertised, and within a week I found myself wandering around southeast DC looking for a guy named Slim who had supposedly witnessed a robbery. It was a disaster. Alabama Avenue in the mid-1980s might as well have run through Alabama itself. It was rural poverty writ urban — as if the tumbledown homes of the Deep South had been shoved together by some huge earthmover. There were low concrete bunkhouses with doors swinging from one hinge, playgrounds filled with dust or mud depending on when it had rained last, and people everywhere, crowding the little cement slabs that served as ground-level verandas, sitting on decaying chairs or plastic milk crates, huddling around card tables chockablock with dominoes, smoking, drinking, and fanning themselves in the humid summer sun.

I stood out.

It wasn't just because I was white, though that certainly helped, but also because I had the stiff walk of the neophyte and the nervous look of the out-of-place kid that I actually was. No one would give me the time of day. Good luck finding Slim.

Nevertheless, as the summer wore on I began to take to the work. It was endlessly fascinating, exposing me to a world I had never really known — a world where people lived by street names, where drug commerce and violence lived cheek by jowl with working families and hopscotching children, where the first assumption was that I was a cop; the second, a rich junkie looking for a fix; the third, a parole officer; and beyond that the hopped-up kids of Alabama Avenue had no idea what to make of me. In time, as I adjusted to the expectations of Southeast, I began to both love it and understand it. By the middle of the summer I'd learned how to track down witnesses, ask questions, and dig up information that would prove useful in the rapes and murders and robberies I was investigating. I'd learned every street and alley in the Quadrant, and could talk my way into almost any house. And most every night I brought home the fruits of my investigations to the lawyers I worked for — hard-charging, dedicated defenders whose passion for their work inspired me every day to find more, and to dig deeper.

My time in DC transformed me. It turned a college kid's diffuse sense of right and wrong into a focused and rigid moral framework. That first exposure — to the criminal justice system, to poverty, and to the macabre hierarchy of criminal defense lawyers — radically altered the next two decades of my life. It gave me a purpose.

Law school was, for the most part, full of overindulged kids looking to become lawyers either to please daddy or to bring home the big paycheck. Worse, with *L.A. Law* sexing up corporate work every week (Arnie Becker got laid twice a show), the fetid focus of law school life became who could get a job at the fanciest firm. This only compounded the pathological competitiveness of the entire law school experience.

I didn't bother to talk to law firms during my first year. I knew exactly where I was headed for the summer: back to the streets of DC and the Public Defender Service. My second summer, though, was different. My dad, who dreamed of telling his friends about how his son was going to work for a Wall Street law firm, argued stridently that before I went off to spend (read: "waste") my life being a public defender, I should at least explore the opportunity costs.

And that's what I did: Dewey Ballantine is about as fancy and white-shoe as a law firm can be. It also had the distinction, in 1990, of being among the highest-paying law firms in the country. That summer, from my aerie on the forty-fifth floor with the commanding view of midtown Manhattan, I got my first taste of what "legitimate" success felt like — and it felt good. Plied with expensive food and name-brand liquor, I spent a summer wrestling with my identity as I shuttled between Wall Street, Broadway shows, and Yankee games. It's not bad being treated like a king. And as it turned out, I didn't mind making an ocean of money. But the vertiginous experience of being a bit player in the big world of commerce never quite sat right. Partly it was my insufferable lack of deference, partly it was my defiant streak, and partly it was just because, looking around the firm at my high-powered colleagues, with their sophisticated airs and entitled perspective, all I saw were slaves.

In *Discipline and Punish,* the brilliant meditation on the history of penology, Michel Foucault suggests that the more advanced a society is, the more subtle the modes and means of penal control. If a summer at Dewey Ballantine showed me anything, it was just how controlling an advanced society like a law firm could be and how brilliantly, brutally subtle penal control could be. Almost every day, one or another of my bright-eyed colleagues would rush into my office detailing in a barely controlled whisper what partner had assigned what task to what associate, who had gone where, and whose fortunes were rising and whose were falling. It was as if we were back in junior high school, except that instead of gossiping about whether Nadjia Neherniak really made out with Mark Burnett, we spent every minute trying to ensure that no one else was making corporate inroads any faster or more effectively than anyone else. To keep tabs on this, summer associates spent an inordinate amount of energy considering how much "face time" was optimal — "face time" being time spent in the office irrespective of whether or not one had work to do.

In between visits to client-subsidized shrimp bowls, Broadway shows, and box seats at ball games, I reflected on the meaning of the experience. I concluded that though it was undeniably tasty and lucrative, to me it was all lifestyle and no life.

It was that realization that animated my stride in November of 1990 as I walked into the offices of the Criminal Defense Division of the Legal Aid Society of New York City and announced, with more confidence than I felt, that I was there for an interview.

"Second or third?"

The woman behind the desk glanced up for a fraction of a second, taking my measure with practiced disdain. The question completely puzzled me, and at first I wasn't even sure what she was talking about.

"There are three?" I asked, my too-cool-for-school laconic delivery quickly giving way to a more familiar boyhood school-yard panic.

"Yeah . . . three," said the receptionist, not at all impressed with my performance so far. "Who did you interview with on campus?"

"Ahhhh . . ." I stalled. "I don't think you come to Wisconsin. I just sent in a letter and résumé and was told to show up today."

This unusual way of doing things seemed to flummox her, but after taking my name, motioning me to a chair, and mutter-ing into a telephone for a few seconds, she managed to say what I'd hoped to hear at the beginning of our conversation: "Some-one will be right with you."

The "someone" quickly morphed into four people, who led me into a nondescript room and mercilessly fired contentious questions at me for forty-five minutes. It was utterly unlike the law firm interviews, which seemed to be structured around the idea that no question was too stupid and no topic too inane to elicit a warm smile and a firm handshake. The people around the table (half of them in jeans) seemed to suggest that I had a lotta gall comin' in to their office on Park Row in New York City and asking them for a job. *Who the hell was I?* each one of them wanted to know.

It was, in short, my kind of interview. And sitting there in the cramped room stuffed with too many chairs and a table two sizes too big, staring out a window that looked out into a sooty air-shaft, I understood, implicitly, that this was my home and these were my people.

"Here," said one of my interlocutors, pushing a set of stapled papers across the table at me like a detective presenting a pre-pared confession. "We'd like to have you back for a second interview. You'll need to deliver a summation. This is the fact pattern."

"Work out your summation during Thanksgiving," said another, "and we'll see you back here at ten thirty Friday morning." Her tone left no doubt that I'd be there at 10:30 and be prepared.

And so while grandma was basting the turkey and my mother and sisters squabbled over mundane Thanksgiving-related matters, I was given the gift of homework. More than content to skip everything about Thanksgiving other than the meal, I holed up in a small bedroom poring over the facts of a faux robbery case, preparing my very first faux summation.

I was back at the offices first thing Friday morning, my heart pounding, certain I was actually going to die as I stood to face my four-person jury. But despite my nerves, my voice was strong and clear as I explained with a few rhetorical flourishes and dramatic gestures why my imaginary client was innocent. The summation lasted about twelve minutes, each one of them floating by me like an iceberg off the bow of a lumbering ship, each moment crystalline, weighty, and portentous. It was the first time, but by no means the last, that I heard myself sum up without understanding a word that I said, some deep part of my limbic system taking over the words while the conscious part of me was left abstractly appreciating the rhythms and sounds, completely divorced from the meaning of any of it. I supposed this was what it was like when an athlete spoke of being in the zone, of doing without thinking, of a deep and golden attention to one's heartbeat, the smell of the arena, the chill of the late fall, the ball slowing as if thrown through honey.

Once done, I was led around to an office on the other side of the building and ceremoniously introduced to Ivar Goldart. Ivar wasn't actually the big boss — that was a guy named Bob Baum. But Bob was out of the office, as was one of his deputies, and so, for my third interview, I got Ivar. Ivar was a lanky man who walked with a pronounced limp — the uneven lope gave him a weird gravitas, as if somehow no guy with such an affliction would ever say anything frivolous or stupid.

"What can we do," Ivar asked me, "to get you to come work for us?" There was a long pause. In truth, it had never occurred to me that I'd get to ask for anything, and I was utterly unprepared for the question. But as I sat there in Ivar's office, with its partially obstructed views and proximity to city hall, it was instantly clear to me that there was really only one thing I wanted. "Being from Wisconsin," I explained, "I always kind of envisioned New York as being bound by the East River and the Hudson, and I'd really like to stay in the city I imagined." In other words: Manhattan. Ivar fixed me with an ingratiating smile: "Oh, no problem," he said. "That's where we send most of our out-of-state people."

And with that, then and there, in the narrow Park Row building across from city hall in downtown New York City, on the Friday after Thanksgiving 1990, I made up my mind: I'd turn my back on the filthy lucre of Wall Street and spend my life being down, dirty, and righteous with the Legal Aid Society of New York.

Ivar and I shook on it.

Less than six months later, after the bar exam, along with seventy-one other newly minted legal aid lawyers from around the country, I shuffled in and out of the College of Insurance Building (around the corner from the World Trade Center), where I learned things like "how to win speedy trial motions" and "just how much community service is a misdemeanor worth?" I went through day after day of lectures, demonstrations, and exercises designed to ensure that when we actually strode into court on behalf of indigent clients, we wouldn't hurt them too badly. Six weeks came and went in a haze of astonishingly cool topics — each more real and practical than the next — all things I was desperate to learn. And like a kid in a samurai film who yearns for the day he can trade the bamboo stick for the tempered-steel sword, I gobbled up every day's lessons hungry for the moment they'd finally cut me loose to do some real battle.

When it was finally assignment day, the Friday before we were to head to our waiting offices, one of our instructors wandered down the aisles calling out names and handing out our assignment slips.

"Enjoy," John said, handing me my little white slip.

I took the little piece of paper and unfolded it distractedly. AP-3 — Brooklyn. *Brooklyn?* I felt a little rush. Surely there's some mistake, I thought. Me . . . Brooklyn . . . impossible. They promised to send me to Manhattan. *I don't even know where Brooklyn is!* I felt my face start to flush. I looked up. John was grinning at me.

"See you across the river," he said, hooking a thumb east over his shoulder.

At that point, everything I knew about Brooklyn I had learned from *Welcome Back, Kotter.* But despite my ignorance and my horror at being relegated to what I considered a third-rate borough (the Bronx was at least sexy in a hard-core kind of way), my first year across the river was revelatory. Unlike almost all the other lawyers I knew back then — the ones I'd left in the towers of Wall Street, the smart people elbowing to succeed at big law firms — when I arrived at work every single morning of that first year, I was utterly happy. The host of *Morning Edition* had barely gotten to his last name by the time the covers were flung aside and I was headed for my tiny bathroom, almost skipping with the realization that I was headed *back* to work. The sheer exhilaration of knowing that in an hour or so I'd be in court, standing beside the poor and bedraggled, the violent and the innocent, the people who never wanted me as their lawyer in the first place was intoxicating. That the Criminal Defense Division of the Legal Aid Society would even pay me to do the work seemed, at the time, like a gift.

The limits of that gift soon became apparent. I got a raise for passing the bar and in one fell swoop went from making a paltry $29,500 a year to a whopping $31,000. I celebrated this by treating myself to coffee in the morning and toppings on my pizza at night. That ate up the raise.

My nutrient-deficient diet was just one of the scary aspects of my new life. Frankly, everything was terrifying. Every day of walking to court; finding my way around; memorizing the names of the judges, the assistant DAs, the court clerks; questioning whether I pled someone too soon or too late, whether the fine was too high, or whether I'd needlessly ruined someone's life by giving them a criminal record — it was constant stress and confusion. And every day was a battle. Some were mere skirmishes, others Iwo Jima. Sometimes I saw them coming; other times I was blindsided like an American pedestrian crossing a London street against the light.

⇥⇤

Survival was something Eddie Mayr knew a little something about. Eddie had spent three tours in Vietnam and considered all of life to be just another form of jungle combat. Every Friday afternoon he'd march the first-year lawyers into his office to do "simulations." Lecturing us on the need to keep attacking, even when he'd angrily shot us down, he'd torture us for hours, making us get up and deliver opening statements, formulate cross-examination questions, or try our hand at voir dire (the questioning of potential jurors before a trial). I happened to like this sort of trial-by-fire approach, and I often stayed after school along with most of the other lawyers to decompress — that is, drink heavily — in Eddie's office. As the evenings progressed, the conversation usually turned to who did well and who fucked up during the week. This was often unpleasant. After all, Eddie's thousand-yard stare and vicious nature lent a certain harshness to his critiques. But it was an effective way to learn to be a better lawyer, and I wanted very much to be a better lawyer.

And so, in Brooklyn, under Eddie's watchful eye, I learned to be a public defender — mostly by supplying him with Budweisers and listening to him rant. It was the best sort of law school I could imagine. At the time, I was juggling between 100 and 125 cases — an ocean of pleas, arraignments, motions, and trials. Every day I traversed the monolithic gray stone court building on Schermerhorn Street, defending poor people charged with misdemeanors — train hopping, pot smoking, meat boosting (meat, along with batteries, aspirin, and Pampers, is often stolen because it's easy to resell), or prostitution. Misdemeanors help you get your court legs, help you learn the mechanics — where to stand, what to say, how to read a judge. The legal aspects of the misdemeanor cases that occupied all of my time were seldom complicated, which was good since the judges who presided over them seemed to have only a rudimentary understanding of the law.

Once a young lawyer has been mired in misdemeanors for a year or so, having handled between four hundred and a thousand or so of them, a supervisor can begin the process of "felony certification." With this supervisory approval, one can start doing low-level felonies, cases in which people are looking at a few years (rather than ten or twenty) — purse snatches, gun possession, car theft.

Although the certification system is fairly rigid, the actual assignment system is very porous, and enthusiastic kid that I was, I soon began sneaking felony cases — something my overworked felony-certified colleagues were more than happy to ignore. With felonies, I got to go to Supreme Court, where courtrooms are bigger, cases are fewer, and the tone of the proceedings is much more formal. Because Supreme Court adjudicated more serious cases, the standard bargaining unit jumped from days in jail to years in prison, and I began meeting new and different kinds of clients and spending more time in jail cells.

Just behind an unmarked door on the ground floor of the Supreme Court of Kings County there was a nondescript corridor that led to the "pens" — courthouse slang for jail cells. The corridor ended at a door, conspicuous for its weight, with a small window cut at eye level and a red-and-white sign that made clear that you were now entering a secure area. The sign also listed a large number of potential infractions — any of which could get you banned from the pens, arrested, or, if you were an inmate, additional time behind bars.

Just behind the door was a corrections officer who, nearly every day, perfunctorily examined my Legal Aid Society ID and motioned me lazily toward the back. Around the corner were the pens themselves, three huge cells, each the size of a racquetball court and crammed with prisoners waiting to be seen. The men were standing, sitting, or sleeping under the steel benches bolted to the walls.

Supreme Court cases usually last longer than misdemeanors, and therefore they afford a lawyer a greater opportunity to form a long-term relationship with a client. From the beginning I loved most of the people I represented. There was the defiant Hasidic Jew from Borough Park who tried to refuse a dismissal, screaming at me, his peyos bouncing in consternation. "I don't want ACD," he told me. (ACD is an adjournment in contemplation of dismissal — the closest thing there is to an outright victory and something almost no one, and certainly not this guy, should turn down.) "I want full vindication at trial! Nothing but full vindication at trial!" And there was the Rastafarian client who promised me that when he got out I could come to his house in Flatbush to "it sam fine-food, mon." Almost every day brought me into contact with an astonishing array of people, all of whom desperately needed my help.

Oddly, the fact that they were needy seldom translated into gratitude for being helped. That was something I had to get used to. It took a while to really, viscerally understand that helping people has to be its own reward — that if, as a public defender, you expect any appreciation from your clients you'll never survive, because the unfortunate truth is you'll rarely get it. This was a lesson made explicit for me one Thursday night in the back of Callahan's Bar and Grill, the Irish dive bar next to the office. The bar was split the usual way — prosecutors in the front room, defense lawyers in the back, and there was almost no movement between rooms, except to get to the turkey. The turkey — usually a twenty-plus-pound behemoth — was set out around 7:30 P.M. and usually rendered a bony, picked-over carcass by 7:37. For a bunch of underpaid prosecutors and legal aid lawyers, Callahan's turkey was a way to spend some limited resources on liquor and still get some food in your stomach.

I spent a lot of time at Callahan's.

Among the experienced attorneys who occasionally bought the younger lawyers drinks, Paula Deutsch was my favorite. A hard-drinking, brilliant true believer, Paula was the kind of elegant woman who, despite her graying hair and mild lisp, had the sultry sexiness of a librarian in a skin flick. She tried some of the toughest cases in the office while seeming to love both the work and her clients. One night, after a particularly rough day, an hour or two after the turkey, Paula told me something I'd never forget.

"Thing is, Feige," she said, leaning forward, shaking her head, and fixing me with an urgent glare, "you gotta lawyer *for you.*"

The sentiment seemed strange coming from her, and I must have looked at her blankly, because she smiled bemusedly and continued.

"If you're doing this work because you think people are gonna love you, or appreciate you, or admire you, you're fucked. Your clients, they got no reason to appreciate you, and if you think they're gonna just sit up one day and realize you're the best lawyer they've ever had, you better just hang it up right now. And prosecutors — they think you're shit on a good day, and that ain't never gonna change. And judges . . ." Paula made a whistling sound as she exhaled. "You can be as smart and persuasive as you want. You can bring all that beautiful passion and that big brain of yours to bear every single day. They ain't gonna care — they're still gonna fuck your client anyhow. So if you're working this job looking for appreciation, you're never gonna last." She paused for a second to parse my distraught look. "Feige," she said, leaning closer, trying to convey that there was a point to this lesson in tough love, "it's gotta come from here" — she clapped my shoulder and gave it an almost maternal squeeze — "you gotta know deep down that this is the most righteous work there is, that even though we lose and lose and we get creamed every day, even though we watch them take our clients and haul them off to jail, you have to wake up the next morning and fight your heart out, looking for those few times we can stop it. Not because you're looking for appreciation, not because you want someone to say, 'Thanks, Feige, you saved me,' but because, at the end of the day, no matter what anyone says, you know that what you're doing is right."

➤━◄

I actually got felony certified several months after I started sneaking felonies. By that time I'd already tried and won a few bench trials — an innocent kid swept up in the mayhem of the Crown Heights riots (I called his priest as a character witness) and the front man in a turnstile double-up ("He just slid in behind me — I don't even know him" was his legitimate defense). I'd also dabbled in the terrifying world of the misdemeanor jury trial. In a DWI case, I began my opening statement by saying, "It was a dark and stormy night. . . . I've always wanted to start an opening statement with those words, and now I have. But you know — it's actually true." It was the road conditions, I argued, not the alcohol that caused the car to slide. The jury acquitted in fifteen minutes.

My first big loss was a young kid named William Valentine. William was short and squat and handsome. A light-skinned Hispanic with Schwarzenegger's square jaw, William possessed the toned physique of an aerobics instructor — which, in fact, he was. A huge hit at a local Brooklyn health club, William was doing well in the world until he was charged with rape.

Under New York law, there are two statutes that cover the acts most of us imagine as rape. One, called "rape in the first degree," is a class B violent felony. It is defined as "sexual intercourse by forcible compulsion" and is punishable by up to twenty-five years in prison. Almost any defendant convicted after trial of what the system calls "rape one" is likely to spend a few decades behind bars. There is another sex crime that also covers rape, though. It's called "sexual misconduct." Technically defined as "sexual intercourse without consent," the crime, at first blush, seems different from rape in the first degree. It's not. As it turns out, lack of consent is actually defined as resulting from "forcible compulsion." Nevertheless, sexual misconduct is a class A misdemeanor, punishable by a fine, community service, or up to one year in jail. Rape in the first degree and sexual misconduct are the same crime — the distinction exists solely to give prosecutors discretion in charging. In a cruel twist, however, defense lawyers cannot argue to a jury that they should convict a client on the misdemeanor rather than the felony. The charging decision begins and ends with the prosecution.

Linda Liotta was the kind of Italian Catholic girl most Jewish boys dream about. Long and lithe, with pale skin and dark eyes, she came from the kind of tight-knit, restrictive family that still thrives in Brooklyn neighborhoods like Dyker Heights, Bay Ridge, and Bensonhurst. Linda could be fiery and independent, and seemed to yearn for a life away from her family. She moved out just after her nineteenth birthday. And for her first weekend alone, she called her aerobics instructor and asked him out on a date.

They had a good dinner by all accounts, chatting amiably, going for a short walk, and driving around near the boardwalk in William's car. They never went out again, though Linda continued to take William's classes — sometimes twice a day.

The phone calls started about six months later — Linda asking to talk to William, leaving messages two and three times a day. She still took his classes — as many as eight or ten a week, standing right in the front of the room, often dead-center. Club management got concerned about the situation when the calls and messages started to interfere with William's class schedule, and eventually, they asked her not to phone so much. William had another girlfriend by then, someone he was serious about, and she thought Linda's calling was distracting and unhealthy. Club management agreed, but the calls continued. There was a meeting, and eventually Linda quit the club.

It was nearly two years after their only date that Linda Liotta told the police, for the very first time, that William had raped her. Despite the two-year-old complaint, the total lack of physical evidence, and Linda's odd behavior at the health club, the police went ahead and did what police do — they arrested William.

This wasn't surprising. With the advent of Special Victims Units and domestic violence prosecutors, most anyone able to enunciate the word *rape* can almost always get someone else arrested. Sometimes, of course, there is a real basis for the arrest, but there are also plenty of people manipulating the system. Worse is that oftentimes there is minimal investigation beyond the allegation itself. Delayed outcry is explained away, lack of physical evidence is taken as a nonissue, and problems with memory or an inability to recall details are excused under the theory that rape is such a traumatic experience that the usual rules don't apply. Whether all of this is a good thing or a bad thing depends on which side of the accusation you're on. For a belated accuser with vague memories and no physical corroboration, it's great. For someone surprisingly accused of a two-year-old crime, faced with losing his livelihood, job, girlfriend, and freedom, it's pretty far from great. And for prosecutors unsure of what or whom to believe but required to take a rape allegation seriously, the complicated cocktail of facts can lead to baby splitting — a misdemeanor rape prosecution, which is precisely what happened to William.

William's account differed substantially from Linda's. They had driven around for a while, parked near the boardwalk, and started making out in the car. The making out led to more significant making out and then, eventually, to consensual sex. But in Linda's version, after a little making out, William had climbed over from the driver's seat, tilted her seat back, and raped her.

William was a wonderful client: he was sweet, prompt, thoughtful, and kind. Though he was not particularly bright (he did, after all, make his living jumping around in a tight-fitting outfit in front of a room full of sweating women), he was astonishingly considerate and willing to listen. "You never know what can happen at a trial," I told him. But William was utterly resolute. He wasn't going to plead guilty (he was offered three years of probation) to something he didn't do — particularly not a rape. He wasn't a sex offender, and he wasn't going to say he was just because he was scared of jail. He'd take his chances.

After cross-examining the prosecution's expert in rape trauma syndrome — the DA's attempt to explain why someone wouldn't report a rape for nearly two years — and after delivering a powerful summation, I felt good. The jury may have been out for three days, but I had gotten precisely the jury I wanted — six men, no women. And so, as I rose to face the judge, to take the verdict that had left me sleepless for nearly fifty hours, I believed that William would be acquitted. I believed, after all, that he was completely innocent.

"How do you find as to the first count of the information, charging the defendant with sexual misconduct?" asked the clerk of the court.

There was hardly a pause: "Guilty," said the jury foreman simply. My shoulders slumped, William's girlfriend gasped, and Linda's parents, who had come to comfort her, harrumphed with satisfaction as Judge Michael Gary ordered that William be hauled off to Rikers Island.

"Defendant is remanded," he said before I could even open my mouth.

And as the words tumbled out, the burly court officer behind William seamlessly slipped the cuffs over his wrists, grinding them home — the ratcheting sound of the metal etching itself into my mind like an acid-tipped brush searing a copper plate.

I'd made one of the worst rookie mistakes there was. No one had bothered to tell me that no one in his right mind picks an all-male jury in a rape case. The reality is (or at least I believe) that when it comes to rape most men spend their time in the jury room trying to validate themselves by demonstrating how sensitive they are to the victim. Consequently, men are uncomfortable acquitting someone on a sex charge, and this is acutely true with an all-male jury. It takes a woman in the room to corroborate their skepticism, to make their disbelief okay.

They took William away, and outside in the wide hallway with the ugly brown linoleum and clanking half-painted radiators, I sobbed. I knew abstractly that as a public defender, at the end of the day, depending on whether I did my job well or not, my clients would either go home or be carted off to jail. And I knew that no matter what happened to my clients that I would go home to my little apartment on the Upper West Side, safe and sound in a life full of good choices.

But what I didn't know until that day was how devastating William's loss would feel to me, or how, as I watched those court officers take him down the hall, my throat would constrict and I would feel as if someone had just dropped an elephant on my chest, and that I would think of William Valentine every single day he was incarcerated. I had had a chance to speak on William's behalf, and what I had said and done in that capacity had actually meant the difference between life and whatever it is that you call a year behind bars — and I had blown it.

⇒►◄⇐

And along with the specter of Angelo Tona, it is the horror of blowing it, of making a mistake and then having to watch someone led off into the deafening brutality of prison life, that finally gets me out of bed and into the shower this cold winter morning.

It is now nearly 9:00 A.M. No matter how hot I make the shower, it cannot wash away the ghosts. But there is no more time to think about William. It is time to get dressed and head north yet again, to the battlefield, to the apocalypse, to the end of the world.

To the Bronx.

Two

9:22 A.M.

S OMEONE PISSED ON MY DOORSTEP. Because my apartment
building is slightly recessed, it provides excellent cover for
the inebriated Yuppies who stagger home from the bars
down the block late at night. The result: several mornings a week
I'm greeted with a little olfactory premonition of the day to come.

I step over the little puddle and into the flow of businessmen
in expensive English bench-built shoes flooding toward the subway station and the cute new moms carrying yoga mats, ducking
into the Bikram yoga studio a few doors down.

My neighborhood is affluent by any standards, with even
small apartments commanding prices suburbanites might pay
for a freestanding structure and a lawn. There are four nice bak-
eries within a block or two — offering decaf cappuccino and a
selection of baguettes and croissants that would make a French-
man envious. At the Tasty Bakery on the corner, the friendly
Slavic woman is already pouring my decaf by the time I order.
Once I cross the river, the only places that have decaf are the
Dunkin' Donuts and the gas station. The Bronx is not a decaf
kind of town.

Weaving my way up Broadway, I pass the fresh fruit display
in front of the Fairway grocery store — plums and grapes and
nectarines and strawberries shimmering red and purple, a world
of fancy produce just a block away. My car is wedged into a spot
on Seventy-fifth Street — a "must be out by 11:00 A.M." spot.
Those of us who can't afford the several hundred dollars a month

it costs to garage a car in Manhattan study the intricacies of New York City street-parking regulations like the Talmud. During my career I've been late for court, late to dinner, late to the movies, and late to parties, but I've never risked missing a parking spot deadline.

Heading toward the car, coffee in hand, I think hard about Cassandra. There are people you meet in my job who are so helpless, so hopeless, and so sad that it slices your heart up, people whose stories are so dire and desperate that they stay with you — a wound that never heals. Cassandra is one of them.

Cassandra is big and round and overweight, with a puffy, moon-pie face. Her eyes are set deep, and they betray no expression at all — ever. She speaks in a halting, childish monotone with the kind of bluntness that suggests she has long since given up trying to hide anything. Cassandra has just about all the problems a person can have — she's drug dependent, deeply depressed, homeless, suicidal, and mentally ill. To look at her is to see someone utterly lost.

I first met Cassandra in 1997, when she was arrested for an attempted arson that was as much a suicide attempt as anything else. It took all of two minutes to figure out that like many people, Cassandra had needs well beyond what the criminal justice system could handle. So while she sat in jail, I started the long and complicated process of trying to get her into a residential mental health program.

Things went well at first. With the help of a social worker in the office, I found a suitable program. Cassandra pled guilty to reckless endangerment (arson convictions usually disqualify someone from residential mental health programs) and was released. More than six months went by without a hitch. But then, as they so often do with Cassandra, things began to unravel.

Cassandra got herself thrown out of the program. We got them to give her another chance. She got ejected again. We tried a different program. She didn't last there either. This cycle continued for more than a year as we went through program after program, finally finding a place that she liked and that could deal with her. For a few years, everything was stable.

Until I got the call.

"Hello . . . , David?"

I knew her voice immediately.

"Cassandra. Hi," I said. "How are you?"

"I'm fine."

"Where are ya, darling?"

"Uh . . . I'm at the precinct." She delivered this news with her usual lack of inflection.

"Sweetie, why are you at the precinct?"

"I robbed a taxi," she said plainly.

"Okay, okay, Cassandra, I want you to listen really carefully. You know the police are going to arrest you, right?"

"Yes, David. I know."

"Okay, I understand what you did, but I don't want you talking about it right now. Do you understand?"

"Yes, David."

"Okay, now I'm gonna come right down there, and then I'll be there again for you when you get to court, okay?"

"Yes, David."

"I want to talk to the policeman now. Can you put him on the phone?"

"Okay."

I learned from the detective that Cassandra was charged with using her index finger to try to rob a livery cab driver. I told the detective that I'd be her lawyer and that he should not question her, and to call me if there was going to be a lineup.

When I saw her later, after her arraignment, I asked her why she'd done such a silly thing.

"Well, I did it once before and it worked," she answered simply.

"But, sweetie, why try it in the first place?"

"Oh," she said. "I wanted money — I was feeling depressed and sad and I wanted to go buy a little alcohol or maybe some crack or something, to make me feel better." She nodded and raised her eyebrows, and shrugged as if apologizing for her depression.

In junior high school civics classes we're taught that all Americans have a fundamental right to a speedy trial. In fact,

big-city justice often means epic delays and months in purga-
tory — which in Cassandra's case was more like hell. She was
kept locked up in jail for almost a year. It was a year punctuated
by court dates designed only to momentarily release her so that
we could drive her to interviews with psychiatric programs
around the state. This time, no one would take her, and so at the
end of the day we'd surrender her back to the judge, who would
put her back in jail.

As his final official act at the Bronx district attorney's office,
an assistant district attorney agreed to let Cassandra withdraw
her guilty plea to a felony and plead guilty to a misdemeanor. He
knew how hard we'd been trying to find her a program, and he
felt bad that she was sitting in jail because there were no programs willing to accept her. There was no weapon, and no one
was hurt, so he figured the year she had already been in jail
should suffice as a sentence. The plea deal meant that Cassandra went free again. Over the ensuing years, I saw Cassandra
regularly: acting as her post office box when she was homeless;
storing her eighty-nine-dollar check (her share of an uncle's
estate) until she could collect it; trying, as often as possible, to
provide a stable, reliable place where she could feel welcome.

And then, just three weeks ago, Denise, one of our social
workers, caught me at the door. I was coming back from a har-
rowing day in court — I'd just had a client handed the maximum
sentence after he'd been acquitted of all the most serious charges
in his case. The judge could have given him probation — instead
he gave him up to fifteen years.

"Guess who's here?" Denise asked.

"Let me guess." There was something in her voice that gave
away the answer — a schoolmarm's disapproval of a disappoint-
ing pupil. "Cassandra?"

"Lorraine let her sleep in the interview room," Denise said
with a frown.

"Okay, good," I murmured, lugging my trial bag up the stairs.
"Let her sleep for a while and keep me posted."

"Only because she's yours, David," Denise declared in a
chiding tone. "She's homicidal and suicidal, with attempts as

recent as yesterday, and she's intoxicated. If she were anyone else's, I'd have already called the crisis team. But she said she wanted to talk to you, only to you, and she doesn't want to go to the hospital — at least not one where there are any men."

"Yeah. That's a thing of hers — not really a big fan of men."

Three hours later Cassandra was awake. The smell in the interview room was almost unbearable. Coming down the stairs, I could see her through the glass of the door before I ventured inside. Her hair was matted and nappy, and she was bundled in three mismatched coats.

"Sweetie," I said, "I thought we sent you to detox?"

"Yes, David." Her big brown eyes were glassy, and it looked as if she'd lost some weight. Her face, usually soft and round, had hardened into something more akin to an oblong.

"Well, what happened?"

"I didn't stay."

"Well, why not?"

"They kicked me out," Cassandra explained, her voice dropping — a descending piano scale, every word one note below the last.

"I understand that, darling, but why did they kick you out?"

"I didn't like them," she said, nodding. "There were men in there."

"And you don't like the men."

"Riiiiight." Cassandra nodded softly. "They look at me . . . you know."

"I know, darling. I know." Since she watched her father murder her mother when she was a little girl, men had been a complicated issue.

"I've been sad." Cassandra nodded again, as if it was news to her too.

"And what have you been doing about that?"

"I tried to kill myself — get AIDS, lie in the street. It didn't work." She said all this matter-of-factly, as if describing last Sunday's weather.

"Honey," I asked, "why were you trying to get AIDS?"

"I thought they would take care of me then," she said blandly.

"I had sex with a man — he had AIDS. I told him not to use a condom. Didn't work. I layed down in the street too — thought maybe a car would run over me. It didn't — they were nice. The police. Took me to the hospital."

"Sweetie, I think we need to get you back into a program — I think you need someone to look after you a little more than I can."

Cassandra's face should have betrayed some emotion. Instead it was blank.

"I know, David," she said flatly. "Not today though."

"Honey," I said, trying to sound firm, "you know you can't just show up and crash here."

"I know, David, I know." She nodded gravely. "But I been on the streets for a while, and I was real tired, you know?"

"I know, sweetie, but we're going to have to do something about this."

The odor was nearly intolerable — opening the door, I could see some of the kids from the youth program in the next office wrinkle their noses, look up in alarm, and retreat down the hall.

"Okay, sweetie, you know I love you," I told her, leading Cassandra to the door to the courtyard, "but I need you to wait in the courtyard with me while we figure out what we're going to do. 'Cause you're a little bit stinky, and I can't really have you inside right now, okay?"

"Okay, David," she said with a resigned smile. "I know. I do have an odor. I do. I admit that." She nodded as if considering the whole situation. "I've been on the streets for a lot of days too. Begging and drinking . . . people are nice you know . . . they give me soup sometime. And money too, real nice . . . everyone's real nice."

As I led her from the client interview room, the stench followed us through the library and out into the fresh air. Passing through the library, I noticed for the first time a little blister on her lower lip.

I was at a loss — I hadn't seen Cassandra this disheveled in ages. From what I could tell, over the past six years we'd tried almost every program and shelter we could think of. Hospitals were unlikely to keep her for any more than a day or two; shelters and programs were essentially out. I could turn her back to the streets, of course, where her suicide attempts would continue, or she'd find herself back in jail, possibly for a long period of time.

Carefully positioning myself upwind of her, I proposed a radical solution — something that goes against everything I believe.

"Sweetie," I said, "do you think a little time might help?"

I had never, in my entire career, *tried* to put someone in jail, but I had also never had someone whose mental health and addiction problems were as intractable as Cassandra's. Downwind, Cassandra seemed to consider the question seriously, and there was a long pause before she answered.

"Yes, David," she said, "I think so — maybe two or three weeks, a month maybe, just to clean up, to sleep."

The idea filled me with self-loathing and a profound sense of failure — personal and systemic. It was bad enough that there might not be any better solution than locking Cassandra up at Rikers Island, but worse was that *she* could see it as a viable solution to her life's problems. I felt tears welling up in my eyes.

"Is there anything you need right now?" I asked.

"Maybe some soup?" Cassandra said simply. "I'm a little cold."

Raiding the food usually kept for the hungry kids in the youth program, I found a can of Wolfgang Puck's egg noodle and chicken soup — a fancy last supper in a can.

With Cassandra considering a jail stint, I started thinking about just how to get her in. I needed to think of a crime minor enough that I could control the outcome, but serious enough that a cop who might not otherwise want to arrest a malodorous homeless person (rather than just issue a summons) would actually have to take her in.

First I considered a ploy I learned from another homeless guy who used to come through the system at the beginning of almost every winter. When it got too cold and too hard to survive on the street, he'd take himself to a rib joint near Times Square — and order himself a feast. He'd eat slowly and deliberately, savoring his meal. When the check came, he would quietly but insistently refuse to pay or leave. When the police came, he was unfailingly polite, standing up and placing his hands dutifully behind his back so they could cuff him. When he saw the judge, he'd always plead guilty right on the spot despite his lawyer's attempts to keep him from doing so — sometimes even asking for a little extra jail time, just enough to ride out the worst of the winter.

Sadly, there wasn't any place Cassandra really wanted to eat, and she was so smelly and disheveled there wasn't any place likely to serve her anyway.

"Is there something you'd like to do since you are going to get arrested anyway? Any crime that might at least bring you some joy?"

"No, David," Cassandra said in her flat, vacant tone. "I'll do what you say."

Maybe turnstile jumping is the way, I thought.

"Okay, we'll go down to the train station together," I told her. "I'll find a police officer and try to explain that he needs to watch because you are going to violate the law. And then when I say so, but not before, you try to climb over the turnstile."

Cassandra just nodded.

Just before we set out, I went over the pre-arrest checklist.

"You know they're going to search you when you get arrested," I warned her, "so I want you to go through all your pockets right now and make absolutely sure that there is nothing in them that can get you in any extra trouble — it's really important that we don't have any surprises."

Digging around in one of her many pockets, Cassandra came up with a small, round chipped piece of glass. The crack pipe was short — around three inches long and about the width of the barrel of a ballpoint pen. The end was blackened and sticky from the flame and the tarry residue of crack, the rest smudgy but transparent.

"I think we'll need to throw this away, sweetie." I sighed.

After rummaging through the rest of her pockets, Cassandra came up empty — seventeen cents and some rough deli-counter napkins, all she had left in the world.

"Cassandra, I want you to think really, really carefully now — have you been arrested since I saw you last, or have you gotten any tickets that you were supposed to go to court for but didn't? Are there any warrants out for your arrest for any reason at all?"

A long pause.

"I think I got some tickets," Cassandra said, nodding.

"Do you remember what they were for?"

"For loitering and having an open beer, I think, and maybe one for sleeping in the park."

"Did you give them your actual name?" I asked, suddenly seeing a perfect way out of the whole problem.

"Yes, David."

Ten minutes later, I was on the telephone with an incredulous sergeant at the Bronx Warrant Squad.

"You're her lawyer?" he asked.

"Yes."

"And you want us to come and arrest her?"

"Right."

"You don't want to turn her in voluntarily?"

"Right — she's here now, and if we wait until tomorrow, I'm likely to lose her to the streets again."

"And she knows she's gonna be arrested?"

"Yes. That's what we want."

"And you want me to call you when she's in court?"

"Right. And make sure that the lawyer doing her arraignment tomorrow gets the letter that I'm going to give her."

"Okay, Counselor, you got it. Gimee your address and I'll send a team over."

"Thanks, Sergeant. I appreciate it."

"Be about twenty minutes."

"Perfect. Thanks."

Hanging up the phone, I turned back to Cassandra.

"What medications do you need and in what dosages do you need them?"

"Ah . . . I'm not on my medication, David."

"I know, Cassandra . . . but when you get to the jail, they are going to put you back on them. That's the point."

"Ooooh . . . okay," Cassandra said slowly, then listed the particular drugs and specific dosages she should have been taking. After jotting all of it down, I headed upstairs and typed out a quick letter to accompany Cassandra on her journey through the system — a letter I hoped would ensure that at the very least she'd get her medications and that I'd be notified before she saw a judge. I printed three copies — two for Cassandra (in case she lost one) and one for the detectives.

The Warrant Squad arrived as promised. There were three of them — one African American man and two white guys — all big and muscular with cold gazes. I led them to the courtyard and introduced them to Cassandra. I explained that we'd decided that she needed to spend a few weeks in jail and that I'd hoped that they'd help me out by making sure that when she got to court her attorney got the letter I'd prepared. The African American cop offered to take the letter. "It has a list of the medications she needs, my home and cell numbers, and a specific request that the judge set five hundred dollars' bail and adjourn the case for two weeks," I told him.

"Counselor," one of the white detectives said, "your client . . . ah . . . she knows we're gonna have to cuff her, right?"

I told him we knew.

Just before the white guy reached for his cuffs, the African American detective interrupted. Turning slightly away from his colleagues, he leaned close. "You know they're gonna search her when we get to the precinct — are we okay or do you need a minute to, ahh, talk to her?"

I smiled up at him, grateful for his decency. "We're okay," I told him. "Already took care of it — we're good to go."

"Okay, Counselor," he said, nodding to the others. "Thanks."

"Ms. Stallings, could you turn around please?"

Cassandra stood up, put her hands behind her back, palms out, thumbs touching, and waited to be handcuffed.

"B-Bye, David," she said, and then, seeing the look on my face, she added, "it's okay, I'll see you tomorrow. Thank you, David." And with that she was gone.

Today, I realize as I sip my coffee, is the day Cassandra comes out.

—➤◄—

Every morning it's the same — up the West Side Highway past the procession of cars stuck in traffic streaming toward midtown, across Harlem, along the ridge at the top of Sugar Hill, and eventually down a long viaduct and across the Macomb's Dam Bridge into the Bronx.

Three clients and three murders are going to start my day. One of them is certain to be my next trial. I just don't know which one. A hint would be nice.

All three homicides are pending before the same judge, and having them together allows me to get a sense of which prosecutors are pushing for a trial, how the judge sees each one, what I can expect. All of this will help me prioritize. Having all three on the same day also means that I can spend some time in the pens with each client. And so, as the 155th Street cemetery glides by, surrounded by an army of trucks crammed with movie equipment, I make mental notes on each case to be sure I won't forget anything later.

Just past the cemetery, from the top of Sugar Hill, the Bronx spreads out below me. Yankee Stadium, abandoned for the winter, dominates the landscape. Above it, perched on the Grand Concourse, its golden windows shimmering in the winter light, I can make out the Supreme Court building, home to all three of this morning's murders.

The Bronx is a world unto itself. Known, like Watts or Cabrini Green, as much for its crime rate, violence, and poverty as anything else, the Bronx is amazingly diverse: from the palaces of Riverdale to the working-class neighborhoods near the Whitestone Bridge, there are parts of the borough that utterly defy the stereotypes. Take a drive through the very northern edge of the

Bronx, where it fades seamlessly into Yonkers, and you'd think you had stumbled into Dublin — you'll find pubs filled with rowdy locals watching soccer, stores filled with Irish delicacies, and accents so thick they are almost incomprehensible. Similar enclaves exist in other areas too. The fabled Italian restaurants of Arthur Avenue, in the heart of Belmont, are surrounded by the kind of small butchers, fishmongers, and fruit stands you might find in Tuscany or Palermo. And it's not just the ethnically ghettoized enclaves that persist. City Island, a small strip of land connected to the rest of the Bronx by a long, narrow bridge, sports marinas and clam shacks that could fool you into believing you were in a New England fishing village. In huge swaths of the Bronx, Jamaicans, Dominicans, Italians, Irish, and African Americans live side by side in comfortable, stable neighborhoods.

But not down south. From Mott Haven to Hunts Point, from Morrisania to Castle Hill, there is much of the Bronx that really does reek of the violence, pestilence, and poverty of stereotypical urban decay.

As you drive south on the Bruckner Expressway, away from Westchester and the ever-greener neighborhoods and suburbs above, toward the heart of the industrial South Bronx, on your left, just before the Colgate Scaffold yard, you'll see the hulking cement-frame towers of the Soundview Houses. Built a half-century ago, Soundview is one of the most violent housing projects in the Bronx. Cut off from the main bulk of the Bronx by the highway, Soundview is a study in contrasts: neat single-family houses occupied by solidly middle-class folks push up against the rat-infested projects of the immobile underclass. It's a place where the successful people are drug dealers or sanitation workers rather than corporate tycoons or investment bankers, and it sits just ten miles from the skyscrapers of midtown Manhattan, a place many residents have never even visited.

I know the projects pretty well, and since one of the crimes I'm dealing with today took place there, I've been thinking about them a lot. I've represented some local celebrities, and walking around the hulking buildings, I'm likely to be recognized. "Yo, you was my lawyer!" is a common refrain, and "Hey, you Bemo's lawyer, right?" is a close second. Kevin Bethea, known around the neighborhood as "Bemo," was a Soundview legend. He had a rap sheet that ran to thirty pages and a crack addiction to which he had completely surrendered. He was bald, with the thin, resilient frame of a man who has spent many homeless nights seeking shelter in out-of-the-way places. A scar covered half his forehead — either the result of a gunshot or a close encounter with a jar full of lye.

Bemo was a notorious gangster in his youth, but crack turned him into a charming but perennially petty criminal. He was single-handedly responsible for most of the neighborhood's car break-ins, and, as with so much in the projects, everyone knew it. But there was something compelling about him. A detective I know told me that he once saw Bemo walking down the street with a few car radios that still had the wires hanging out of them. Bemo walked over to the detective's car, carefully put the radios down, and put up his hands in an exaggerated gesture of surrender: "Okay, Garcia, you got me again." He was so funny about it the detective couldn't bring himself to arrest him.

"Go, Bemo," he ordered, "and get rid of that shit before someone you can't charm comes along."

Bemo was gunned down two weeks after I got him out of jail for the fifth time. A citizen with a rifle, uncharmed by his antics, shot him in the head as he broke into yet another car, trying to steal yet another radio. Unlike the other times he'd been shot, this one was fatal.

When I'd first heard about the shooting, I was terrified that Bemo would be buried in Potter's Field — the massive paupers' grave often tended by inmates from Rikers Island. He had, so far as I know, no relatives in New York. But for the anonymity, such a lonesome cemetery might have been a fitting place for Bemo — surrounded by so many others from the neighborhood who had no one to claim them, no one even to identify their remains, his unmarked grave watched over by the guarded gardeners of Rikers Island.

But Bemo wasn't destined for Potter's Field at all. Within the tiny world circumscribed by the sweep of the Soundview Oval, a

U-shaped drive flanked by drably identical project buildings, Bemo was a kind of hero. For days after he was shot, kids — for some reason it was mostly kids — swarmed through the tall project buildings with buckets, collecting dollar bills and spare change to cover the funeral home bill. And within hours of his body being carted away for evidence, a shrine went up at the corner of Randall and Rosedale, across the street from the little ghetto grocery store — a favored hangout of hustlers and drunks.

The shrine was a cardboard box cut in two, with Polaroid pictures of Bemo taped to or propped next to it. One could see Bemo when he was young, mean, and gangstery, or when he was older, the small, scarred bald head cocked slightly to the side, his bright, dancing eyes sizing up the camera. There were flowers too, huge stacks of cheap deli flowers, their dyed blooms fading in the afternoon sun. And candles, of course — nearly two dozen of the colored votive candles the Dominicans love, lit for peace or serenity or safe travels — faded decals of second-tier saints curling off the glass as they flickered down to nothingness.

The Oritz Funeral Home on Soundview Avenue is a dingy building crammed amid the jumble and decay of the neighborhood. Ortiz does a brisk and unusually young business — ODs and murder victims, slain gangsters and kids caught in the cross fire. The expertise helped: I'd never seen Bemo looking so peaceful as he did lying in the casket in his prom-style tux, his small, twitchy face smoothed to a consistent, if waxy, pallor, his hands crossed demurely over his chest. The brutal fury of the bullets — their entry into and exit from his body — was nowhere in sight.

I spoke at Bemo's funeral, as I had so many times in court, my brief remarks sandwiched amid the testimonials of family and friends, former drug addicts, and recent crime partners, all celebrating a life — regularly violent, certainly criminal, and often tragic — led entirely within the confines of the projects.

The cops, keeping a respectful distance, watched the comings and goings closely, shooting me a quizzical look when I stopped near the shrine for a moment of reflection. Two reporters were circling, looking to understand the strange phenomenon of a beloved neighborhood thief. Their questions betrayed an ele-

mental confusion, the same one that pervades the criminal justice system — how can a criminal actually be good?

This is a question that surfaces almost every time I talk
about my work.

"He's a thief!" my friend Diana said to me once, her blond
curls bouncing slightly. "Doesn't that creep you out just a little
bit?" We were standing in a crowded SoHo bar in the middle of
an otherwise restrained birthday celebration. I was about
halfway through my third glass of overpriced, mediocre
Cabernet when I'd mentioned Bemo.

"I mean, how can you actually like them?" she persisted.

"They're people, Di," I replied, wondering for perhaps the
thousandth time why being a lawyer for the poor somehow
anointed me ambassador for the despised. "They have lives
and wives and loves just as poignant and real and compelling
as yours."

"Well, I don't go around robbing people," she sniffed as I
managed a wan smile and changed the subject.

For some reason when it comes to my indigent ghetto clients,
it becomes easy to forget that people, including those who break
the law, are complicated and often charming. That they too contain multitudes. Oddly, no one has trouble understanding the
humanity of white crooks. We mythologize them all the time —
Bonnie and Clyde, John Gotti, Carolyn Warmus — all are complex people we find ways to relate to and even admire. At the
movies we cheer for Butch and Sundance, Scarface, or *Ocean's
Eleven* crew. The fact that John Gotti was a ruthless killer who
wreaked havoc on far more lives than any of my clients ever
touched never eclipses the public memory of him as big, handsome, and defiant. People loved Gotti's resistance to governmental authority. But put a black face on Gotti and no matter how
dapper a don he is, the press, the prosecutors, and the public
only read menace. I've often represented people as "big," "handsome," and "defiant" as John Gotti, yet when I invoke the
humanity of these faceless robbers and killers, it sends most listeners from the land of mere confusion to that of utter incomprehension. To this day, I wrestle with where this understanding

goes off the rails. Fundamentalist Christians constantly speak passionately about seeing the possibility of redemption in everyone, and no one bats an eye. But make this same point in the secular context of the criminal justice system, and rather than praiseworthy piety it is heard as liberal gibberish.

⟶⟵

As I pull up to the office, pondering Bemo and Soundview and today's murder cases, I glide past boarded-up buildings and carefully tended community gardens: a world of cracks in the wall.

There used to be plenty of street parking on the block around our office, but as we've grown, parking has become more and more scarce. The real problem is that there is only one marginally safe block to park on if you want to have any assurance that your windows will be intact when it's time to go home. Our building sits on Courtlandt Avenue between 160th and 161st Street, and while our block of Courtlandt is well traveled, the rear of the building — the one that abuts 160th — is a strip of vacant lots, burned-out buildings, and community gardening projects. It's not often used and, as a result, is an invitation to the crackheads who often wander down it looking for cans to recycle or, not infrequently, an easy radio to poach.

As usual, I'm late, so I'll have to trust my car to the gods or demons of 160th Street. With a bad parking spot, I figure my chances of being broken into are about one in forty. Over the years, I've had my windows smashed, my radio stolen, and my side-view mirrors swiped. For a while, Robin Steinberg, my boss and friend, had the turn signals from her Volvo stolen almost weekly. (It turns out that you can just pop the blinkers out of a Volvo and resell them to a parts place for $30 each. They're $170 new, and the places that buy them hot resell them for $50 or $60, often to the victims of the theft.)

I finally make it through the door and into our cheery reception area at about three minutes after ten. When clients walked into my old office at the Legal Aid Society in Brooklyn they were greeted by a thick grease-smeared sheet of bulletproof Plexiglas — and if they were lucky, a frustrated receptionist behind it. The clients, of course, are used to this; everywhere they go — welfare, housing, parole, SSI — they get crappy injection-molded chairs, bulletproof Plexi, and the kind of service that wouldn't be tolerated at a ghetto McDonald's. At the Bronx Defenders, by contrast, from 8:00 A.M. to 6:00 P.M. clients are greeted by our receptionists Lorraine and Jennifer — and, consistent with the philosophy of the office, not from behind Plexiglas. Instead, one of them is sitting at a curved modern desk in a cool waiting room strewn with children's toys and comfortable couches. Both women are bilingual and unceasingly chipper, professional, and cool.

Unlike the Legal Aid Society, the Bronx Defenders is a relatively small public defender office. With about thirty-five lawyers and a few dozen social workers, investigators, support staff, and interns, the office is responsible for handling about 12,500 criminal cases a year. Most of the staff are divided into interdisciplinary teams presided over by a senior lawyer known as a "team leader." Other than Robin, the founder and executive director, there are only two lawyers who aren't officially on a specific team — the legal director and the trial chief. Florian Miedel, a former appeals lawyer whose Teutonic good looks often prompt "golden boy" jokes, is the legal director. Miedel is responsible for the technical, legal side of the work — motions, legal briefs, and legal arguments. I'm the trial chief, providing guidance on handling complex cases and help with trial tactics and techniques. I'm about the facts; Florian is about the law. Florian helps the lawyers win before judges; I help them win before juries.

Heading past the reception area and through the lunchroom on the way to my office, I run into Branford.

"Wassup, Feige?" he says, giving me a street handshake and a warm hug. He's decked out in shiny black shoes, a perfectly pressed white shirt, and nicely tailored slacks. The only hint of his past is the thick gold chain around his finely sculpted neck.

Branford was fourteen when he swallowed the bullets, .22-caliber rifle shells — live, long, and lethal. Branford was running with an older crew then, selling drugs, robbing people, and running the streets. The shells matched a sawed-off that the crew had ditched just after a shooting not far from one of the most violent spots in Soundview — a blood-bathed strip of pavement perched at the top of the Oval at the intersection of Randall and Rosedale Avenues, and referred to by the neighborhood kids as Kozy Korner.

When the cops had rolled up, Branford had the bullets in his jacket pocket. So as the cops worked their way down the long line of kids, tossing one after the next, Branford, with a furtive look to his left, slid the bullets from his inside pocket and started downing them. It worked: they pinched another kid for the gun. Branford walked.

The X-rays were pretty astonishing — five rounds of live ammunition working their way through the duodenum of a fourteen-year-old boy. Even in the overcrowded emergency room overflowing with gunshot wounds and accident victims, the attending physician called the residents together to admire the film. "It was a dare," Branford explained, opening wide his transfixing eyes. "I just wanted to win the bet." The assembled doctors nodded, credulously accepting his explanation. *Stranger things have happened in the Bronx,* they probably thought to themselves.

A laxative and twenty-four hours later, Branford was back on the streets. The other kid wasn't so lucky. He spent about a year in jail for a crime he didn't commit. When you grow up in the Soundview projects, that's the kind of lesson you learn, usually the hard way: the kids who'll swallow metal walk; the ones who freeze go to jail.

Branford understood this. He was fearless, itinerant, and lethal. In time, though, the life catches up to you. Like virtually everyone else in the game, Branford eventually went to prison.

Once released, Branford came to work at the Bronx Defenders, devoted to the idea that he, unlike so many of his brothers from the street, was never, ever going back. Almost all ex-cons start out this way. Jimmy Seelandt, another ex-inmate we hired, did well for almost a year before lapsing back into addiction. By the end of his second summer of freedom, Jimmy was dead, a needle in his arm.

Freedom is tough.

In a certain way, it's only the worst, most successful criminals that ever have a chance to make it in the straight world. The transition is so alienating, the cultural transformation so complete, that only those with unimaginable willpower really stand a chance. The temptations are everywhere, the signals are constantly crossed, and restraint has to replace reflex in a way few can manage. When quick thinking and violent reactions often save your life, it's hard to hold your fist, let alone your tongue.

Branford, though, has made it more than five years, and though it hasn't always been easy and he still has moments of thuggish stupidity — mostly in inappropriate clothing choices (it was years before we got him to surrender the huge, golden faux-diamond-encrusted hand-grenade pendant) and his religious insistence on driving a fancy car that he can't really afford (it's what he always dreamed about in prison) — Branford has actually succeeded in making the shift.

"What you got today, Feige?"

"The usual shit," I tell him. "Three murders in Moge's part though."

"Yeah?"

"Yeah — and Clarence's one of 'em," I tell him.

Branford knows Clarence. Everyone in Soundview knows everyone.

Clarence Watkins is charged with murdering Shamar Hardy. Clarence was raised in 1715 Randall Avenue, two buildings away from the crack house where Bemo slept. He has a handsome, elegant face set off with big, expressive eyes. He is utterly innocent.

Number 1715 is one of the hulking buildings arrayed around the Soundview Oval. Clarence lives on the second floor, down a dirty, poorly lit hallway, in an apartment he shares with his mother. Clarence is not a particularly magnetic guy, but he's not particularly offensive either. He doesn't do drugs or run with gangs. He is sweet, shy, and almost demure. He knows the neighbors in the casual way of those who have lived in the same building for years. Clarence, though, as almost everyone who knows him will tell you, doesn't talk much. He prefers to keep his own company.

At thirty-seven years old, he has lived in Soundview for nearly his entire life.

Though a hustler for a short time in his youth, Clarence had pretty much avoided trouble as an adult. He'd joined the navy, and after his service, when he couldn't find a job, he'd gone to Israel to proselytize. That didn't work out so well, and after about eight months he returned to New York and to Soundview, where he was slowly working his way through college, holding down various jobs to get money for classes, and getting good grades.

Until he was arrested and charged with murder.

A semiautomatic .380 is a small but deadly weapon. Petite enough to fit in the palm of a large hand, the .380 may not have the stopping power of a larger-bore handgun, but it is often more effective. When you divorce bullets and bodies from the pain and loss and suffering, the former causes the latter — weapon choice becomes a complicated compromise between stealth and lethality. In the Bronx, it's not easy to sneak up on someone with a huge .44 Magnum in your hand — and certainly not if they're also armed or anxious. The gun is just too big. A .44, and even its slightly smaller cousins, the 9mm, .357, or .45, is also likely to raise police suspicion.

A .380, by contrast, is a weapon of stealth. Easily concealable and capable of firing more rounds than a standard police revolver, a .380 has a reputation on the streets as a perfect mixture of small and dangerous. Generally lacking the power to fly completely through a body, smaller caliber bullets will often bounce around inside those unfortunate enough to be shot by them. The bullets are slowed by tissue and deflected by bones, and the wound tracks left by a .380 or its smaller cousins, the .22 and the .25, are often tangled freeways of physical destruction. This is especially true when a little slug winds up in someone's head. The thick carapace of bone in the skull will absorb so much energy that the bullet can't escape. The result: a deflection off the other side of the skull and scrambled brains as the bullet ricochets inside the skull cavity. Not surprisingly, mothers and doctors hate small-caliber weapons.

It was a .380 that killed Shamar Hardy in December of 2002. He was gunned down inside the cramped lobby of 1715 Randall Avenue — four feet from the mailboxes, eight from the elevator. The building lobby, like most in the projects, was built small, the architecture of low-income housing dictating that common areas be intentionally hard to hang out in. The foyer was barely large enough for four people to stand in, and when Shamar's dead body came to rest there, it stretched half the distance from the vestibule doors to the elevators. Shamar took six shots: five to the body, one to the head. Shell casings were sprinkled around like metallic potpourri. His clothing soaked up much of the blood.

When the police came, just minutes after the shooting, the shooter was long gone. Knocking on doors, they got nowhere. The crime scene unit came up with nothing other than some spent shells. No one would admit to having seen anything. There were rumors that a couple of people had been seen running from the crime scene, but no one could provide much information, or if they could, they wouldn't. That wasn't terribly surprising to the night-watch detectives who showed up well after EMS had carted Shamar's body away. In the projects, no one sees anything, or at least few people say they do. The fact that local drug dealers live by their own rules, and often die by their rivals' guns, is a matter for gossip and speculation, but not, in most cases, court testimony.

Edmundo Rulans was drinking the night of the shooting. He and Mary, a friend who also lived in the building, had gone through several forty-ounce beers before hearing the shots. Edmundo isn't the most stable of people — even according to his wife, he's drunk much of the time, medicated nearly all of the time, and what she calls "very imaginative." Still, what he told the police set everything in motion: "I saw Clarence shoot Shamar." Those five words put Edmundo Rulans in the middle of a murder prosecution and sent Clarence Watkins to jail.

Edmundo's statement to the detectives, made a week after the shooting and a week before he himself was busted for drugs, was the only thing that linked Clarence to the murder. The police, though, didn't need anything else. Clarence Watkins was arrested and charged with Shamar Hardy's murder.

There are times as a public defender when you can just smell innocence. It's easy to spot weak cases or tenuous legal theories, and the naive among us regularly have the waft of innocence in their nose to begin with. But when you've been a public defender for a long time, the smell of innocence is rare and unwelcome. Clarence reeked of it.

Defending the guilty is easy. Not all clients are classically pleasant, of course. Some are defiant, others pathetic, some terribly needy, others inalterably enamored of the gangster life. But every client has a story — not a story about the crime or charges, but a life story that is by turns tragic, compelling, and unique — and getting to know clients makes them easy to defend. It's easy to want to protect someone you know from the horror of prison — even if they've done something criminal.

But God help you when you have those innocent kids. Nothing good can happen when you represent an innocent client. If you beat the case or the client is acquitted, it is precisely what everyone expects — no joy there, just the relief associated with avoiding a terrible injustice. And if you lose, the case haunts you, so that in the middle of the night and until sunrise you wonder what you did wrong, what you forgot, what you could have said or done — how such a thing could have happened. It is a searing, guilty pain that can last for years, if not forever. It's the innocent ones that drive you out of the work.

It is precisely this problem that leads many criminal defense lawyers to shut out questions of guilt or innocence. The responsibility for the innocent can simply be too much. Sometimes it's better not even to wonder.

When Clarence sat down across the battered table from me in arraignments, not far from the stinking cells that hold the dozens of people waiting to see a judge for the first time, I knew this was going to be one of those "God help me" cases. It wasn't his rap sheet that made me think he was innocent — he was a twice-convicted felon. And it wasn't the strength of his defense either: "I was at home with my mother when the shooting happened" is one of the worst defenses imaginable. Everyone believes that family will lie to protect family, so jurors never believe the "I was at home with my mother" stuff. Often it's better not even to introduce it. This is especially true when being at home puts you thirty seconds from the scene of a homicide.

Still, I believed Clarence almost immediately, and as I sat there, the woozy fear set in.

It was because Clarence smelled so innocent that I began to think for the first time since Gillian Sands that a grand jury would toss a murder charge. It wouldn't be easy, but it seemed like a risk worth taking.

A grand jury story is like tissue paper — gossamer thin and nearly translucent. When done right it explains the client's innocence and lets the jurors see the person inside. When done wrong, it's a thunderously painful disaster. Take, for instance, Alonzo.

"I'm gonna tell 'em my side, yo!" Alonzo sputtered in the midst of a vitriol-laden tirade in which he attacked my legal acumen, impugned my manhood, and suggested rather stridently that I was seeking to "get paid" by pleading him guilty.

"Ah, right, Alonzo."

"*My* side!"

There was something almost charming in his furious predictability, the way he'd roll his eyes when I'd come upstairs to the pens to visit. The way he'd swagger his way into the interview room as if by sitting down with me he was doing me a huge favor. The way he'd snort before I'd even opened my mouth, as if to say, *I gotta listen to your damn fool nonsense again?* In fact, I could barely get past a friendly hello before he'd unleash a generous stream of invective concerning my "bullshit cocksucking cop-out bullshit" (Alonzo was never one to skimp on repetition).

Alonzo didn't want to be in jail, and despite my counsel he had decided that the best way to go free was to testify in the grand jury. Any attempt to suggest that this might not be such a grand idea prompted an inventive concatenation of curse words, which, simply translated, meant: "I'd prefer not to heed your advice."

My advice, though, was based on the fact that Alonzo seemed to believe that his simply not *wanting* to be in jail constituted an effective legal defense to the robbery charges he was facing.

"Alonzo," I had said patiently, steering clear of the cocksucking cop-out bullshit, "you can do whatever you choose. If you want to testify in the grand jury, I'll make sure you can, but it's really important that you at least tell me what you're going to say, so I can help you prepare."

Alonzo looked at me as if I was speaking Latvian: "I'm gonna tell 'em my side, yo," he said simply.

"Right, Alonzo, I get that, but what *is* your side?"

"It's. My. Side. Yo."

"Right, but what is it? What *is* your side of the story?"

"I just told you, fool — it's MY SIDE!"

"Okay, so try to tell *me* your side, just like you would in the grand jury."

Alonzo rolled his eyes. "Yo, I ain't got time for your damn foolness," he said as if rather than being in jail, he had a packed social schedule. "I'm going to the grand jury, an I'm gonna tell 'em my side."

I tried one last time: "*Right,* but what is *the essence, the point, the story,* if you will, that constitutes your side?" I asked, thinking maybe, just maybe, he'd get it.

Alonzo fixed me with a withering stare: "It's *my side,* yo," he said simply.

We never got beyond this impasse. Two days later, sitting in front of twenty-three grand jurors, Alonzo said, "I'm here to tell you my side. I got a damn fool lawyer who don't tell me shit, and I don't even know why I'm here."

The grand jurors weren't impressed. They indicted.

At least I knew what Clarence's side of the story was: he was at home, upstairs with his mother, when Shamar was murdered. Moreover, I believed it. There was something else too. Because grand jury cases are so abbreviated, likability plays an important role — often a far greater role than at a trial. And Clarence (unlike Alonzo) was, in my view, very likable.

Apparently not likable enough, though. The grand jury indicted him too. And because of that indictment, Clarence is facing a murder trial today.

Reaching my office, I drop my bag, hang up my coat, and log in to the computer. I have ten unread e-mails and, according to my phone, four new voice mails. The cheap clock across from me, a relic from my old office, reads 10:08 A.M.

Three

NIKKI CALLS.

Nikki is tall, slender, and almost model beautiful, with deep brown eyes and a face the color of wet sandstone. She's almost twenty now and still as fresh-faced as the day I met her — a sixteen-year-old girl charged with murder.

"Hi, David," she says in her naive, singsongy voice.

Nikki is calling just to be sure she's not going back to jail when she comes to court next month. She spent almost a year and a half at Rikers Island before I got her out, and even though I explain that she's pretty much done all the time she's going to do, she gets understandably nervous before each court date. I remind her that eventually she will have to step back into a prison cell for a few weeks so that she can then be officially released on parole — but not this time.

"Promise?" she asks me.

"Promise," I say definitively. Then we hang up.

From the moment I walk into my office until the time I shut out the lights in the evening, the phone is always ringing. It's been like this for years. Whether I was in Brooklyn, Harlem, or the Bronx, the pace of inquiring phone calls has been just as relentless.

"What are my chances on appeal?"

"Is there an offer on my case?"

"My son just got arrested."

"You a shitty lawyer! You ain't done shit on my case."

Most of the hours I'm not in court or out in the field investigating are filled with responding to stuff like this. Some clients are constant callers, while others never call at all — either they're content to show up in court and deal with their fate, or unable to muster the juice it takes to get to the gang-controlled phones at Rikers Island. (In many of the facilities at Rikers each gang controls a particular telephone, and lonely inmates longing for a friendly voice must either be aligned with a particular gang that controls a phone — the Bloods, Nietas, or Latin Kings — hustle to get access to one of the very few nonaligned phones, or pay a gang member dearly for the privilege.)

LeShawn Jones was one of those rare inmates who had no problem getting to the phone at Rikers Island, but he had no one to call when he did. The result of that strange coincidence was the series of calls that eventually yielded my old nickname at the Legal Aid Society: Mista Fudge.

I represented LeShawn in a gun case. There was little that was unusual about it, other than LeShawn himself — a client who literally couldn't get over the fact that somehow he found himself in jail. As sweet as he was, our attorney-client relationship never really developed beyond a constant conversation about his continuing incarceration. His calls were so relentless and so tragic that LeShawn eventually became a legend in the office. Here's how it went.

"Hello. David Feige."

There was a short electronic beep — indicating that the call from Rikers had been connected. And then, with no preamble at all, LeShawn's voice would come tumbling out as if he'd been holding his breath, waiting for the beep, ready to explode with the revelation he'd just had.

"Mista Fudge, it's LeShawn Jones. I'm in jail, Mista Fudge. I'm in JAIL!"

"I know that, LeShawn," I'd say evenly. "You've been in jail for five months already."

"Mista Fudge, please." His whereabouts seemed to be a source of continuously pained astonishment.

"Yes, LeShawn."

"I'M IN JAIL, MISTA FUDGE. IN JAIL!"

"Right, LeShawn."

"MISTA FUDGE, I'M IN JAIL!" LeShawn would shift his emphasis from *I'm* to *in* to *jail* as if this recombination might better convey the magnitude of his suffering.

"I. Am. In. Jail! Mista Fudge. *IN. JAIL.*"

"What would you like me to do?" I'd say, feebly aware that there was little I could do to help him come to terms with his predicament.

Frustrated, he'd hang up, only to call two hours later with the same startled realization.

"I'm in jail, Mista Fudge. *In Jail!*"

My colleagues noticed this telephonic ritual, and eventually, over the months and the dozens of identical conversations, LeShawn became a macabre joke, an embodiment of the deep pathos churned up by the justice system. His calls were eventually transferred to speakerphone as a small crowd of amazed young public defenders gathered around to hear him say his magic, tragic words. As for me, forevermore Mista Fudge it would be.

By the time I'm done with Nikki and the accumulated e-mails it's 10:25 A.M. and I'm already absurdly late for court, and just as I start to get moving the phone rings again.

It's Alvin. He needs to ask me for the twenty-fifth time about his upcoming sentencing. Harsher than I should be, I tell him I can't talk and if he needs more reassurance he'll need to call me at four. He keeps talking, and I put him on speakerphone while I head toward the two rows of hooks behind my office door.

I loathe suits. But with Alvin still on the phone, I grab a vaguely frayed chalk-striped suit, and what I hope will be a matching tie, and do the quick change, leaving my jeans in a crumpled heap under the desk. Pulling a plain blue cotton oxford over my head, I tune back in to Alvin. He is still talking, having segued into a story I've heard a dozen times about why he needs a note from me to show to someone else so that person can write a note to a third person who will help him get a non-driver's-license ID, which he can use to get another document, which in turn has something to do with his SSI benefits. His is a complicated life, one I've been dealing with for more than six years, but this morning, like most mornings, I can't give Alvin the answer he's looking for, and so, having let him fulminate for three or four minutes, I finally say the only thing that works: finger poised above the speakerphone button, I say as calmly as I can, "Alvin, I love you, but I'm hanging up now. Call me at four."

On goes the jacket. Down goes the finger.

Click.

→·←

It's a ten-minute walk to court — out through our library, past a small white table filled with lawyers and social workers talking in hushed tones to huddled clients and their concerned families, past Lillian in her usual spot, clutching the plastic bag of grimy papers that she sorts and resorts almost every day, sitting alone at a table at the end of the lunchroom. "Hi, Lil." I smile as I go by her, heading toward the door. "Hi, Dave," she says haltingly, eyes darting around the room — guarding her precious papers. And finally past the reception area, where two kids in matching red do-rags and desultory looks lounge on a couch in affected tough-guy poses.

Outside, just up the block, I pass the Gaseteria, with its oil-caked pavement and rickety pumps, and the weird car lot where Robin and I parked for a while after the weekly turn-signal thefts began.

I usually make the hike to or from court at least twice a day, sometimes more often, and it's the rare day that I don't pass someone I know — someone like Ms. M., whose kids are almost always in jail. I've represented two of the three and helped out on her third son's case. Every time I see her she gives me updates: this one's coming home, that one just got a little sentence, the third has been taken by the feds. She's a sweet woman and loves those boys, and I tell her to send them my love and then continue up the block past Frank, a former client, who is selling incense on the corner.

José, with his two blue Latin King teardrop tattoos, waves from a car, shouting to me that he's doing good — gone legit, working construction and raising his son. He smiles and gives me the thumbs-up. I'm not sure whether he's legit or not, but with his record, any new violent felony and he'd be facing a life sentence.

There are people lounging around the bodega across the street. Several kids, invariably attired in the street uniform of un-cannily clean clothes and immaculately maintained shoes, keep watch on the vestibule of the project building directly across from them, on my side of the street. The complex is called Morrisania II — as if it's the QE II's cheap housing-project cousin.

Next to the bodega, several large women jam themselves into what might arguably be the most cramped nail salon in the known world: Honey Nails. Built into an embankment, more like a missile silo than a commercial establishment, Honey Nails sports unwashed windows plastered with faded posters of outra-geously elaborate fingernail designs. Though I've seen people inside, I have yet to see anyone enter or emerge.

I'm nearly two blocks from the office.

Almost every time I cross Morris Avenue I have a pang of nostalgia for the old Bronx Defender offices. Built in a renovated ice factory, they felt like a massive, superhip downtown loft. With its thirty-foot ceilings and totally open floor plan, "the Ice House" (as it was known) was dreamily spartan and chic — a message to clients and staff alike: this is no ordinary public de-fender office. Sadly, the Ice House lasted less than three years. In a generally unnoticed bit of irony, it was demolished to make way for a new courthouse.

The skeleton of that new courthouse stretches two full blocks now, and the humming of cranes and clanging of burly workmen using their hugely outsized wrenches to bolt I beams together masks the reggae music the guy selling pirated CDs is playing on a boom box powered by electricity conspicuously stolen from the adjacent lamppost. The block is always crowded: welfare, parole, and the Administration for Children's Services are all housed in the massive, dreary brown brick building that takes up the entire block across from the construction. As I weave between the people, my backpack or litigation bag barely avoiding collision, my brain takes in the snippets of almost invariably angry overheard conversation: "he cut me off . . ."; "waited there for four hours . . ."; "locked him up for bullshit . . ."; "he don't know shit."

The swirl of voices thins as I come alongside the tall black wrought-iron fence of the incongruous mall across from the criminal court building. The mall was where we started out. Eight of us, committed to creating a new kind of public defender office, opened the Bronx Defenders for business on September 1, 1997, in a tiny office sandwiched between the Radio Shack and the Rent-A-Center.

The "mall," of course, is not what most people who are used to seeing shopping centers imagine. There is no glistening glass. There are no elegant escalators. There are no department stores, no bookstores, no quaint jewelry carts in the middle of regularly swept corridors. The main mall attraction is a food court composed almost entirely of fast food — McDonald's, KFC, Arthur Treachers. There is one set of escalators that leads to the underground movie theater and only works sporadically. I once saw someone collapsed there on the immobile top step, still bleeding from a bullet wound.

The mall has a few other stores too, mostly down-at-the-heels retail joints selling low-grade electronics, sneakers, and knock-off jerseys. The biggest tenant by far, taking up one entire side of the open rectangle, is a grocery store, fully stocked with the culinary preferences of a predominantly immigrant community. On the other side is a vaguely linear crowd of about two dozen people.

They are waiting to see their probation officers.

⇒•⇐

Because I'm late, I quicken my pace. I hurry across the street and up the hill, past Twin Donut and the always-smiling shoe guy; past Farooque's sandwich shop, which is chock-full of annoying assistant DAs; and past the fraying offices of a few old-time criminal defense lawyers, until the majesty of the Supreme Court comes back into view.

Perched at the corner of the Grand Concourse and 161st Street, the imperious old Supreme Court Building still cuts an imposing figure. With its bas-relief elevator doors and cavernous courtrooms, the building evokes the majesty of a different era — both for justice and for the Bronx. It is 10:39 A.M. as I bluff my way through the attorneys' entrance, bypassing the snaking line of people at the metal detectors. Since September 11, attorneys are technically required to have a new high-security pass in order to avoid the line. In the intervening years, almost everyone complied, submitting to the indignity of a background check and registration, but like a few others, mostly the older or more radical lawyers who had been in the Bronx for years, I found the new requirements offensive — after all, they only applied to defense attorneys. Assistant district attorneys, clerks, court officers, and judges were exempt.

So I never bothered to get the new card but persisted in using the attorneys' line as if it were my God-given right. Usually I walk right in, though a few sergeants, knowing full well who I am, delight in the petty exercise of making me submit to the line and a nice, slow, thorough search.

Nestled in a corner of the fourth floor of the Supreme Court, part 20 is known rather cryptically as the "Standards and Goals" part — "Standards and Goals" being a neat court euphemism for "old case," "part" being just another term for courtroom. Once an incarcerated client has spent fourteen or fifteen months lolling around Rikers Island waiting for a trial, his case is likely to be shipped out to part 20. It's the fast track to trial, and all three of today's homicides are already there.

Inside, Judge William Mogulescu is likely to be exasperated, as usual. Mogulescu is fair and smart, but few lawyers please him. They all seem to be late, foolish, or unprepared. At just over six feet with a thick black mustache, he has the gaunt good looks and subtle dismissive wit of the lefty defense lawyer he used to be. Mogulescu is one of the few judges who wound up on the bench despite having represented radicals and protesters in many of the politically charged cases of the seventies and eighties. Named to the bench by Mayor David Dinkins (the first African American mayor of New York City), Moge is an artifact of New York City politics and an object lesson in the importance of judicial appointments. For years, many of the city's judges were hacks — overwhelmingly white, politically connected former prosecutors, they terrorized both defendants and the lawyers who appeared before them, meting out justice that was informed more by the code of the streets than by any actual legislation. They were, basically, crazy.

"All the Jews up against the wall!" That's what Judge Michael Curci once bellowed at a startled panel of jurors sitting patiently in his courtroom. Looking confusedly at one another, several men and women rose slowly from their seats. "You're all excused!" said Curci, his pale, flabby arm extended toward the exit from his courtroom. "All Jews, out!"

To Curci, a former Republican state senator, this was a matter of expediency and not anti-Semitism. A completely Looney Tunes jurist, with an Elmer Fudd face, a Casper the Ghost complexion, and a wisp of hair that seemed drawn out of his scalp, Curci was known for his utter unpredictability and his wonderfully inventive vocabulary. Court officers and stenographers assigned to his part kept a running glossary of his hilarious malapropisms and incomprehensible phrases, such as "dangerosity," "the psychic transmogrification of the Gestalt," or "assidulosity" — as in "I will sign your subpoenas with great assidulosity, Counselor!"

An old-school jurist, the kind that wound up on the bench by slipping the right person thirty-eight thousand dollars in an envelope, Curci read *Soldier of Fortune* with great assidulosity and loved nothing more than to play with guns. Once, during an attempted murder case, he famously instructed a court officer to hand him the alleged murder weapon. "I assume this is unloaded?" said Curci, jacking the slide commando-style and pointing the weapon in the direction of the defendant while half the courtroom ducked. "Uhhhh, I sure hope so, Judge," said a petrified ADA.

A beat as Curci considered.

Gazing at the gun longingly, he sighed. "This portends great dangerosity," he said, and then, handing the gun back to the stunned court officer, "Take this weapon back to the robbing room and discharge it if necessary."

What had set Curci off on his get-out-the-Jews rant was a succession of mild-mannered people patiently explaining that if they were to be chosen as jurors they'd need to be absent on the Jewish High Holidays. Curci apparently wished to work on Yom Kippur, and so, to minimize further delays by others with the same problem, he saw fit to order them all up against the wall.

As odd as he was about picking a jury, Curci was just as crazy without one. In one legendary case, Curci subjected a defendant who'd been foolish enough to waive a jury to a full-court mock deliberation. "If this were a jury trial, I'd instruct on self-defense," Curci reportedly told the defendant. Then he spun his high-backed chair toward the courtroom wall, leaped to his feet, and declared, "The record should reflect, I have now charged myself with self-defense." Plopping his squat little body back into his chair, he spun back around and faced the parties in the court-room. "I am now deliberating!" he said, swiveling round and round in his chair.

The prosecutor, defense lawyer, and defendant all watched as the plump judge switched directions and spun back the other way. Around and around he went. "I'm *still* deliberating!" Curci said merrily as the defendant waited tensely to find out if he was going to prison or not. The seconds ticked by while the court-room stared at him, agog. Finally Curci's chair ground to a halt. Cocking his head like a retriever who can't find a ball, he fixed the defendant with a solemn stare as he declared in his tinny little voice: "That's it. I'm hung. Send it out!"

Mogulescu is no Curci. And he is in part 20 for a reason. He hates excuses and browbeats lawyers into either trying cases or pleading them out — NOW. Mogulescu is one of my favorite judges. As difficult as he can be, he is unusually thoughtful and almost always fair. But he is also a big bully. Moge does what he does because he believes that you have to be a bully in the criminal justice system to get anything done. To his credit, it's also true that what he wants done is usually the right thing.

Years of my life have been spent navigating the dangerous reefs of a belligerent judiciary. Half of being a good lawyer is learning how to anticipate and cope with the idiosyncrasies of various judges: Darcel Clark, who can't stand being interrupted; Barbara Newman, who requires a soothing, confident tone; Joseph Dawson, whose hot button is tardiness; or old Muriel Hubsher, who just wants to have a nice chat about fashion before sentencing a client.

But while knowing judges' foibles is one thing, being immune to their vitriol is quite another. It's hard to stare down a judge. They have enormous power — not just to jail you but also, as my early encounter with Tona taught me, to hurt clients.

The result of this power is a constant deference that turns many judges into spoiled divas who can't stand even a hint of disrespect. Judge Carol Berkman once called me up in the middle of a hearing. "Mr. Feige," she said, "let me be perfectly clear — my life is a living hell, and one more question out of you and I'll make your life a living hell. Now shut up and step back." I was also there when Judge Edward Rappaport, once a silver-tongued dean of the Brooklyn defense bar, spewed, "Fuck you too" to a manacled defendant who wouldn't accept his suggested plea. Self-important judges can be surprisingly nasty.

It is also true, though, that many nasty judges are all show. Take Blog the Cave Judge. Blog's real name was Alan Lebowitz, and way back in 1992 he taught me a valuable lesson about pushing the limits.

Blog was trembling. His face was red, and he was doing a lizardlike thing with his tongue — flicking it just outside the left corner of his mouth.

"Ooooh, Mr. F-Feige," he was stammering, "do *not* tempt me."

His tiny courtroom was packed. The two-dozen mismatched

chairs were filled with lawyers and misdemeanants awaiting his adjudication. It was nearly 3:00 in the afternoon, and there were at least a dozen cases left to go.

It had already been a long day, and by the time I got to Blog, I'd had enough. Enough of petty judicial tyranny, enough of my clients being mistreated and incarcerated for no good reason, enough of stupid prosecutors and lying cops — enough already. I was one very young, mightily pissed-off public defender, and Blog the Cave Judge was not about to back me down.

"Judge," I said sharply, trying to interrupt him. We had been arguing for several minutes.

"No, Mr. Feige. No!" He cut me off. "Not another word from you." My client gaped at me. He'd wanted a lawyer to fight for him, but he could sense that this was getting a little out of hand.

"Mr. Feige," Blog warned, his tongue flicking like an iguana's, "I am telling you now, do NOT tempt me. There is no one I'd prefer to hold in contempt than you."

The idea that he would not only hold me in contempt for fighting for my clients, but would enjoy doing it was too much for me to bear. Slowly, defiantly, I turned completely around, placing my hands behind my back, one wrist flush against the other, thumbs almost touching. It was the "cuff me" pose — utterly familiar to anyone who had spent time in the criminal court system. There was an audible gasp in the courtroom. The seconds ticked by in exaggerated slowness as I waited to feel the steel.

"Oh, no, no, no, you don't!" I heard him say. "Oh, no, Mr. Feige." I still wouldn't turn around. "You will NOT goad me into holding you in contempt, sir!"

I felt my shoulders slump slightly.

"No," Blog exclaimed, "you will not!"

I turned around to face him, slowly, deliberately, and he was smiling at me, his head shaking slightly. It was a bemused smile, almost as if he couldn't believe what I had just done. And all of a sudden I understood it: I had won. In that moment I knew that he'd *never* hold me in contempt, that for all his bluster, he was all bark and no bite. He had no power over me after all. More-over, I realized there and then that unless a judge was really will-ing to put me in jail, so long as I was willing to feel the steel I had far more power than I'd thought. Looking at Blog, I saw that he knew it too and that the balance of power in the courtroom had just shifted from him to me. In his smile was the recognition that I'd called his bluff and he had folded, and that my appear-ances before him would never be the same. It was, almost, a smile of approval.

"What do you say we adjourn your case until May, Mr. Feige?"

"That seems just fine, Your Honor," I said, still flush with the knowledge of what had just happened. "How's the twelfth?"

"That seems like an excellent choice," Blog said, still shaking his head.

⇥⇤

It's 10:44 when I finally stride through the worn wooden door, keeping my head low, scanning the audience for Clarence, hop-ing Moge is too busy berating someone else to chastise me for my characteristic tardiness. As the door closes behind me, I look up and see that Moge is midsentence, seemingly focused on the lawyers in front of him. I'm heading straight for the podium where the clipboard with the day's calendar is when I spy Clarence, give him a nod, and start looking around a little less furtively, sizing up the scene in the courtroom.

"Ahhhh," Moge says, interrupting the case in progress before him, "it's Mr. Feige!" The mockery is as biting as it is routine. "So very kind of you to join us today, Mr. Feige." Moge is glancing at the clock at the back of the courtroom, preparing to continue his chiding: "And before eleven o'clock too! What a treat." Some of the other lawyers look down, pleased that they've been spared the treatment.

Looking up from the clipboard, I fix Moge with a warm smile. "Nice of me, isn't it?" I ask, while the judge shakes his head in mock annoyance. "Imagine me gracing you with my presence," I continue. "Must be your lucky day."

"Excuse me, Mr. Feige," the judge says, "but I have a case going on here." He nods at the lawyers in front of him as if to scold me for my rudeness in not noticing them, and then, having had enough, he goes back to actually dispensing his special form of justice.

The arrangement in Moge's part is pretty standard: on the left, four assistant DAs; one supervisor, and three line assistants from the Trial Division. On their wide wooden table — the one closest to the jury box — their files are spread out, dozens of legal-size, preprinted manila folders lined up in alphabetical rows stretching from one end of the long table to the other. Behind them, shoved into a corner near the jury box, are the metal mesh handcarts the DA's office uses to lug all that paper around. The front row — reserved for lawyers, cops, and the press — is only about half full. With Clarence present, what appears to be a short line, and the fact that almost everything I have in Supreme Court today is in Moge's part anyway, I decide to risk it and stay, as opposed to leaving for a while to get some other work done.

For some reason, in every courtroom I've ever been in, the prosecutors get to sit next to the jury box — something most lawyers understand to be a significant advantage. Leaving aside the obvious issues, like when the assistant DAs ostentatiously leave inadmissible evidence lying on their table, plainly visible to the jury (or in one instance I remember, a file marked in thick black ink: SUPPRESSED EVIDENCE), being close to the jury allows a lawyer greater dramatic impact and an easier time of watching a juror's reactions. While the defense is almost always farther from the jury, in some courtrooms just outside the city the defense actually sits behind the prosecutors. I learned this tidbit while chatting with a colleague who was second-seating a trial with a burned-out veteran in his office.

"Objection!" the grizzled vet would shout seemingly at random throughout the district attorney's presentation, causing the pretty young assistant DA to leap up in protest. "What's the objection?" she'd demand, flummoxed.

"Overruled," the judge would murmur blandly before anyone had a chance to answer.

"So, why *are* you objecting?" my colleague eventually asked in a whisper, after yet another completely frivolous objection. Surely, he thought, this being a murder case and the veteran being such an accomplished trial lawyer, there had to be some subtle reason he just wasn't grasping. Leaning in conspiratorially, the old guy nodded sagely and gestured toward the young assistant DA trying the case in front of him. "You know, every once and again," he said with a shrug, "I just like to look at her ass."

⟫━⟪

There are very few judges who will ever consider releasing someone charged with murder. It is, quite simply, an unacceptable political risk. Judges live in fear of "soft on crime" headlines, and one of the surefire ways to wind up on the front page of the *New York Post* is to release an alleged murderer, whatever the evidence or lack of evidence.

"You know," Judge Ralph Fabrizio said to me sotto voce as I peered up at him during a bench conference one evening, "the first thing they teach you in judge school is that no one ever got bounced off the bench for setting bail too high." I've heard this theme a dozen times over the years from various jurists, and it disgusts me. Over the years, one judge after the next has confessed their moral failings to me. *Please,* they plead, *you have to understand. I can't just do what's right — I have a job to protect.* This sort of moral equivocation is precisely why I loathe so many judges. If you can't do the job, if you can't be strong and stay above the fray and do what's right, get the hell off the bench and make room for someone who can, I always want to tell them. Sadly, knowing full well that my condemnation will make no difference, I usually deliver a far milder rebuke.

I'll trade a lot for a simple sense of moral conviction and the courage to implement it. And that Moge has in spades. He's one of the few judges who seems to rule without fear. This makes being in front of him, dealing with his wry derision and constant condescension, worthwhile.

And having Moge today truly is the luck of the draw. Back when he was still in jail, about three weeks after the grand jury indicted him, Clarence appeared for the first time in Supreme Court to plead not guilty to the indictment voted against him. It was there that a court clerk spun a big metal wheel to determine which Supreme Court judge would hear Clarence's case. "Spinning the wheel" is one of the most stressful moments in a criminal case, since the judge you draw has as much to do with whether you're eventually locked up and for how long as almost any other factor. As the clerk pulled the little white card from the wheel and read the name printed in black block letters into the record, I couldn't believe how lucky Clarence and I were.

"Moge," I told Clarence, "is the kind of judge who might actually release you if we can convince him you're innocent. He's the best draw we could have gotten."

Clarence was bewildered. "Why wouldn't *any* judge release me if they thought I was innocent?" he wanted to know. "Isn't that what they're supposed to do?" This is a tough question and one that deserved a longer and perhaps more honest answer than I was prepared to deliver while standing on the filthy side of the graffiti-scarred door that separated the courtroom from the barred pens of the Department of Corrections.

"Trust me, Clarence," I told him, "if there is a way outta here before the trial, Moge is the best chance we've got. You just need to hang in there until we can get to him and really put our best foot forward."

"Let's go!" a burly corrections officer yelled.

"Just hang in there, buddy," I said, trying to be cheerful.

Shaking his head forlornly, seemingly searching for some untapped reserve that would see him through another stretch of incarceration, Clarence turned to shuffle up the worn staircase.

He emerged again twenty days later, in his very first appearance in Judge Mogulescu's corner courtroom on the fourth floor of Bronx Supreme Court. Just after noon, two white-shirted court officers led him in, his face just a bit thinner, his eyes betraying an almost panicked sadness, to face Moge.

"I understand you have a bail application to make, Mr. Feige?" the judge said.

"I do, Your Honor," I replied, taking a big breath and offering up a little prayer to the gods of judicial kindness.

Armed with witness statements, psychiatric records, and the presence of much of Clarence's extended family, I made my pitch. A single witness had identified Clarence as the shooter. That witness, drunk at the time of the shooting, hadn't seen what he thought he saw. Indeed, I argued, he was contradicted by other people and undermined by a psychiatric history that included hallucinations. There was no physical or forensic evidence to link Clarence to the crime. Moreover, my investigation revealed that three witnesses had described two males fleeing the scene — Clarence, though, lived upstairs. I also had two alibi witnesses that were willing to testify that Clarence was home when the shooting happened, and we'd uncovered evidence that suggested that the decedent had been involved in a drug-related murder two weeks before he himself was shot. Even the DA's office conceded that Clarence was not involved with dealing or gangbanging, and was, therefore, far less likely to be the shooter than someone in one of the rival drug gangs who actually had a motive. Finally, we had a petition, signed by dozens of residents of the building where both Clarence and the decedent lived, insisting that Clarence was innocent. Outlining each fact, I kept looking up, scanning Moge's face, searching for a cue. None came.

Assistant District Attorney Paul Rosenfeld went next. Sure, he allowed, he had some information concerning the previous shooting, and it was under investigation, but other than a weak familial alibi, the defense had provided nothing real, nothing substantive that proved Clarence was innocent, just a sad assemblage of conjecture far short of justifying a defendant's release on bail in a murder case. Moge was still impassive.

"So, what do you suggest I do, Mr. Feige?" he asked me. The judge's question was calm but warning too, telling me, in essence, make your pitch but do it right, don't ask me to do something stupid here, be measured, be responsible . . . think.

"I'm asking you to set a partially secured surety bond of one hundred thousand dollars," I said calmly, suggesting a kind of bond that requires several people to promise to pay but only requires them to put up a small amount of cash (it is a section of the bail statute that is almost never used).

There was a pause as Mogulescu nodded, lips slightly pursed. I couldn't tell whether the expression was deliberative or approving.

"And so I'd assume you have suitable suretors?"

"Yes, Your Honor," I said quickly. "And they are available to sign surety affidavits and post the cash portion of the bail today."

"Judge!" the assistant DA tried to interrupt, worried that things were going my way.

"I understand your arguments, Mr. Rosenfeld," Mogulescu said, raising an eyebrow slightly and looking over at me to make sure I knew what was coming. "I'm going to grant the application."

Three hours later, Clarence was free.

⇒⋆⇐

Today, Clarence is sitting in the fourth row. His collared shirt is neatly pressed and carefully tucked into his pants. Wagging my finger toward the door, I silently indicate that he should come outside with me for a second. Moge is still torturing the lawyers in front of him.

The moment the doors swing closed behind him, Clarence turns to give me a big hug. He's happy to see me, but he's also agitated and has a whole bunch of questions. Clarence *always* has questions. Now that he's out of jail I have a lot less patience with Clarence. Normal questions feel cloying, and reasonable expectations feel disrespectful. I know they shouldn't, but Clarence doesn't seem to get what a big deal getting out of jail on a murder case is, and even though I don't expect gratitude, his insistent belief in his own innocence seems to be danger-ously close to denying the reality of the system — something I always feel duty-bound to correct.

"David," he says urgently as we huddle across from the doors to the courtroom, "I can prove I'm innocent — really I can!"

"That's great, Clarence," I tell him. "How?"

I've gone through this kind of conversation many times. Clarence constantly believes he's one court appearance or one little realization from vindication. From his point of view, he's so obviously innocent that no moron could fail to see it. For me, on the other hand, getting him out of jail was the first step in an arduous two- or three-year process of what I hope will be his eventual exoneration — for me, that process is fraught with terrifying pitfalls, any of which could lead to a lifetime in prison.

"It's the gun," Clarence whispers, nodding vigorously as though he can't wait to reveal the secret he's uncovered this time. Clarence has clearly been spending a lot of time figuring out just how to present this proof of innocence to me, and I can tell from his quavering voice he's about to make a big presentation.

I'm nonplussed.

"Clarence, let me guess," I interrupt him, furrowing my eyebrows just a bit, conscious that my tone is a bit too harsh and powerless to tone it down. "You're about to tell me that gunshot pattern proves it was an execution — right? You've been reading the autopsy report, and you saw the head shot."

Clarence looks stunned. "You know about that?" he asks me suspiciously.

"Yes, Clarence," I say with exaggerated patience. "I know about that, and I understand why you think it's consistent with innocence, but I'm telling you — it's not the silver bullet you think it is."

"David" — Clarence is insistent — "it was a hit — the first shot was like point blank in the head — it was a drug hit just like we always thought it was."

The first time I read the autopsy report I had the same feeling. And within weeks of the shooting, my investigator, Ben, had turned up several spades full of dirt on Shamar Hardy. He was a drug dealer who ran with a notorious crew in Soundview, and a widely circulating rumor suggested he had been involved in a murder just a few weeks before he himself was shot. Shamar, it was whispered on the street, had been the setup guy in the Baby Angel murder — a drug-related homicide that went down at the base of the Soundview Oval.

Street gangs are as much a part of the life of the Soundview projects as crack and poverty — and undoubtedly related to both. Much of the gang activity in Soundview surrounded a gang called the Bloods and a particular "set" of Bloods known as Sex Money Murder (SMM) Bloods. Partially founded by "Pistol Pete" Rollack in the 1980s, Sex Money Murder was responsible for much of the drug trade and some of the violence in Soundview. Prosecuted aggressively by the federal government, most of the old SMM leaders were eventually murdered or incarcerated (among them Bemo's son, known on the streets as "Baby B"). And while that kind of turnover might have put an end to a lesser organization, gangs, especially those with the mythic status of SMM, are remarkably resilient. Factions quickly sprang up, all claiming a part of the SMM legacy, and from what I could tell, if he wasn't an official member, at the very least Shamar Hardy ran with a group of drug dealers affiliated with an SMM faction.

Of course, no one from Soundview would ever say such a thing in court. The culture of silence that surrounds the drug game runs way too deep. Still, if it was true that Shamar had lured Baby Angel to his death (and I had every reason to believe that it was), that fact was very important for Clarence — it was an obvious motive for a rival gang to retaliate. And given that everyone agreed that Clarence was not a gang member, it squarely suggested that someone else was likely to have been the shooter. Add that to the three witnesses Ben turned up who saw two young men sprinting from the scene, mix in the brazen nature of the shooting, and it certainly had the drug rub-out vibe. Throw in the autopsy and I guess I could understand Clarence's excitement.

Reading autopsy reports can actually be quite fun — sick, but fun. Unlike gruesome crime scene photos, which are almost always gut-wrenching, autopsy reports are slick and concise and clinical. Dense with pallid descriptions of organ weights and wound tracks, as well as dry commentary on the composition of bile or vitreous humor (the fluid inside the eyeball), autopsy reports almost always yield magical secrets for the inquisitive criminal defense attorney. Unfortunately, many criminal defense lawyers — even those able to do homicide cases — fail to spend much time on the autopsy report. That is a terrible mistake. In nearly every case there is something lurking in the autopsy. It's rarely obvious; it's not something like whether the decedent was high or drunk. It's usually something else, something not always having to do with the cause of death: the angle of the knife wound in a stabbing, the disparate number of entry and exit wounds in a shooting case, or, as in a child murder case I once did, an abnormally high concentration of salt in the bloodstream. It's these details that can crack a case.

In New York the medical examiners are designed to be neutral finders of fact. They don't technically work for the police, and they don't technically work for the prosecutors. What that means, in practice, is that unlike all the other witnesses in a criminal case in New York City, the medical examiners (MEs) will actually meet with a defense attorney and go over the autopsy report (just as they do with prosecutors). Sadly, though, their vaunted neutrality and willingness to meet — which initially seems like a boon to a defense lawyer struggling to understand a complicated medical issue or explore a theory — masks a more pernicious reality: that meeting will almost always get quickly reported to the prosecutor's office, along with a description of what the defense lawyer was interested in. Defense lawyers never get such calls after a medical examiner's meeting with a prosecutor.

The snitch factor is one of the reasons I never meet with the medical examiners, relying instead on friends or the help of a forensic expert. I'll meet the ME on the stand.

That's a long way off, though. Right now what's important is talking Clarence out of insisting that I march into court and make a stink about how the autopsy report proves his innocence. I've also got to make sure he doesn't go back to one of his other crazy ideas — that what he really wants is a quick trial.

"Listen to me, Clarence," I say very slowly, looking him straight in the face, "I know this was a drug hit. I even think I know who might have done it. I know that the autopsy report shows stippling, and I know, therefore, that the shot to the side of the head was a contact shot — fired at point-blank range. I understand that it looks like an execution-style murder. . . ."

I trail off to make sure he's with me.

Clarence is nodding emphatically as if he's in complete agreement — so far.

"BUT," I say, "what that autopsy doesn't show is whether the shot to the head was the first shot or the last. Moreover, given the way the body was facing and the placement of the head shot, it could be that someone was lying in wait for Shamar and stepped out of the stairway that leads to the vestibule. Isn't that right?" Clarence looks at me skeptically. "Clarence," I insist, "doesn't it make sense that Shamar could have been shot by someone coming out of that stairwell? It's narrow in there, he fell with his head facing the elevator, the bullet entered on the left side of his head — so it looks like he's leaving the building when he's shot." I can see Clarence's mind turning.

"Yeah," he says tentatively.

"Clarence," I say, giving him a hard look, "that's the stairway that leads to your apartment."

I try hard not to let the kicker sound as if I doubt his innocence, which of course I don't — though as usual, that's right where Clarence goes.

"David" — Clarence's eyes are wide — "you know I'm innocent, right?" I just stare at him, and he continues. "I know you say it doesn't matter to you, but it does to me." Clarence is still searching my face, and using the ambiguity of my own beliefs to leverage him into choosing to do what I want him to do, I lean toward him and put my hand on his arm, drawing him toward me.

"Listen to me now," I say. "I already got you out of jail; I'm gonna find a way to beat this case. But you gotta calm down, you gotta shut up, and you gotta give me the time to find a way to do what we both want — prove your innocence. Now we're gonna walk into that court, we're gonna shut up about the autopsy report, and we're gonna adjourn this case for another month while you continue to stay out of trouble and continue to do all the good things you've been doing since you got out . . . understood?"

I see him nodding, his eyelids drooping slightly in partial defeat. "Yes, David," he says quietly as I turn to head back into the courtroom.

Four

FOUR MURDERS LURK among the fifty-six cases on Moge's calendar today. Three of the four are mine. Each case is different, bound together only by the fact that someone died in every one. One is a twenty-three-year-old homicide that the Cold Case Squad just closed by arresting my client Alberto Collado, an older Hispanic guy who walks with a cane and is already serving a seventeen-year sentence for an unrelated rape. The second is a crack-house stabbing. The third is Clarence.

After a few years of being a public defender, you begin to see the world as being made up of two states of being — in and out, incarcerated or free. Somehow, against this essential dichotomy, every other distinction pales. Black and white, rich and poor, vicious and passive all fade next to the basic question of self-determination. Of my first three cases of the morning, Clarence is out, and Reginald McFadden and Alberto are in.

Two court officers are lounging by the defense table, just a few feet from the podium. One of them, a heavyset sergeant with a distractedly disapproving look, has a pile of tattered blue cards arrayed before him. The Department of Corrections uses the cards to keep track of inmates. Every time an inmate — known in the argot of the courthouse as a "body" — is "signed out" (that is, transferred from the custody of the Department of Corrections to the court officers or vice versa), a blue card gets handed over. No card, no body. The result is that cards become synonymous with clients. So instead of asking the corpulent sergeant whether Mr. Collado and Mr. McFadden have arrived from Rikers Island yet, I lean over the rail of the courtroom and say, "Yo, Sarge, you got cards on Collado or McFadden?"

"I got everybody," he murmurs derisively, looking up from his magazine — *Guns & Ammo*.

A beat to ogle the money shot of a 9mm Ruger.

"You want 'em down?"

"Yes, please. Both of them," I say, taking a seat in the front row to wait.

I've been sitting less than five minutes when my cell phone starts vibrating madly. It's the office, calling to tell me that I have two clients waiting for me over in criminal court. The problem is, I'm in a different building, and having ordered the cards I've pretty much committed to doing my cases in Moge's part first. I step outside, waving to the clerk to indicate that I'm just making a phone call, and call Lorraine. "Just tell them to be patient," I say. "I'll try to get there before the lunch break." Even as I say it, though, I have the nagging feeling that I'm almost certain to disappoint one if not both of them.

Calendar management is one of the most important skills a public defender can master. When you have a caseload of between 75 and 120 cases pending at any given time, the simple matter of where to be when becomes one of the most complicated and taxing puzzles we face. It's not unusual to have six, eight, or even ten different courtrooms to go to in a single day. Once you start picking up felony cases, those courtrooms are spread out on different floors of different buildings, occasionally requiring a full-on Edwin Moses–like sprint, dodge, and hurdle just to get from place to place on time. The challenge of getting everything done becomes both a mental and physical chore, and so, in my spare moments, when I'm not plotting revenge against Angelo Tona or one of his evil brethren, I'm plotting my path through the courthouses.

Whatever the floor, whatever the judge, nearly every court appearance a defendant or public defender makes will end the same way — in an adjournment that postpones resolution to a future date. Quite simply, the system is not designed to mete out the kind of speedy justice that any normal person would expect. Pleas are adjourned for sentencing; trials are adjourned because the police don't show up, or the defense isn't ready, or motions that should have been filed weren't. Cases are adjourned for plea discussions and then, more often than not, for more plea discussions. It's a vicious cycle, chronically resistant to change, born of consistently overtaxed resources.

Because of this crush, zipping a case through the system is virtually impossible. It is also, generally, not a good strategy for an out defendant. Leaving aside the terrible waste that goes hand in hand with delay, from a purely strategic point of view cases usually get better for the defense with age: witnesses move away or forget details, ADAs get sidetracked by other trials or leave the office, bad judges get transferred or eventually happen to have such a good day that they have a miraculous, if fleeting, moment of compassion. The downside for an in defendant, though, can be a terrible stretch in jail waiting for a trial. The relentless volume of cases ensures a brutal schedule of court appearances — so many that they are nearly impossible to manage. Becoming a good client juggler is something that every public defender has to learn in order to last.

Adding to the challenge, unlike many federal courts, in which all parties are instructed to show up to court at a certain time, Bronx courtrooms work like a casting cattle call — first come, first served. This policy is enforced through the use of sign-in sheets, on which a lawyer with a ready case will sign the case in by calendar number and defendant's name, usually indicating whether or not an interpreter is required and whether the defendant is in or out.

Once a case is signed in, a court officer responsible for calling the cases (the "bridge man" or "bridge officer") lines up the case files in a long row, scratches them off the list, and starts calling them. The rule is that once a case is signed in, the lawyer is not supposed to leave the courtroom, but the reality is that once a case is signed in, it can be an hour or two, sometimes even more, before it gets called. This is especially true with slow judges. If I see Judge Seth Marvin briskly dispensing with cases, it's likely I'll be in and out of the courtroom in fifteen minutes. On the other hand, if I walk through the courtroom door to find sweet Eddie Padro, who, partially because he grew up in the neighborhood, used to come down off the bench to give little personalized lectures to the kids appearing in front of him; or George Villegas, whose hilarious back-and-forth with defendants could add two or three hours to a 120-case day; or Judge Judy Lieb, once a fancy private lawyer turned federal prosecutor, whose precision and formality ensure lengthy discussions with unprepared assistant DAs and defense lawyers, I'll know it is going to be a *long* time before my case is called. Faced with a slow judge, there is only one rational thing to do — break the rules: sign up the case, talk to the client, slip out the back, and go do something else.

I tried to explain the importance of this sort of rule breaking to Jason Miller one fall afternoon. A young lawyer with a thin frame, a mop of brown hair, and oversized glasses perched on a prominent nose, Jason was not a natural candidate for the role of office dandy, but along with his cutting sense of humor he brought to the Bronx a wardrobe of thick, well-tailored shirts and bright, daring ties. From early on it was clear that he would be a good lawyer. It had nothing to do with the Ivy League pedigree — that hurts as often as it helps, since much of the day-to-day public defender work is intellectually simple but emotionally complex. But Jason had an astonishing ability to use his awkward delivery and his deadpan sense of humor to reach clients utterly unlike him, quickly absorbing the culture of the courthouse and acclimating to the pace of the work.

We were standing in the capacious hallway between four of the largest courtrooms in the criminal court building in the crush of a crowded day when he astutely popped the question: "How do you keep up?" He seemed a little nervous that whatever the answer was, it wasn't going to be good. "I mean, how do you play by the rules and still get to every case?"

"Just be like a shark," I told him.

"I gotta be like a shark?" His glasses hid a look that could have been bemusement, admiration, or contempt.

"Like a shark," I persisted, "you gotta be in constant motion. You see, the problem you're gonna have is that you're gonna want to listen to the judges and court officers: to respect them and not piss them off."

There was a pause as Jason digested this critique.

"Ah . . . yeah," he said, his face suggesting that he thought there might indeed be good reasons to not piss off judges.

"Can't do it," I told him. "Not if you want to be effective. You gotta do exactly what they forbid you from doing. Gauge the line, sign in the case, and then leave."

"I thought we weren't supposed to do that?" Jason said warily, as though he was trying to decide whether I was just setting him up to get hurt.

"You're not," I told him, "but it's the only way you're gonna thrive." You swim, you live. You stop, you die.

⇒•⇐

Everyone assumes that as citizens we should respect the criminal justice system. What is often overlooked is that the system should respect the citizens as well. Behind every case there is an anxious client who has taken a day off work, or who needs to pick up her child from day care, or who is nervous about an appointment with the welfare office or a meeting with her parole officer. All of them have a life that has been put on hold until they get to see the judge — and all are counting on us to be there, to help them, and, perhaps most important, just to get them out of there and back to the lives they've briefly, tensely checked at the courthouse door. I wanted Jason to understand that following the rules would waste not only his time but, even more critical, theirs, that the only moral and logical thing to do in a system whose rules make your job impossible is to reinvent the rules.

Sadly, not every public defender does this well, and much of the burnout young public defenders experience is the simple result of too much rule following. I'm always skeptical of lawyers who are sitting on their asses in a shabby criminal courtroom waiting while fifteen other cases are called before theirs gets heard. Almost to a person, they're the ones who won't last. I can see it in how they talk to clients, the glazed look that comes from seeing the tedium of patterns instead of the specifics of people — the sense of futility that comes from knowing that to every client the criminal case pending against them is one of the most stressful things in their lives, that they want, more than anything, to have it over, but that you'll be essentially power-less to end it. You play by the rules, but what does it get you? Hours in limbo while the rest of your clients wait, their lives eroding away. Play by the rules and the only way to survive is to turn off entirely. Rule breaking is a way of eking out some tiny sense of power in a system that leaves defenders utterly disem-powered.

Burnout has a dangerous but predictable progression — first you draw lines between lawyer and client; then you start blaming the clients; then you just stop caring. Most people make it less than three years before they fry. Some get over the hump and live to six. A few, and only a few, stay sharp, focused, and com-mitted for more than a decade, fighting the unwinnable fights, defending the impossible cases.

Assistant district attorneys rarely have this problem. Unlike us, they have cases rather than clients. Sure, there are victims and a system of laws that ADAs claim to uphold, but they're on the winning side, the popular side, the side glamorized in a thou-sand *Law & Order* episodes. And while they may know their complainants, they spend the bulk of their time with cops, not citizens — and certainly not citizens facing incarceration, disso-lution of their families, or the orphaning of their children.

Even more significant is the fact that in the Bronx few of the relevant ADAs are even around when most of the mundane non-sense and interminable adjournments are taking place. Because their system is about cases rather than clients, it relies on having certain ADAs assigned to specific courtrooms, playing zone as opposed to man-to-man: rather than run around, ADAs just distribute their cases to whichever colleague is, in courthouse speak, "covering the part." Unfortunately, since most ADAs are shockingly bad at the simple chore of annotating their files or ensuring that the necessary information is available to the colleague who actually stands on the case, more often than not the prosecutor in the courtroom knows almost nothing about the cases he or she is ostensibly prosecuting, making it even harder to ever get anything done.

From all indications so far, I'm not going to be getting much done myself this morning. I thank Lorraine, flip the phone closed, and step back into the courtroom to assay my progress.

>→←<

It looks as if there are only one or two cases in line in front of me, and as a nearby court officer shuffles through the pile of blue cards on the table in front of him, I offer up a little prayer, hoping that the next batch of inmates to be brought down will include Alberto or Reginald, or maybe both.

Reginald McFadden's case is interesting partly because of how hard it will be to get rid of it. Reginald's record is so bad that almost any plea would mean a life sentence. On the other hand, this is a classic plea case — one in which the weapon was a kitchen knife, there was only one stab wound (something that makes a murder rather than a manslaughter conviction unlikely), and all of the witnesses, as well as the dead guy, were high on crack. (Crackhead witnesses have an astonishing habit of disappearing just before trial.) But I can't think about Reginald just yet — I still have to hustle Clarence through this adjournment.

The clerk is looking agitated. "Where've you been?" he asks in a slightly hostile tone. "Just outside," I say, vaguely annoyed that he didn't recognize my obvious signal to him. Mercifully, before the exchange can go any further, Moge uses his free hand to motion Clarence and me straight up to our places at counsel table. Standing there, Clarence shoots me a nervous glance. It's always scary standing before a judge. And no matter how routine an appearance is, no one is safe from the creeping fear that something could go awry — that somehow, with the wrong move or a bad argument, the court officers standing just a few feet away could reach for their cuffs and, with a nod from the judge, lead you away, back toward the door by the jury box, to jail. Clarence feels it, and I do too — this is just another chance to blow it.

I give Clarence a reassuring smile and pat his back gently with my right hand. An ADA steps up, and everyone is in his place.

"Remember about the autopsy," Clarence murmurs insistently.

"I'm not mentioning the autopsy, Clarence," I whisper back. "You gotta shut up and trust me here." Clarence looks down, chastened.

I've always believed that one of the best ways to foster a client's trust is to provide them with every bit of paper associated with his or her case. There are many lawyers who either don't bother or prefer not to send the case file, the motions, and the police reports to their clients. But supplying clients copies of all the paperwork gives incarcerated inmates something to do while they spend a year or two waiting for their trial, and it gives clients a sense of the case against them — something tangible to pore over, to think about. The not unexpected result of this paperwork empowerment, however, is an enormous number of conversations like the one I seem to be perpetually having with Clarence.

"Look," said a client of mine charged with burglary just a few weeks ago, "it says here that no one was home. So how could they know it was me *if no one was home?* Huh?"

Jimmy was a skinny white kid, with beady eyes and an amphetamine-fueled inquisitiveness. He was the kind of kid who was proud of his insight into the criminal justice system and would spout off confidently to other inmates in the cell, finding power in dispensing often-erroneous legal advice. We were sitting in the dank interview room on the sixth floor of Supreme Court, where general population interviews take place. Jimmy was so skinny that he barely filled the gray plastic chair he was sitting in. His eyes were narrowed, his face flushed, his hands folded on the table — fingers interlaced in a "let us say grace" kind of pose — leaning in at me, challenging me to disprove his brilliant theory.

"Well, Jimmy," I said, smiling back at him, "they're not relying on anyone *saying* they saw you — they're saying that when they stopped you down the street, you had the complainant's Discman on you and a credit card with her name on it."

These sorts of conversations take patience and caring, and

without really understanding that most clients are terrified and desperate, it can become insufferable to have to listen to the arguments — especially those aggressively propounded by jail-house lawyers like Jimmy.

"That's bullshit," Jimmy said firmly. "I know the law, and if they got no witness, they got no case."

"Jimmy," I tried again, trying to be calm but firm, "that's not true. They can prove your identity circumstantially . . . that means by evidence other than direct observation."

"No they can't," said Jimmy simply.

"Yes, Jimmy, they can," I insisted. "Look, if they had your prints inside the house, would you cop out?"

"*IF* they had my prints," Jimmy replied, fixing me with a tough stare and uttering the *if* in a way designed to accentuate his skepticism. "Yeah — a course I'd cop."

I gave him a smile. "But they only got your prints — not a witness."

"Yeah, but if my prints are there, I gotta have been there," Jimmy explained to me.

"Exactly," I told him. "That's *circumstantial* evidence of your presence."

"Yeah?" Jimmy asked.

"Yeah," I said emphatically, "just like the goddamn credit card with her name on it in your pocket ten minutes after the burglary."

"But I coulda *found* that," Jimmy said, a little fight still left in him.

"Sure, you could of," I said sweetly, "and if we go to trial that's what we'll argue — that in those few minutes the real bur-glar ran up to you and just handed you the lady's credit card and Discman, and that you took them 'cause you didn't know what else to do, and then the guy ran off just as the police came."

"Yeah — that's right!" Jimmy said, enthused that I'd properly asserted his defense.

"Jimmy, all you gotta ask yourself is, are twelve people gonna believe that story? 'Cause one might hang the jury, but all twelve gotta agree before you walk."

"Sure, why not?" he asked.

"Most of all 'cause it sounds like bullshit," I explained in the most legal of fashions, "but if that's how you wanna go, you need to understand that's what we'll do. But you also need to know that if you get convicted, you're gonna get football numbers — like fifteen flat when we go down."

"Oh" was all Jimmy said. Then, after a long pause, his eyes darting around the room, his narrow face screwed up into a mask of concentration: "And what they offerin' me?"

I tilted my head back, slowly and soberly, being careful not to show that I knew he was about to cave. "Three flat," I told him. Holding his gaze, I waited patiently for the reaction I knew, with that public defender instinct, was coming.

"Okay, I'll take it," he said, nodding as if we had just agreed on the purchase price of a 1984 Volvo wagon.

⇒⇐

"Number sixteen on the calendar, indictment number thirteen of 2003, *People of the state of New York versus Clarence Watkins*," the clerk intones, officially calling Clarence's case into the record.

"David Feige — F-E-I-G-E — of the Bronx Defenders appearing for Mr. Watkins," I say as Moge looks down impatiently.

"So," Moge inquires, looking at the ADA, "are we ready for trial today?" Moge already knows that I'm not ready, that I'm still searching for the information that will conclusively vindicate Clarence. This is his way of putting the ADA's feet to the fire and taking the pressure off me. I appreciate the gesture.

"Where are we on this case, People?" Moge demands.

"The People are not ready, Your Honor," admits the ADA, sounding resigned to the tongue-lashing he's about to get. "As I explained to the court earlier, Mr. Rosenfeld is on trial in another matter."

"Ah, yes, Mr. Rosenfeld again," Moge says sarcastically of the ADA assigned to the case. "And when did we agree Mr. Rosenfeld would deign to try this one?"

He gets no answer, so he turns to me. "And you, Mr. Feige?" he inquires as Clarence shifts nervously.

"Given the situation, how's the twenty-sixth?" I ask non-chalantly.

Moge is good to me today. He raises an eyebrow slightly and says, "Twenty-sixth, People?"

"That's fine," says the ADA, a note of relief in his voice too.

"See you all then," Moge says, smiling.

On to the next case.

Five

11:03 A.M.

A S CLARENCE HEADS OUT the front door, a court officer comes through the rear one — the one that leads to the back hallway and the stairs to the bull pens. I can see that he has blue cards in his hand — a sure sign that an incarcerated defendant or two is about to be brought in. I'm hoping to see Alberto, Reginald, or maybe even both.

Reginald McFadden is a killer, a thief, a drug user, and an all-around badass, and I love him. Reginald went to prison for the first time just before I was born, five years in '64 for an offense lost to time (record keeping wasn't so great back then). Paroled in 1968, Reginald caught his first murder case within a few years, and sometime in the early seventies — his rap sheet was quite clear on this point — he got ten years for manslaughter. Eventually released after serving that sentence, Reginald filled the eighties with a series of robberies, parole violations, and a few drug cases. All told, Reginald had been sentenced to prison on six separate occasions. He was, according to almost anyone's calculus, a bad man, or by mine, a man with a very bad record.

Reginald is charged with stabbing a crackhead. One poke, right in the heart. With a heart wound (in this case a little nick to the aorta) the blood comes fast and furious. The dead guy was found splayed across a cheap mattress laid casually in a corner, the thick pool of blood soaking his shirt, trickling down his torso, inching across the plastic sheeting that covered the mattress, and pooling on the dirty linoleum floor. In cop lingo, he "bled out."

Reginald was arrested months after the stabbing, after the police released the first few guys they charged. From what I can tell, there is not much of a case against him. Though the cops have the murder weapon, neither Reginald's fingerprints nor his DNA is on the knife, and the bloody footprint left on the floor in the house seems to belong to a shoe far larger than any Reginald would have worn.

I was there the night of his arrest.

Long before Bronx Homicide moved to the stately renovated manor house that eventually held the marquee assignments of Bronx copdom — Special Victims, Sex Crimes, and RIP (a special robbery squad) — the Bronx Homicide Task Force was jammed into a small squad room on the second floor of the run-down forty-eighth precinct. Buried under the hulking pylons of an elevated section of the Cross Bronx Expressway, the 4-8 was a dingy but vibrant station house built in a style that would have made a Soviet architect swoon for its brutal, unadorned efficiency.

The entrance, facing the underside of the highway, opened into a reception area reminiscent of the station on *Hill Street Blues:* a large central desk, filled with baskets of forms, surrounded by milling uniformed cops and presided over by a disaffected desk sergeant. On the side, more cops, pairs and trios gathered around corkboards jammed with flyers, union messages, wanted posters, and row upon row of recent regulations.

Walking into the Homicide Task Force office on the night Reginald was brought in, I passed through knee-high swivel gates — saloon doors for Lilliputians. It felt like stalking into the Wild West.

A homicide detective named Infante was waiting.

"He's over there" is all he said, hooking a thumb toward the cage where Reginald was sitting.

It was 7:35 P.M.

"Mr. McFadden," I said, walking over to the bars and slipping a card through them. "My name is David Feige, and I'm gonna be your lawyer."

I hadn't yet seen Reginald's rap sheet and had no idea whether or not he'd been through the system before, so I started with the basics: "Mr. McFadden," I said carefully, "I don't know much about what's up here, so all I can tell you is this: they're looking at you for a homicide, they wanna do a lineup, and that means we gotta be serious and we gotta be careful. Now I don't know if you've said anything to them yet, but —"

Reginald cut me off. "I'm familiar with the process," he said evenly. "It's all right . . . I understand. I haven't made any statements. . . ." He trailed off, and I smiled.

I liked the guy already.

Interviewing clients at a precinct can be a dangerous proposition. Most of the time they're desperate to explain their side of the story, naively certain that they can talk or explain their way out from behind the bars. Reginald did not seem to have this problem. Unlike him, most clients have already made statements to the police, and some are baffled as to why the explanation hasn't proved sufficient to set them free. Faced with a lawyer, many clients wrongly think that reiterating their statement will help, and that once the lawyer is convinced it's a simple matter to set them free.

In that, as in many things, they are wrong.

Generally, I preempt any such discussion. "I don't want to discuss anything about what might or might not have happened right now," I told Reginald, leaning farther into the bars, "so everything we talk about tonight is just gonna be about procedure."

"No problem at all," he said.

"And by the way, Mr. McFadden." I nodded as my right hand, palm down, snaked through the bars, fingers covering the cigarette pack below. Reaching out, knowing exactly what was going on, Reginald held my gaze while gently taking my hand, relieving me of a sealed pack of Newport 100s.

"Thanks for coming down." He smiled.

Newports are a surefire way to start off on the right foot with a client. A sealed pack (sealed to protect me against any allegation of passing real contraband) is an unspoken proclamation of empathy — *I know you're stressed out. I know being in a cage really sucks. I know you want answers that I can't provide. But I know the drill; I'll bend the rules, and right now this is about the most I can do for you.*

Cops use them as well. They are (or were until they were banned from Rikers recently) a favored form of jailhouse currency — worth favors and commissary all around the island. Slipping someone a pack (assuming the client is not fresh faced and scared, in which case they'll just get jumped and robbed of the cigs) will put them in good stead for their first week or so on the inside.

Ten minutes went by. I handed Infante a written request asking him to do the lineup a particular way; he threw it in the garbage.

"I'm gonna do this my way," he said.

His way seemed to be the slow way, and three hours after I arrived, five men walked in, herded by two uniformed officers. They ranged from five foot six and 150 pounds to six two and 235, and seemed to have little or nothing in common with my five-ten, 210-pound client. The men filed by. Twenty minutes passed before Infante was ready.

I took out my 35mm camera.

"You're not taking pictures of my lineup," Infante said. "You can have copies of the Polaroids."

This is another cop trick. Not all detectives do it, but many do. Just before a lineup takes place, a detective will snap a few tiny Polaroids from far enough away that facial features become indistinct. They further ensure that this is all the documentary evidence there is. The advantage is that when a judge can't see the problems in a lineup, he's unlikely to suppress. Refusing to allow decent pictures designed to document a deficient lineup is the kind of overt manipulation of the system that should be punished. But in all my years, I've never seen a judge even blink when the cops overtly acknowledge that they prevented the defense from taking pictures, opting to rely instead on their crappy snapshots. Some confident cops and particularly seasoned detectives who are secure about their lineups will actually allow the defense to take better pictures — and in those rare instances I'll insist that the investigator take a dozen shots (a closeup of each face, pictures of each pair and each threesome, and several of the whole lineup). But those situations are the exception, not the rule.

I headed into the lineup room, but Infante stopped me, preventing any discussion with the fillers — the guys, usually homeless, getting ten bucks to stand next to Reginald in the lineup. In most instances, the defense is at least allowed to ask the men for their precise height, weight, and age — not today though.

Infante's the one with the gun.

The cage was opened up, and Reginald was walked into the lineup room. We chatted for a few minutes, and he sat down in position number four. A sheet was draped over everyone, obscuring each from the belly button down. Several of them had gray sprayed in their hair, a few others had ridiculous-looking fake facial hair rubber-cemented into place. Reginald was, even by Infante's questionable calculus, fifteen years older than the next-closest person. Half of these guys might as well have been white for all they resembled Reginald. Of course, with the Polaroids, even a judge with a magnifying glass would have trouble seeing the differences.

"Everybody ready?" Infante asked. And then, without waiting for an answer, he turned and headed for the viewing room.

And there, in the narrow room, my back pressed up against the wall, two extra detectives crowded in, I got my first look at the witnesses against Reginald.

"See anyone you recognize?" Infante asked coolly as a wan-looking woman scanned the lineup.

Seconds ticked by in agonizing silence as she looked back and forth among the men before her.

"Take your time," Infante said. "No one can see you."

"I don't see anyone."

"Take your time," Infante said again, an edge in his voice.

A few more seconds.

"I don't see anyone," the woman repeated feebly, seeming confused.

"Just try to remember." Infante again. It had been forty-five seconds, maybe more, and the tension was palpable. Infante was trying to force a pick.

"She just said she doesn't see anyone," I said sharply.

"Quiet, Counselor!" Infante snapped.

"Sorry," the witness said simply before being led out. The blinds came down. Infante glared at me.

Another detective from the squad brought in the next witness, a man this time, a tall African American with darting eyes.

"See anyone?" Infante asked.

The man, stooping toward the window, started to make a light humming sound, as if he was thinking.

"Take your time," Infante urged. The man seemed as though he was going to say something at any moment. His lips were pursed, and he continued to hum. I counted the seconds off, trying to keep track of how long it was taking him, and he finally muttered something.

"Nope."

That was it. Infante was visibly upset.

"Look again!" he said sharply. My heart was racing as I tried to decide whether or not to interrupt again, the prospect of two no-hits in a lineup making the entire evening seem like a very worthwhile temporal investment. Another twenty seconds slid by. It'd been more than a minute since the guy had spoken.

"Are you sure?" Infante said. "No one can see you . . . don't be afraid."

The man shook his head, though Infante's urging seemed to fluster him. He took one more look — almost exaggerating the motions of attentiveness — when I finally said, "Seems like that's a no."

"Yeah," agreed the guy. "I don't see no one."

"Thanks for coming in," Infante said, but the tone made it clear that the unspoken end of the sentence was "you fucking skell."

The lineup room door was opened. Reginald was escorted back to the cell. The fillers relaxed, tearing off their fake mustaches.

I asked Infante for copies of the lineup Polaroids.

"Forget it," he snapped, "you'll get 'em in discovery."

I fixed him with a serious gaze. "Detective, with two no-hits and no further witnesses, I assume you'll be releasing my client?"

Infante ignored me.

Another detective ambled over. "What happened?" he asked.

"Two no-hits," Infante said.

The other cop raised an inquisitive eyebrow, but Infante hooked a thumb toward the cage where Reginald now stood.

"Book him anyway," he said.

That was eighteen months ago. Reginald has been in jail ever since.

On the one hand, Reginald's record is so awful that it is unlikely that the DA's office will be interested in working out a plea. On the other hand, from the paperwork, it appears that there is no real case against him. This is just the kind of intractable situation that usually results in one of the rarest events in the criminal justice system — a trial.

Trials, though they capture the imagination of the public and inspire young people to become lawyers, almost never happen. Though I handle hundreds and hundreds of cases a year, if I try three of them it will have been a busy twelve months; almost every case is resolved through dismissal or plea. The statistics, particularly in the Bronx and particularly regarding misdemeanors, are staggering. Of the more than fifty thousand misdemeanor cases processed in 2003, *twenty-three* resulted in jury verdicts. More felonies go, but still not too many. For all the drama of a courtroom title fight, most everything is actually decided before weigh-in. That being said, trials usually involve a select subset of cases — the very innocent people and the very bad guys.

Innocent people go to trial mostly because they're naive. Like Clarence, almost all of them tragically believe that the system will work and will exonerate them. In their minds, it's only a matter of time. And no matter how many times I explain that innocent people can get convicted, I'm regularly confronted by the touched smile of the truly innocent. It is a look that is similar, though not identical, to the calm of the true sociopath.

The preternatural calm of the truly innocent is disconcerting and disorienting: precisely the people who should be most furious, most incensed at the injustice of the system are often the least belligerent and the least angry — even when they are wrongly in jail. They evince confusion rather than anger, devout in their faith that the process can be counted on to exonerate them. Their certainty, of course, does nothing to help my anxiety.

The other chunk of the trial docket is made up of bad guys and serious cases. The reason serious cases, especially murders, are overrepresented in trial statistics is that despondent clients figure, *I'm gonna do twenty years if I plead, so I might as well go to trial.* This is a tough attitude to combat, and I've spent years of my life working with clients to overcome just this kind of coun-terproductive (if not entirely irrational) thinking. What they often ignore is that a trial loss will almost inevitably result in a much longer sentence (known in many courthouses as "the trial tax"). Still, twenty years can seem like a lifetime, especially to a kid, and given how hard life on the inside is, it may well be. In those cases, just like in the ones with the confident, innocent clients, sometimes you just gotta stop arguing and pick a jury.

But the truth is, if you are actually trying a case, you've already lost. It's not that you can't win the case, or even that a trial wasn't the right move. It's just that being on trial means that your other skills — negotiation or clever legal maneuvering — have failed, and there is nothing left to do but gamble with someone else's life. It's what I'm about to do with Reginald.

Glancing up at the court officer by the back door, I realize I just got lucky. Reginald strides in — his white knit kufi perfectly covers his handsome shaved head, his gait is smooth and delib-erate. He flashes me a smile when he spies me. Right behind Reginald, Alberto hobbles in — hands cuffed to his crutches. I have no idea why Alberto is always hopping. He's a tough guy, so a jailhouse assault is unlikely. I think he's had a broken leg since I met him.

The two of them, handsome Reginald and hobbling Alberto, are led to the defense table. I take up my place just behind them, waiting for their cases to be officially called into the record. It's 11:35 A.M.

Many people charged with murder wait two or even three years for a trial. In New York, there is no statutory right to a speedy trial in a homicide, and as a result (and because murder cases are complicated and usually prosecuted and defended by very experienced and very busy lawyers) the mere allegation can land you in jail for a few years.

"Hey, Dave," Reginald says as he inclines his head slightly. "If you got a second, can you come on up and see me afterwards?"

I nod.

The clerk clears his throat.

"Number nine on the calendar, indictment 3209 of 2001, *People versus Reginald McFadden,*" he says as Reginald steps up to the table.

"Good morning, Your Honor," Reginald says, smiling at Moge.

"Always a pleasure to see you, Mr. McFadden." The judge nods.

This is another one of Mogulescu's strengths — he actually interacts with the defendants before him in a decent, civilized manner. Most judges berate them, urging guilty pleas while their lawyers stand there like idiots. Some, like Ruth Sussman, a Smith girl turned prosecutor and then judge, are so obviously disdainful and aloof it seems as if they are hardly aware that there is a human being in front of them.

But there are a few — like Moge, or Caesar Cirigliano, a once-jovial, heavyset, cigar-chomping legal aid lawyer turned by a heart attack into a svelte, healthy-living judge — who are constantly aware that they are judging cases involving living, breathing, complicated people. Moreover, they realize that their judicial decisions are important not just to their own careers, but to the lives of the defendants, the victims, and the community. These are the judges it is a pleasure for clients to appear before. And the truth is, they are also the judges who are better for all involved, not just the defense, because they actually care. Bad judges may seem tougher, but in the long run, their generic, bureaucratic, reflexively proprosecution decisions undermine confidence in the criminal justice system. This is particularly true in the poor African American communities that provide many of the system's complainants and defendants. What they want, more than anything else, is a fair system, but what they perceive, whether from the perspective of a juror, defendant, or dark-skinned citizen walking the streets, is a system in which the powerful bend the rules to fit their own agendas.

It was judges like Alan Broomer that gave them this idea. A former bodybuilder and long-time prosecutor, Broomer was a sadist in a robe. Broomer's body looked like a blow-up Mr. Universe doll that someone had let the air out of. Though he reputedly worked out for hours every day, age had larded Broomer's broad body with flesh that seemed to drip from his still-powerful frame. Broomer's courtroom was not so much a temple of justice as a Starr chamber. Broomer was so pro prosecution that he'd help assistant DAs with their questioning and would regularly depart from the approved jury instructions to explain his own take on a case. This sort of behavior often got Broomer reversed by appellate courts, which dryly cataloged his sins by way of rebuke.

Judge Broomer, they'd note, "delivered a lengthy charge in which he instructed the jurors on the importance of harmonizing their views and avoiding emotions. In the midst of this charge, the court stated: 'And when you examine it logically, if you were twelve computers, you'd all reach the same results because you all have the same knowledge of the case. None of you knows anything about the case more than the others. If you have twelve computers and they're all identically programmed and you push the verdict button, the verdict will be guilty.'"

The verdict will be guilty? That guy got a new trial.

Broomer once discharged a juror for farting; the defendant in that case got a new trial too. As the appellate court wryly noted: "A number of jurors complained of another juror who emitted a foul body odor and was flatulent. The court found that the juror had thereby engaged in misconduct of a substantial nature as contemplated by CPL 270.35 and discharged the juror without having interviewed him." Oops. Chuck an alleged farter without even asking? That's a new trial. And so is explaining the delicate question of identification by citing musical theater. Broomer did that too.

"You know how in that song 'Some Enchanted Evening' someone looks across a crowded room and sees a face that changes their life that they never forget?" Broomer asked in an identification case. "This case is like that." Wrong again.

"So what are we doing with Mr. McFadden's case?" Moge demands.

He's looking at the district attorney's table. There, the same assistant DA who will handle Alberto's case is once again flipping through the long line of white-flapped folders that line the prosecution's table.

"How about two weeks?" pipes the ADA, asking for the default, I-don't-really-know-what's-going-on-in-this-case adjournment period.

"Work for you?" Moge asks me, citing a date in January.

"Sure," I say. What else can I say? Since there is no speedy trial right in a murder case, the DA's office sets the pace.

"Done," Moge says, jerking his head upward and to the right, his expressive eyebrows leading the way in a get-out-of-my-courtroom nod. But I'm not leaving just yet.

Six

ALBERTO HOBBLES UP. I've barely spoken a word to him in months.

Alberto is charged with a two-decade-old homicide and, according to the DA's murmurings, may be a suspect in two others. A short, graying Cuban, Alberto has spent most of the years since the Mariel Boatlift in prison. In Alberto's case, unlike in nearly all of my other cases, I'm not fighting for my client's freedom; no matter what happens in the murder case, Alberto's still got another fifteen years to serve on a rape.

Alberto wants a trial. Why, I have no idea — the entire case is built around a confession he signed while already in prison. He called the detectives himself. It seems he wanted to implicate a former partner in crime who'd stopped sending him commissary money — the cash inmates rely on to buy (usually at obscenely inflated prices) basic prison necessities like soap, deodorant, and candy. Apparently, soap was something Alberto never intended to do without. And so a few years into his seventeen-year sentence for rape, Alberto decided that he was going to inform on his old female acquaintance. He called the Cold Case Squad and told them he had information about a twenty-three-year-old murder.

For his efforts, they charged *him* with the crime.

Alberto's predicament dramatizes a core principle: making a statement to the police is never — *never* — in a criminal defendant's interest. Talking to the cops is generally a bad idea, even if you're the one who called them. This is true whether you are Martha Stewart, who secured a jail term when she foolishly decided to make a voluntary statement to the authorities, or Alberto, who fancied himself a clever jailhouse lawyer, confident that he could get even by manipulating the cops. It is one of the few things that every criminal lawyer will agree on: in the crucible of police interrogation, the police will always win.

In most states, including New York, when two or more people set out to commit a felony and someone dies in the course of their committing that felony, even if the death may not have been part of the plan, pretty much everyone involved in the crime can be prosecuted for what's called "felony murder." Alberto didn't seem to realize this. And as a consequence, a statement like the one he signed, one that read "*we* went to rob the payroll, and then Angie shot the clerk," presented far more than a pronoun problem for him. The *we* was a tight little noose, and by using it Alberto obligingly handed prosecutors the business end of the rope they could use to hang him for a good long time.

I have told clients a thousand times: if the police try to talk to you, just stay calm, ignore everything they ever tell you, and ask for a lawyer. Repeatedly. Insistently. Relentlessly. And hard as it is to believe, this is the best course of action *whether or not* you are guilty of anything. No one should talk. But nearly everyone does, and almost everyone regrets it.

Having procured a signed confession from Alberto, the prosecutors need to do two simple things in order to use it against him and potentially convict him of murder. First, they have to notify me that they intend to use the statement, and then, if I properly challenge the admissibility of the statement, there will be a suppression hearing in which I can press my challenge by arguing, among other things, that they got the statement in violation of Alberto's *Miranda* rights.

The notice requirement is easily satisfied. Criminal Procedure Law Section 710.30 (1)(a) explains that within fifteen days of arraignment the DAs have to tell the defense about any statement that the prosecution intends to introduce in their main case. This is done in different ways in various jurisdictions.

In the Bronx, this is done orally. That is, when a case is first before a judge, the DA will say, "710.30 (1)(a) — the defendant stated in sum and substance at the time and place of arrest . . ." and then read for the record the statement they intend to introduce. In Brooklyn, however, these notices are in writing. There the prosecution hands over an actual piece of paper (in triplicate) that describes the statement they intend to introduce. Back in Brooklyn, I had posted some of the more colorful statements on my office wall.

> Please take notice that at the time and place of arrest the
> defendant stated in sum and substance: I am a warlock,
> and all who fuck with a warlock must die.
> [obstruction of governmental administration]

> I didn't rob him: he robbed me.
> [robbery]

> Worth it? Clearly you ain't never had my blow jobs before.
> [prostitution]

Not all statements are amusing, of course. Many are tragic; a few are unsettling. A client of mine, for example, once distractedly explained: "She didn't have the money, so I shot her in the head. Then I went back to Brooklyn." The banality was nearly as chilling as the crime itself.

The more serious the case, the more covetous the police become about getting a confession. They press harder in murder cases than in commercial burglary, harder in robbery cases than in simple assaults. And the more mentally retarded, naïve, or young the defendant, the more likely it is that there is a full videotaped confession. I have yet to see a case in which a young kid, thirteen, fourteen, or fifteen years old, is charged with a serious crime in which there was not a statement — sometimes written in the detective's crabbed scrawl, but more often a damaging admission caught on videotape. In murders too (other than Reginald's), self-incriminating statements are commonplace.

Alberto only speaks Spanish, and since my usual little check-in patter comes off as halting and stiff when filtered through an interpreter, I don't really bother. As the clerk calls his case, Alberto struggles up, leaning on his crutch and hopping the last few feet to the counsel table.

Given that he's already serving a lengthy sentence and that the case against him is already almost twenty-five years old, adjournments really don't matter much in Alberto's case. As with clients like Jimmy, Alberto's self-defeating jailhouse lawyering seems to know no bounds.

"You know," he said gravely the last time we met, looking at the interpreter with a canny smile, "when they arrested me, no one read me my rights."

Nearly every week some client tells me that. Like Alberto, most of them think not reading you your rights means that the case has to be dismissed. Nothing could be further from the truth. "Reading me my rights" is, of course, an allusion to a famous Supreme Court case, *Miranda v. Arizona*. It was that case that codified the speech we've all heard a thousand times in every cop drama ever made — "You have the right to remain silent, etc." Unfortunately for my clients, *Miranda* is essentially a dead letter. The politics of statements are such that over the years judges have found myriad ways to ensure that anything defendants say will somehow be used as evidence against them.

For starters, *Miranda* doesn't even apply unless a prosecutor wants to use a defendant's incriminating statements against him at trial. Exculpatory statements — things like "I didn't do that" or "the sex was consensual" — aren't subject to *Miranda,* and aren't even admissible by the defense. It's why talking never makes sense — the prosecutors can use the bad stuff, but the defense can't use the good stuff. Also, because *Miranda* is not so much about being arrested as being interrogated, there is an additional category of statements to which *Miranda* doesn't apply — something called noncustodial questioning. Judges try to wedge open this unrestricted space as wide as they can, often finding that an interrogation isn't custodial until the cops snap on the cuffs or lock the door. Open your mouth before then and whatever you say is almost certain to boomerang.

The travails of another client of mine provide a good example of all this. Taken from his building and placed in the back of a squad car, in which the locks are controlled from the front, James was brought to a police precinct, where he was marched in past the desk sergeant, up a guarded set of stairs, down a short corridor of scuffed linoleum, past a series of armed police officers, and into a tiny interrogation room in the middle of the Homicide Task Force detective area. There he was questioned about a robbery and shooting. The room had three chairs, a long heavy table pressed up against the wall, the obligatory one-way mirror, and a door that bolts from the outside. And there, behind closed doors, his chair pressed up against the wall, with two detectives leaning in — one sitting across from him, the other sitting at the edge of the table effectively blocking his exit — James was interrogated for four and a half hours.

And did he talk? You bet he did. Just like almost everyone else I've ever represented. Isolated and alone, terrified by the surroundings and the detectives, pretty much everyone talks. The idea that anyone encircled by armed detectives and shut up in an interrogation room of a police precinct feels free to leave is a bit absurd. In fact, the overwhelming experience of clients I've spoken to is feeling trapped and frightened. And to a person, they believe (rightly) that if they tried to get up and walk out, they'd be physically stopped and possibly assaulted.

But judges hate to suppress confessions, so when it came time to argue that James's interrogation was "custodial," and thus his statements should be suppressed, the response from the ADA, buttressed by sworn police testimony, was sadly familiar: sure the door to the interrogation room was slammed shut, they admitted, but it wasn't *bolted* shut, so James had been "free to leave at any time" (in the cop's own words on the stand). The judge (as they all do) found this shameful argument compelling.

Of course, there are many situations in which someone is clearly arrested at the scene of the crime. Being placed in handcuffs right away might seem to end the argument as to whether or not the defendant was in custody. But porous *Miranda* carves out exceptions for this situation too by exempting what are termed "spontaneous statements." These are generally understood to be things just blurted out by the defendants. Some of these are devastating and others hilarious. A favorite of mine in a drug possession case in which an officer fished four vials of crack from a client's pocket: "These are not my pants."

Explaining these legal distinctions to clients like Alberto is hard — his understanding, reasonable for anyone but a lawyer or inveterate cynic, is that the rules simply mean what they say. It's hard to explain that under the twisted law of the admissibility of statements it doesn't really matter whether or not the cops read him his rights.

Of course, explaining that the cops are actually allowed to lie is even harder. As it turns out, police officers are perfectly entitled to deceive suspects in order to persuade them to confess. Cops love this fact, and veteran detectives are often proud of their inventiveness when it comes to tricking people they consider stupid perps into confessing. Lying about evidence found at the scene, falsely suggesting that a codefendant is fingering them, or fabricating the existence of nonexistent eyewitnesses — all have been sanctioned by judges and are regularly used to extract statements from clients.

Given all these exceptions, pretty much anything a defendant ever says during an encounter with the police will ultimately be used as evidence against him. The impact of this fact, like so much else in the system, falls disproportionately upon the criminal defendants who don't have a lawyer on retainer, or don't know who to call when they get arrested. They are the ones most prone to relentless interrogation, most fearful of the police, and least able to call upon professional help. And as a result it's their statements from every step in the process that come back to haunt them come trial. Alberto will be no exception.

The court officers uncuff Alberto from his crutch, and he leans forward awkwardly — an aging man, eyes narrowed by crow's feet, clutching the battered wooden counsel table for support. Up on the bench Moge seems momentarily out of steam. This makes things easy. Standing at the table with my hobbled homicidal client murmuring to me in Spanish, I get a quick adjournment, glance at the clock, pat Alberto on the back, give Reginald the thumbs-up, and sprint for the door, hoping beyond hope that I can get some cases done over in criminal court.

I'm halfway down the hall when I remember that Reginald wanted to talk.

Going to the cells upstairs is a twenty-minute investment, and I've got half a dozen people waiting over in criminal court. It's closing on noon, and if I don't get to criminal court quickly, it is almost certain I'll wind up spending the entire afternoon there. I do the calculus quickly — Reginald can get to the phones at Rikers pretty easily, and at least three clients have already called the office to complain about waiting. On the other hand, Reginald doesn't ask for much, the pens above Moge's courtroom are easy to get to, and one of my favorite corrections officers sits the desk up there. She'll probably give me a few minutes with Reginald in the high-security area. That'll save some time, I think, pivoting toward the unmarked door that leads to a dingy staircase that ends in a gray steel door behind which my incarcerated client waits.

It's usually noisy on the inside — inmates yelling between cells, corrections officers shouting out names — but today things seem almost placid. Officer Cordero takes my ID and smiles when I ask her if I can talk to Reginald around the corner rather than go all the way up to the general population interview area on the seventh floor. "Sign the book," she says, inclining her head toward the back with a slightly exasperated smile.

"You're the best," I tell her as another corrections officer goes to get Reginald from the big cell where two dozen men wait for their few minutes in court or brief legal visit.

From a cell: "Yo, Feige."

It's Shamar — a kid I represented years ago. Shamar has gotten big since I saw him last. Gone is the skinny kid with the devilish smile and smooth delivery. In his place is a bruiser with a tough-guy face and cold eyes. Sha is lounging conspicuously in his cell, ostentatiously taking up more space than he deserves, the other inmates — four or five of them, old and young — crammed into the small cell, making room by perching on the edge of the bench or sitting on the floor. On seeing me, Shamar hops over to the bars, his perfectly white sneakers signaling a man well taken care of on the inside. Leaning into the bars and affecting a conspiratorial tone, he says to me, "You gotta take my case, man — I ain't seen my lawyer in months. I'm telling you, months!"

"Sha," I say firmly, "I ain't takin' your case. Who's your lawyer? I'll call him for you — tell him you need to talk to him."

"Nah, man." Sha is insistent. "I already called him. I need you, Feige — c'mon, you know me. I need you."

It's always nice to be liked, even when the admiration is the desperate, transparent hustle of a kid facing a life sentence. In a world that rewards a mien of tough callousness, subtle signs of need or pain have to be carefully masked — presented as hustle rather than weakness. Sadly, taking the time to figure out which is which is a luxury I can seldom afford. There are certainly times when begging works on me. There are a large number of cases that I've taken just because an old client asked, or the sister of an old client called, or someone thrust themselves against the bars and told me a tale that made me want to listen, despite the bruising caseload, screaming judges, and constant phone calls.

The funny part about Sha's pitch is that it is almost certainly true — that he, like many jailed clients, actually *hasn't* talked to his lawyer in months. Even in a reasonably well-funded system like the one in New York City, this is a common complaint. Between the daily crush of the courtroom and the pressure to get cases done, lawyers often don't bother to see clients — some adjourn cases without even bringing them up to the courtroom. It's called "waiving a client" — that is, waiving a client's right to be present for the mundane proceedings against him — this is a tradition in criminal court, and a decision almost always made based on the vagaries of the lawyer's schedule rather than the client's needs. In fact, it's often done without consulting the client at all.

Unfortunately every court day, whether they're going to see their lawyer or not, Shamar and thousands of other incarcerated clients like him are woken up at four in the morning, piled onto rickety old school buses outfitted with metal mesh windows, and driven from Rikers Island to courthouses around the city. The New York City Department of Corrections is almost unimaginably vast, housing more inmates on a typical night than the entire prison population of forty states. In shuttling Sha and his locked-up brethren around, the several hundred DOC buses log an average of thirty-five hundred miles every day.

When the inmates actually get to court (a process that, thanks to security measures, can often take several hours), they are off-loaded into huge pens (where assaults abound), which in turn filter into smaller pens arrayed around the Supreme Court building. Shamar, like most incarcerated clients, regularly spends an entire day in a bull pen without ever being called to court or even talking to his lawyer. Inmates call it "bull pen therapy."

"I'll call him for you, Sha. That's all I'm gonna do. I'm just being straight with you, brother."

"Okay, Feige. Thanks."

I shake his hand.

"Good luck with it, okay?"

"Don't worry, Feige. I'll beat it," he tells me with more confidence than I suspect he should.

Around the corner there are three narrow rooms accessed through locked steel doors. The middle one is for lawyers, the outside rooms for clients. The top two thirds of the long walls in the center room are made of steel mesh, allowing lawyers and clients to face each other. Farther down the hall is the Hannibal Lecter cage. It holds a single manacled client behind its thick grate.

The door to the middle room is ajar. Inside is a cross section of the Bronx legal community. In one corner, sitting across from a well-coiffed white guy, is Murray Richman, the self-proclaimed king of the Bronx bar. Murray's stature in the legal community is hard to overstate — he represents rappers (it was his client that went to prison in the Puff Daddy trial) and politicians, hustlers and fraudsters, charging them tens and sometimes hundreds of thousands of dollars for the privilege. He is a self-made guy who glad-hands his way through the courthouse as if he's the mayor. In a sense, he is.

Already past the age of usual retirement, Not-a-worry Murray looks a little like a puffin, resplendent in brash tie and matching pocket square. His expensive double-breasted suit covers a thick midsection, and his hair is combed in a way that suggests a great deal of attention has been lavished on every strand. He has a wide, round face and twinkly eyes, and he greets people with a "howyadoin?" honed by years of ingratiating practice. A charmer, Murray brings a winning theatricality to every sentence he utters. And he is utterly unselfconscious — as if he's completely forgotten that he'd long ago temporarily cast himself in a part written for someone larger, leaner, and more debonair.

A colleague of mine once ran into Murray on the courthouse steps. She had her six-year-old kid in tow and introduced the two of them. "This," she said to her child, "is Murray Richman, one of the most famous lawyers in the Bronx."

"Hi," said the kid shyly.

Leaning in close, his squat frame bulging with self-importance, Murray gave the kid his pitch.

"You know what?" he asked.

The kid shook his head, his eyes wide with interest.

"I'm *the* best lawyer in the Bronx," Murray said. "And I've never lost a case."

"Really?" The kid was impressed.

"Really."

Murray, despite the rather compelling documentary evidence to the contrary, was dead-serious.

Yet if he has lost more than a few cases here and there, and sometimes has a loose grip on the applicable case law, Richman has great sway with both judges and juries. Judges respect him because he is savvy and fearless, but also because he is deeply involved with the politics of the judiciary. Murray gives generously to judicial candidates and is active in local Bronx politics — something never lost on the judges he appears before.

Juries love him too. They like his perpetual tan and his flashy ties, his homespun antics and his theatrical cross-examinations. And he knows how to pick them. Having lived in the Bronx for the better part of a century, Murray knows every corner of the borough like a beat cop.

Seeing him, I smile and give a half wave. He nods back at me without interrupting the sentence he's hurling toward his client — a calm white guy in a wiseguy suit — with utter conviction. And as I sit down and watch him work, I see again the pathological confidence that makes him so appealing.

Sitting with his back to Murray, facing a different client in the opposite prisoner room, is the anti-Murray, Mark Brenner. Brenner is so loony that he once hauled off and kicked a client right in the middle of Troy Webber's courtroom. He also is said to have once pled a client charged with a driving offense to a prison sentence longer than the maximum allowed by law. (Just as scary, Judge Megan Tallmer apparently okayed the plea. On resentencing, Brenner advised the guy to just take the maximum.)

Wearing boat shoes and smudged white chinos, Brenner has his long white hair pulled back into something that appropriates the worst qualities of both a mullet and a ponytail. The overall effect resembles a Daniel Boone cap bleached blond.

Brenner isn't a public defender in the usual sense. Instead of practicing with a criminal defense organization, he's a solo practitioner who gets cases through an "assigned counsel plan." To a client this is a distinction without a difference. To them, any free lawyer is a public defender. That confusion is unfortunate for the rest of us.

Brenner's client is not white, and not calm. "Yo, I know guys who got six flat for a body!" he exclaims. A skinny kid with a shaved head and spindly arms, he smacks the palms of his hands flat on the desk, producing a sharp sound like a punch hitting bone. Brenner, who should have found other work years ago, sits impassively, a look of disgust on his face. I sit down two seats away, trying hard not to listen, hoping that Reginald will be brought in quickly.

"Sha-tak," says Brenner, a note of world-weary petulance inflecting his voice.

"It's Sha-*teeeek*," the kid says loudly, swinging his head violently back and forth: "Sha-*teeeek*," he repeats, elongating the hard *e* sound, holding it for a full half a second. "You pussy-assed motherfucker, can't even get my fucking name right and you asking me to cop out?"

"Hey, Sha-*teeeeeeeeeeeeek*."

Brenner's deliberately mimicking the kid now.

"Sha-*teeeeeeeeeeeek*, fuck you. I don't give two shits what you do. You don't wanna cop out? Huh? Then don't fucking cop out — go to trial for all I fucking care, get your ass forty or fifty years! I don't give a fuck what you do!"

"That's right you don't!" Shateek says, palms up as if he's made his point.

They're screaming at each other now, and the other lawyers huddled in the small space lean in toward their clients, making sure they can be heard above the din. No one interferes, no one tries to calm them down, and lawyer and client go on yelling at each other for another four or five minutes, during which Reginald, with a sidelong glance toward the shouting, takes his place across the wire mesh from me.

The interaction between Brenner and Shateek is more than commonplace — it's constant. Overworked, underappreciated lawyers and desperate clients are a potent mix. Many lawyers see intimate client relationships as superfluous, and the result, as I see every time I spend an hour or two in the cells, is a system littered with fault lines. And when lawyers cease to even try to understand clients, that mix can become disastrous.

It is something I always try to remember, even when I am impatient with Clarence or listening to Reginald when I really should be running to another courtroom. Instead of letting their anger enrage me, I work hard to recall that most of my clients are in jail, enduring daily an almost unfathomable horror. They're angry, resentful, sometimes frightened, and almost always desperate to get out as soon as possible. And they have no one to lash out at. All the anger, fear, and frustration of a steady diet of violence and bologna sandwiches are often hurled at the only available outlet — a public defender they didn't ask for and don't trust.

After a year or two of being the brunt of this sort of fury — continually abused by the people you are spending your life trying to help — it becomes extremely easy to see the entire attorney-client interaction as a power struggle. The problem is, that struggle is astonishingly damaging to both the lawyers, who spend their days fighting the clients they are supposed to help, and the clients, who deride the lawyers whose help they desperately need. Finding a way to build an alliance with a mistrustful client is one of the things that separates the dedicated from the fried.

Murray, and other private lawyers like him, seldom have these relationship issues.

It's about the money.

Those who hire a private criminal defense lawyer are already able to look at their case in ways that few public defender clients ever will. Private clients are far closer to the mythical rational actor. A private client looking for criminal representation will usually do all the things public defender clients are often prevented from doing: they'll probe and prod, ask questions about the case or predicament, listen for that tone of directness and reassurance that gives a client the confidence and knowledge that although everything might not actually be all right, at least there will be someone to protect them and defend them and try his best to be sure that things don't get too terrible. If wealthy defendants are not reassured, they're unlikely to spend their money to retain the lawyer they are talking to. That's why private lawyers do the dance. There is no question too stupid, no hope too faint, no situation too dire to elicit thoughtful, measured answers and a concerned smile — precisely the things public defender clients almost never get.

The ultimate irony is that at the Bronx Defenders, among other offices, clients represented by public defenders get representation as good, and often better, than that provided by most private lawyers. This is because many public defenders, and certainly the good ones, are able to bring in the kind of additional services that make all the difference in a case — social workers, investigators, and experts, precisely the kinds of services none but the wealthiest criminal defendants can afford. Still, even with skilled lawyers and good ancillary services, public defenders are at a terrible disadvantage in creating good client relationships. When alliances are forged in the crucible of need rather than choice, the resultant links are more often fraught with contentiousness having little to do with the skill of the attorney or even the results in a case.

Ignoring the yelling from Shateek and Brenner, who are still going at it down the row, Reginald leans toward the mesh. He wants to go over some of the paperwork I sent him. He's carefully annotated one or two of the DD-5s (the forms the detectives use to record the steps in their investigation). As usual, Reginald's thoughts are measured and logical, and his questions are pointed and smart. He's been thinking about this stuff and wants to be sure I understand the significance of what he's found. We bat his insights around for three or four minutes (something I should have done more of with Clarence), and then I tell Reginald he's great, to hang tough, and to call me in the office after five someday if he wants to talk about this some more. He smiles graciously and thanks me for coming up. Standing up, I nod at Reginald and, making a fist, press the pinky side of my hand against the grate. Reginald does the same.

I retrieve my corrections pass, check the time, and, as the thick steel door swings open, sprint toward criminal court.

Seven

I BREAK INTO A DEAD RUN the moment the bas-relief doors of the Supreme Court elevators open up. I sprint out onto the Grand Concourse and down the street toward the criminal courthouse. It's after noon, and I'm more than an hour late for criminal court.

I shouldn't have gone up to see Reginald. I've kept half a dozen clients waiting, packed into crowded courtrooms, wondering where the hell their lawyer is. In well-practiced fashion, I can usually get one quick call in during the trip from one building to the other — this time it's merely to retrieve another two messages from justifiably pissed-off clients.

The Bronx Criminal Courthouse is a gray, modern box just off the Grand Concourse. Unlike Supreme Court, which deals with indicted felony cases, the criminal courthouse processes mostly misdemeanors. On many mornings the line to get inside stretches to the corner and around the block, the kind of queue that would entice an elderly Russian woman to join just with the promise of its length. But on 161st Street, those in line wait to be frisked, inspected, metal-detected, and ultimately processed through a criminal justice system that dockets more than seventy thousand cases a year in the Bronx alone: juveniles carted off to jail, fathers thrown out of their houses, blank-faced kids who can't explain why they robbed or shot someone, or failed to show up at probation. The apparent calm of Supreme Court is gone; over here, in the assembly-line justice of criminal court, the system's shortcomings are in your face. For starters, criminal court is always noisy: lawyers yell at clients, clients yell at lawyers, judges yell at lawyers, judges yell at clients, and some lawyers even yell at judges. The uncarpeted hallways reverberate with the constant clamor of a thousand urgent arguments. A massive fleet of court officers — the small army of armed men and women who secure the courthouses and the judges — polices the mayhem.

Even getting inside criminal court can be complicated. There are three lines: one for cops, prosecutors, and other people with badges (they walk right in); one for credentialed defense lawyers (again, since 9/11 a "speed pass" is required for defense lawyers; without one you get searched); and one for the general public. There are more than half a dozen magnetometers, manned by more than a dozen uniformed court officers who inspect the thousands of regular people who come in every day.

Just getting through the line and into the courthouse is a trying experience — a little like clearing security at Angry International Airport. This is partly because almost everyone inside the courthouse is in the midst of a personal drama of some sort — scared about going to jail, hoping to see a loved one who was just arrested, or finally seeking protection from an abusive lover or spouse. The tension regularly bubbles over just as people finally reach the magnetometers.

Today is no different. Heading through the doors, still hustling, I veer toward the middle line — the one for lawyers. Just to my left there is a woman who is obviously homeless. She is thin, though her frame is padded by the bulk of several layers of clothing. Her two coats bulge with ratty papers. She's probably been waiting outside in the cold for nearly an hour.

"Empty your pockets," a young court officer barks as the woman approaches the X-ray machine. Slowly, methodically, she begins taking things out of her pockets. Another court officer (his hands covered by plastic gloves) pokes through the junk, pushing most of it through the machine.

"What's this?" he says, pointing to a sandwich carefully wrapped in a clear plastic bag.

"A-ah . . . ," the woman stammers, "that's my lunch."

"Well, you can't bring it in. No food allowed."

"Can I keep it somewhere and get it later?" She has a thin voice, but it's clear and firm. "It's all I have to eat."

"Nope — gotta go in the garbage."

"Can I promise not to eat it and just keep it with me? I'm homeless; it's all I've got . . . please." A plaintive edge creeps into her voice.

"Put it in the garbage. Or leave."

"But . . ."

"I said chuck it or leave!" Several other court officers stride over. One, looking sideways at the young woman, ominously unsnaps the handcuff case at his waist.

"Please . . . , Officer . . . I don't mean no harm. I gotta go to court, and I got nothin' else to eat. I won't eat it inside. I'll leave it here, I'll pick it up later, please. . . ."

"Escort her out," the original officer tells the backup guys. They close in.

"Please, sir, please" — she's pleading now — "I gotta go to court; I can't get a warrant — I'll throw it out, okay? I'll throw it out. Please don't make me go through the line again."

Four officers surround the woman; there are tears in her eyes. Looking up at the burly men, she seems even smaller than she had just a moment before.

"Take her out."

The officers grab her, roughly spin her around, and march her past me, back up the stairs, and out the door.

"Please, sir, can I have my stuff back?" she cries over her shoulder.

"In a minute, ma'am," says another officer. This one is a Latino guy with silky postpubescent facial hair. He's gathering up the papers, coins, and personal items from the far side of the magnetometer.

"What about this?" he asks, picking up the sandwich and glancing at the square-jawed white guy who had made the fuss in the first place.

"It's disgusting," says Square Jaw, "probably a health-code violation."

"I don't know," the Latino guy says, trying to avoid an unnecessary power struggle. It's too late though.

"Chuck it," says Square Jaw, grabbing the sandwich and arcing it toward the industrial garbage can a few feet away. There's a little sigh from a few people in the line. Some shake their head; others scowl and look down.

Near the trash can, another woman glances around and, reaching down, starts to pull the sandwich out. Square Jaw spots her immediately. "Removing food from a garbage can is a health-code violation!" he barks. There's another sotto voce sigh from the line. The good Samaritan, who a second before had seemed willing to lose her place in line to deliver the retrieved sandwich, knows she can't risk being escorted out and banned from the building, or worse, arrested. And so, with a low shake of her head, she ostentatiously opens her thumb and forefinger, and drops the plastic bag back into the garbage.

"Have a nice day," the court officer nearest me says wryly.

➤⫸⫷

As I walk away from the magnetometers, I'm wondering whether I should find out what courtroom the homeless woman was going to so that I can alert her lawyer or tell the judge that she really did try to come to court. But with the swarm of people heading through the revolving doors and the crowd outside, I can see neither her nor the cluster of court officers.

There's nothing to do.

As I head around the corner to the escalators, I pass another court officer. This one is marching back and forth in front of a huge metal pen calling out names through a bullhorn. There are fifty or sixty people standing around listlessly.

"Here," yells a hugely fat Hispanic man with a goatee.

"Yo," answers a kid in a black-and-red velvet tracksuit.

Both of them are waving little pink slips — criminal court summonses. Summonses resemble traffic tickets and charge offenses like disorderly conduct, possession of an open container of alcohol, or truancy. They are adjudicated in the part just to my left.

Summonses are both the least serious and most bountiful of criminal court actions — the krill of criminal court. The summons part, known as SAP-1 or the "SAP part," is in session several days a week, including today, and handles even more cases than the criminal parts upstairs — sometimes over a hundred a day. Although many of the cases are technically misdemeanor criminal offenses, it is an unwritten rule that no one emerges from the summons part with a criminal record. Still, a summons is a summons, and on the days that they are heard, the ground floor of criminal court can become horrifically crowded — hence the barricade/bullhorn system.

Summonses play a starring role in the overpolicing of underprivileged communities, and if you want to understand why so many poor people view the police with animosity and skepticism, you need only examine the role that police and those pink slips play in the lives of poor folks.

In the Bronx it is routine to see hardworking people who earn minimum wage come into court owing a thousand dollars in tickets issued *at the same time on the same traffic stop.* These people, scraping to get by, don't have any problem paying the summons for the rolling stop at the stop sign — in their view, they did wrong, and they accept it. But the fact that they also got a ticket for a crooked license plate, five more for inappropriately tinted windows (a separate one for each window), a seat-belt violation issued *after* the officer ordered them out of the car, a ticket for an improper lane change because they failed to signal while pulling over for the policeman in question, and a bonus ticket for a cracked side-view mirror — well, that just makes them hate the cops.

The police would never pile on tickets like this in Manhattan or Beverly Hills or Highland Park. Outraged citizens wouldn't just challenge every one of the tickets, they'd complain — to the precinct captain, to legislators, to their friends at the DA's office. Cops who police wealthy neighborhoods don't want to risk being reamed out by their captains for being assholes to a friend of a deputy commissioner. And since the police can't possibly know who those friends are, neighborhood and race become proxies for access. This access to the power structure moderates the nature of policing, keeping it inside acceptable norms in affluent neighborhoods. The odds that someone on the Upper East Side of Manhattan knows the mayor are a helluva lot better than the odds in the Soundview Oval.

My clients, of course, have no access to anyone, so if they do complain, they do so to utter deafness. No matter how outrageous the police conduct, the presumption is that the client is whining, gutless, and guilty — certainly not a serious citizen with a legitimate complaint. With no check on their behavior, the cops in the Bronx tend to be a lot rougher and a little faster with the old summons book. For example: Bronx cops give thousands of summonses for open containers of alcohol — a rule flagrantly flouted in most of the tony public spaces where Manhattan's wealthy gather. In Central Park's Sheep Meadow, a popular summer tanning spot for Manhattan Yuppies, beer peddlers wander openly among the sunbathers and Frisbee players, patronized without a second thought. But have a beer after your soccer game in one of the poorly tended green spaces of the Bronx, and you can expect to get a ticket. At an opera in Central Park a bottle of wine is expected and accepted, but listen to some rappers in Crotona Park with a nice cold one and you'll get to spend a day waving your pink ticket at the guy with the bullhorn.

Reality, as many poor people eventually understand it, is that between the rules about truancy, trespass, loitering, disorderly conduct, and dog walking, most any adventure can wind up getting you a summons. And that's if you're lucky.

Michael wasn't.

It all started on a warm August day. Michael Johnson, a quiet nineteen-year-old who worked part-time as a stock clerk at a hardware store, offered to walk a friend's dog because its actual owner had a family emergency.

He made it exactly three blocks. Walking along the sidewalk, dog pulling happily on the leash, Michael was approached by a police officer. Officer Rivera wanted to see vaccination reports for the dog.

"It's not my dog," Michael patiently explained. "But the owner is only three blocks from here. I could go get him for you."

Rivera wasn't interested. He wrote Michael three separate summonses — one for an unvaccinated dog, one for failing to produce tags, and one for not having, on his person, a paper vaccination report.

Now, I have a lot of friends with dogs, and I live near a couple of dog runs. Most every day I pass dogs on the street, dogs in the park, dogs in the elevators. But I have never seen police from any Manhattan precincts interrogating dog owners at any of the fancy dog runs near where I live. Indeed, if the police on Fifth Avenue started writing tickets for absent vaccination papers when the glitzy Pekingese owners couldn't pull them out of their Gucci handbags, there would be hell to pay. But as with the rest of big-city policing practices, the norms for the rich don't apply in impoverished neighborhoods.

Now Michael was a good-natured guy, and he showed the tickets to his friend the dog owner, who graciously offered to send in the vaccination certificate or pay the fine. The only problem was, he didn't. And so, a few years later, as Michael was leaving his house on the way to work, the Warrant Squad arrested him.

Every year, thousands of criminal defendants fail to show up for court. And in New York, there are tens of thousands of outstanding bench warrants, seeking people charged with crimes ranging from disorderly conduct to murder. It's the Warrant Squad's job to find them. There are both good and bad officers in the Warrant Squad. Some start on the assumption that someone simply forgot — and in most minor cases (and even some major ones) they'll call in advance, remind a defendant that there is a warrant out for them, and just meet them at the courthouse to effect a return. Others love the collar, but most of them would rather pick up the little guys than the scary ones — after all, they're less likely to catch a bullet arresting someone wanted for a health-code violation than arresting someone wanted on a firearm charge. That's why, despite the thousands of felony warrants, people charged with minor crimes get disproportionately brought in.

They came for Michael on a Saturday morning, grabbing him just outside the house he shared with his mother and little brother. "We're from the Warrant Squad," they said, and then, without further elaboration, slapped the handcuffs on Michael and took him to jail. Michael tried to explain things to the cops. "Shut up. Tell it to the judge," they said. He spent the day in a filthy cell, waiting to do just that.

People arrested by the Warrant Squad generally get low priority in the system, and Michael was no exception. A court clerk in the arraignment office of criminal court explained the logic to me once. "The system's always crowded," he said, "and these guys already got their shot at going through quickly. They didn't come back — fuck 'em."

Unfortunately, the police department didn't get around to shipping Michael to court. As a result, Michael spent the night on the hard floor of the cell, a bologna sandwich and some Kool-Aid for sustenance.

Sunday didn't go so well either — he waited all day, regularly shuffled from cell to cell. But even though arraignments were going on, no one came for him. No one called his name. He never met a lawyer. He never saw a judge.

Michael tried to talk to the police officers guarding the big pens. He tried to ask them what was going on, how long he might stay in jail. They told him to shut up. Sunday night came and went.

For the second night in a row, Michael stretched out on the tile floor. No one would explain what was going on or how long he'd be there. Every time he tried to tell his story they'd say, "Save it for the judge." But no one was taking him to see any judge, nor would anyone let him make a phone call (in the Bronx, the "one phone call" rule has long since been superseded by the "we'll let you call if we feel like it" rule).

Unshowered and terrified, Michael spent his third day in the cell, waiting for someone to listen, for someone to get him up to see the judge. Around him, people, many of whom had been arrested for serious charges, came and went.

"Johnson," an officer finally called out.

"Here!" Michael barked, and at long last they led him up the stairs to the holding cells that the lawyers had access to.

One of the young lawyers in my office had picked up Michael's case. "Don't worry," the lawyer told him. "This is crazy — these cases should get dismissed, and you should be home tonight."

There was only one problem: Judge Mary Ann Brigantti-Hughes.

Judge Brigantti-Hughes is not known for her legal brilliance. In fact, she's not known for much except her unpredictable rulings and surprising ignorance when it comes to the laws she is called upon to interpret. Though a pol all her life (after graduating from Temple Law School, she worked for a judge before moving on to a job with the state attorney general, eventually becoming counsel to the Bronx borough president), exactly how she wound up on the bench remains a matter of some mystery. Brigantti-Hughes is one of the very few judges who managed to be rated "not approved" by a bar association yet was endorsed by both political parties for a seat in the Bronx Supreme Court.

Brigantti-Hughes is short and pinched and beady-eyed, and she speaks with a clipped, exaggerated diction seemingly designed to hide the vestigial Spanish accent lying just below her vowels. In a survey of judges published in the *New York Law Journal,* Judge Brigantti-Hughes was rated one of the worst criminal court judges in the Bronx. She is irritable and mercurial, the latter making her particularly hard to practice before, since a lawyer can seldom really tell a client what to expect. Brigantti-Hughes can turn on you without warning, even in the most sympathetic cases.

And that's exactly what happened to Michael.

Facing a man who had spent three days in lockup armed with the perfectly reasonable excuse that it wasn't his dog and that his friend had assured him he'd pay the tickets, almost any judge would have either just dismissed the charges (likely) or at the very least sentenced him to time already served (a virtual certainty). Not Brigantti-Hughes.

"If he pleads to the charge, I'll give him three days of community service," she said, peering down from the bench.

Michael's lawyer tried again, repeating the fact that the summonses were legally questionable in the first place, and that in any case Michael had already been in jail for more than three days on a three-year-old misunderstanding.

"Coun-se-lor," Brigantti-Hughes said, enunciating every syllable, "I said he could have three days of community service."

"You won't even give him time served?" the lawyer asked, stunned.

"No," snapped the judge, "you don't want it?"

Michael's lawyer turned to him, trying to explain on the fly why this was going horribly awry, and that he might actually have to come back to court to clear up the tickets. Apparently the thirty seconds of explanation was too much for Judge Brigantti-Hughes.

"Bail is five hundred dollars on each," she said tartly. "Next case."

Michael looked perplexed as the court officers turned him around and steered him back toward the door that led to the jail.

"Judge, please," the lawyer begged, but it was too late.

"I offered him three days, he didn't take it. Bail is five hundred dollars," Brigantti-Hughes said with utter indifference. Three times throughout the night, Michael's lawyer implored Brigantti-Hughes to rehear the case, and at last, well after midnight, she did so.

Back before the judge, Michael was asked again whether he wanted to plead guilty. His choice, according to Brigantti-Hughes, was plead guilty and spend three days cleaning the parks or go back to jail. Michael wanted the plea.

"So you knew you had an unvaccinated dog?" Judge Brigantti-Hughes said, raising her eyebrows and looking at Michael's lawyer with a smug I-told-you-so look.

"Actually, ma'am, it was my friend's dog; I was just walking it and didn't have the papers."

"Fine," said the judge. "I don't accept your plea." She turned to the court officers. "Put him back in — this court is adjourned." And with that, she got up and walked off the bench.

Michael finally lost his composure. "What do you want from me?" he wailed. "I told you I'd plead guilty — what do you want? I'm gonna lose my job. I haven't showered in four days; please let me out of here!" His voice was shaking and cracking as the officers roughly shoved him back behind the metal door, closing it before his lawyer could follow.

Behind the door were sobs. "Let me out of here. *Please.*"

"Court's closed," the officers said firmly, stepping in front of Michael's lawyer.

❧

"You gotta be kidding me?" Judge Joseph Dawson was shaking his head. "For a *dog?*"

Dawson is a criminal court version of Mogulescu — bullying but kindhearted, intemperate but smart, good on the law, and personally charming. He's a big guy, with a round, jowly face set off with a thick auburn mustache and a pugnaciousness born of being a former organized crime prosecutor. Though Dawson loses his temper occasionally, he is a good man who struggles through a tough job, and on the days he can control his impatience, it is almost possible to believe that he is genuinely committed to justice.

After word of Michael's night-court fiasco got back to the office, I had been dispatched to court to get him out of jail. As it turns out, Dawson was presiding over the courtroom where that could get done.

Grabbing an assistant DA who knew nothing about the case (ADAs generally aren't even assigned to summonses), I explained the whole horrifying saga: Dawson just shook his head, rolled his eyes, and tried his best not to dime out a fellow jurist. "Get him out here," he said.

Michael, though, was nowhere to be found. He'd disappeared back into the vast system of cells, and no one seemed to know where he was. I headed down the back stairs, to the main desk behind which the corrections officers responsible for prisoner movement sit.

"Hey, Counselor," Officer Dawkins said. "How you doin'?"

I get along reasonably well with most of the corrections officers. Unlike the police department, which is mostly white, the New York City Department of Corrections is largely made up of Hispanics and African Americans — many of whom have a genuine connection to my clients. As unbelievably brutal and terrifying as Rikers is, unlike most state prisons, it is mostly guarded by people who know firsthand that mistakes are made and that innocent people are often locked up. Corrections officers know how brutal and utterly unforgiving the criminal justice system can be, and many of these guards are willing to help out, especially when there is a real injustice to correct.

"Hey, Dawkins, I got a little problem from last night."

"Yeah? Go ahead."

I told the four or five officers crowded behind the desk the saga of Michael and the dog, of Mary Ann Brigantti-Hughes and the three days of community service, and also, of course, about Judge Joseph Dawson, waiting upstairs to set Michael free.

"No shit," one of them said. "Three days for dog tags? Damn, that's ugly."

"Let's see if we can find him for you," Dawkins muttered, typing Michael's name into the computer.

He looked up a second later.

"Counselor, you sure he wasn't second called? 'Cause we don't have him." If Michael was "second called," it would mean that he was still in the custody of the police department rather than corrections (who technically take over as soon as bail is set).

"Shit. You sure?"

"Oh, yeah — I'm sure," Dawkins said, shaking his head. "If I was you, I'd check with PD."

Back to the stairs, back through the bars, back past the DOC cells, to the police department's holding cells, where three cops and two corrections officers were sitting around watching a

TV at deafening volume. I started to tell the story again, hoping one of them might be sympathetic, but the cop at the computer just scowled.

"Check corrections," she growled without taking her eyes off the TV or bothering to check the computer.

I realized that if I didn't find Michael soon, he was going to be stuck until the afternoon court session.

"He ain't there. Dawkins is sure of it," I told her.

"Well, that ain't my problem, is it?"

Actually it is, but once again they've got the keys to the cells and the printouts and the tracking information. All I had was a sympathetic story, and it didn't seem as if it was going to get me what I needed.

I was stuck and looking utterly defeated, when one of the corrections officers stood up and fixed me with a knowing look.

"C'mon, Counselor," Angela said, "let's go find your man." And with that, Angela and I went cell to cell, peering through the bars of the various cages under police department control, calling out Michael's name. It took us nearly half an hour to find him, and by the time we did, the courtroom upstairs was closed for lunch.

Michael was, of course, in police custody.

I explained to Michael who I was and why I was there. He was frantic. I was halfway through my short introduction when he exploded.

"Please, you've gotta get me out of here — I don't care if I cop out; I don't care about the fine; I'll do whatever they want me to, but I've been here for days and I can't take it anymore. Look at me." He was exasperated, desperate. "I smell, I haven't shaved, I look horrible, I haven't eaten anything except bologna and oranges and Kool-Aid for four days. I know I already lost my job; my mother don't even know where I am." His hands were balled into fists. "You gotta get me out. I'm *begging* you."

"I will, Michael, I will," I said, hoping that my certainty would somehow help calm him down. "We're going back to see a judge — a different judge. This is all going to work out — and soon."

Michael's face, which had read as confused and angry, now betrayed only despair. "I already lost my job over this," he repeated. "I've been here four days: *what do they want from me?*"

I hate being put in the position of trying to justify a monstrous system, and so while I tried to explain, I took pains not to sound in any way apologetic. "Michael," I said, "you got fucked — plain and simple — you got fucked by a horrible judge and an asshole of a friend who shouldn't have ignored those tickets. There's nothing I can do about all the shit you been through already — all I can do is get you the hell out of here as soon as possible, which in this case means about an hour from now. That's what I can do, and that's what I *will* do. Okay?"

Michael took a big breath, half closed his eyes, swallowed whatever he really wanted to say, and nodded. And an hour later, he was free — as Judge Dawson, with an apologetic nod, dismissed each of the tickets.

⇥⋖⋗

"*ALVAREZ.*"

"Here!"

"*JONES*, Tynesha. *Tynesha JONES.*"

"Me!"

"*MENDEZ*, Pablo, *Pablo MENDEZ.*"

"Si."

The court officer with the megaphone continues to call out names. It's twenty-two minutes before 1:00, and if I don't get to a courtroom fast, I'll never get another case done before lunch. Veering away from the metallic shriek of the bullhorn and the listless crowds near the summons part, I turn right, down an escalator, heading toward the tiny courtroom where kindly Judge Robert Cohen presides.

Judge Cohen is thin and slightly stooped, with a sallow complexion and sharp features that light up when he speaks. Near the age of mandatory retirement, Cohen has long, frail fingers and a thin thatch of hair, but unlike almost everyone else in the Bronx, he is always smiling. Cohen is the kindest, most decent jurist I have ever come across. He is the model of what a judge should be. Cohen is so thin that he is almost swallowed up by the bench from which he presides; still, his voice is strong and clear, and he waves his hands liberally while complimenting everyone who comes before him. For Cohen, every plea seems to involve the admirable efforts of the defense lawyer and the commendable cooperation of the district attorney's office. Under his smiling gaze even routine events become opportunities to congratulate, praise, and approve of the work done in his court. Cohen's thanks is so unstinting and so genuine that lawyers, clients, and even prosecutors (who think he's too pro defense) wind up leaving his part with a warm glow. Stepping into his courtroom feels like a holiday from the rest of the building — an oasis of peace on a continent of fractiousness.

"Ooooh, Mr. Feige," Cohen erupts as I walk through the doors at twenty minutes to one. "So nice to see you, sir."

"Thank you, Your Honor."

Judge Cohen presided over the very first murder case I ever handled in the Bronx (a shooting outside a battered woman's shelter caught on videotape). He also handled one of the strangest trials I ever did. It was a long-term drug operation in which my client (alleged to be the seller) was tried in absentia despite being incarcerated. Basically, he refused to talk to me, to come to court, or to participate in any way in his own defense. By the time he was acquitted I hadn't seen him in weeks. I never heard from him after the verdict and never saw him again.

I'm stopping by the part because I need to look at a letter that a dissatisfied client of mine wrote to the judge. I'd taken the case as a special favor — the fifth attorney for a guy facing a mandatory life sentence for a series of robberies — and though things seemed to go well at first, they deteriorated rapidly. My client resolutely refused to recognize the indictment as having the force of law and rejected the authority of the court. He insisted that I was failing to understand that he, as a Freemason, was not subject to the laws of the state of New York (which, additionally, he believed didn't exist).

I've had clients like this several times, but there was something even stranger and more insistent about this one, and after a lot of soul-searching and many metaphysical conversations with colleagues, I decided to have him evaluated for competency to stand trial. He was found unfit to proceed and was transferred to a psychiatric/prison hospital to be stabilized. He never forgave me for believing him to be crazy. He and his family wrote angry letters denouncing my work on his behalf. He refused to talk to me, and in short order our working relationship eroded past the point of no return. Then he sent a letter to the judge.

Handing me a copy of the letter, Evelyn, Judge Cohen's trusted clerk, smiles kindly.

"Don't worry about this," she says. "Thanks for trying."

"Oh, yes, Mr. Feige," the judge chimes in from above. "You were wonderful, and he was lucky to have you — please don't be upset in the slightest. I've found him new counsel, and he'll be fine."

"Thanks, Judge," I say, smiling.

Down the hall, inside the trial assignment part known as TAP-1, Judge Darcel Clark is dispensing justice at a rapid clip. Every available trial judge is already busy, so her job for the rest of the day is to adjourn cases, push pleas, and survive her calendar. There are more than seventy-five cases on it, and even though it is nearing lunchtime, her courtroom is packed. At least a dozen lawyers are waiting to get their cases called, some sitting on the cramped benches in the front row, others milling around or wandering in and out. It takes all of one look to realize that I am never going to get anything called in there by lunchtime. And so, with an apologetic nod to my client, I retreat, heading across the hall to the overflow arraignment part, hoping to catch Cassandra. It's closed.

Next, I consider running upstairs to the domestic violence part — but by the time I get there, it's likely to be closed as well.

I really shouldn't have taken the time to see Reginald.

Heading back up the escalators, I take a mental inventory of what I've done, Clarence, Reginald, Alberto, and also what I have left to do, Najid, Cassandra, Hector, and Jaron.

Upstairs, on the mezzanine, the court officer with the bullhorn is still making a racket. It's still a few minutes before one, and if I leave now, I can just beat the lunchtime rush of frustrated defendants and impatient lawyers. Heading out through the revolving doors into the cold wind whipping down 161st Street, I drop my chin, shove my hands deep into the pockets of my winter jacket, and, trying hard to enjoy the dull winter light, trudge back toward the office.

Eight

12:53 P.M.

UPSTAIRS, BACK IN MY OFFICE, I dump Clarence, Alberto, and Reginald's documents — each in a heavy red accordion file — in a stack on my desk. I'm tired and hungry, and I don't have the patience to update them in our case-tracking system just now. Besides, my phone is chock-full of messages.

Whenever I don't finish up by lunch there are calls from clients who spent their morning waiting in criminal court. They range from the patient to the abusive. I don't resent them — I'd be leaving irate messages too if I sat in criminal court for three hours expecting to see a lawyer who never showed up.

Scrolling through my messages, I carefully jot down the names and numbers of the mothers, uncles, and girlfriends calling me on behalf of their locked-up loved ones. Dealing with a client through a family member is always slightly touchy — technically, client confidences are only totally secure so long as they remain undiscussed with others, but keeping a client's family in the loop is important too, so I spend a lot of time figuring out who it's safe to talk to. Really knowing a client's family can help the client as well as the case. It is an easy way to communicate certain information, particularly with incarcerated inmates — and when it's time for a client to take a deep breath and commit himself to a prison term, having a wife or girlfriend or family member on board with the plea and able to promise that they'll wait makes the deal go down easier. Such things also give a client a future to focus on and a reason to hope — invaluable commodities when facing the misery of prolonged incarceration.

I have too many courtrooms left to cover and very possibly not enough time. To make it everywhere I have to be this afternoon, I should probably be back in court as soon as it opens. And that means lunching at light speed. It looks as though it's going to be a gas station day.

If anything might have converted me to the big-firm life, it was the food. There were few things I loved as much as sitting down to a lavish meal I didn't have to pay for — the daily perusal of menus that included braised short ribs or delicately poached fish — and if I've paid a price for doing the work that I love, it's a ransom denominated in the currency of culinary pleasure. Up near Supreme Court there is a Burger King and the Courthouse Deli — a vestige of a time when the Grand Concourse really was grand and the streets around 161st bustled with Jews — which offers good matzo ball soup and decent pastrami. Inside the deli, judges, court officers, ADAs, and defense lawyers are all jammed together, mirroring the composition of the courthouse just across the street. But by lunchtime the last thing I want to see is more judges, DAs, and court officers, so it's a place I rarely go. Across the concourse from the Courthouse Deli is a food court where the aggressively obese can choose from various fast-fried flavors: Arthur Treachers, Taco Bell, the always crowded McDonald's. Finally, down a bit farther, near my office, is the dirty sandwich deli/bodega — the sort of place that offers up a prayer every day that the health department hasn't come around. I eat at the dirty deli at least once a week. It's convenient on harried days and easy on a public defender's salary.

It hasn't always been quite this bad. For years, I got daily take-out from a tiny Jamaican place. Known as the Feeding Tree, it had all of one table and two metal chairs. Reggae music bounced around the counter while Tony cooked in the back and Janice held court up front. But they demolished the Feeding Tree to make room for a new, even larger criminal courthouse, which is in the process of being built just down the street from the current one. And so now, on a good day, when I don't endure the dirty deli, the British Petroleum station is as good as it gets. The gasoline fumes aren't too bad, and other than the Courthouse Deli, it's the only place around to get a salad.

Most days I have lunch with Robin. She is my confidante, my boss, and the best public defender I've ever known. We were close even before we moved to the Bronx, and when she won the contract with New York City to start the Bronx Defenders, I was one of the first lawyers she hired. Robin has both striking beauty and spectacular trial instincts, and in court we make a strange but effective team: my strength is attacking; hers is understanding. Robin has an unnerving way of knowing what everyone in a room is feeling at any given moment — as if she is privy to a TV signal (the Feelings Channel, probably) that no one else is receiving. This gift makes her a great leader and a subtle cross-examiner. It also informs every aspect of the way she practices law.

⇨⇦

People do public defender work for all kinds of reasons: some resent or fear the power of the government; others believe in the process and could actually either prosecute or defend; and then there are client-centered defenders like Robin who are motivated by genuine empathy and a deep belief in the goodness of people. It is no surprise, then, that the public defender office she established would pioneer "holistic" representation — an approach that focuses on the general needs of the client rather than on the specific dictates of a criminal case. It was Robin who believed that a great public defender office should include a civil action project to help with housing and benefits questions, an immigration attorney to help ensure a client doesn't get deported, a family court unit that tries to keep families intact, and even a community organizer devoted to empowering client communities.

Robin's uncanny sense of what is going on in someone else's head is tremendously practical too. Trying to suss out what a client is really trying to say is one of the most daunting parts of my job. There have been a number of times when a client was trying to tell me something that for some reason I just couldn't hear. This happened most dramatically not too long ago, with a sixty-two-year-old man who found himself charged with shooting his neighborhood coffee-cart guy in the head.

I took an immediate liking to Edward, with his graying Black Power Afro; thick, studious glasses; and respectful, deliberate speech. According to the district attorney's office, despite living a spotless life for more than half a century, Edward decided out of the blue one morning to shoot a random guy in the head and then sit down in the street and wait to be arrested.

That was not Edward's explanation at all.

Looking earnest, if a bit befuddled, he explained that he'd been about to get a cup of coffee when he heard the shots and stumbled into the fracas that followed. He lay in the middle of the street because he knew he was slow and figured that was probably the safest way to take cover. Taking into consideration the weirdness of the case, the fact that the bullet had essentially bounced off the man's skull (causing minimal physical damage), and Edward's five decades of a law-abiding life, the DA offered Edward a plea to three and a half years in state prison.

He turned it down, insisting on his innocence.

I fought his case for a year and a half, searching in vain for some reason that would explain the case or the crime. I found nothing. Time and time again I was drawn back to the scene of the crime — right near a welfare building across from Crotona Park — hoping that I'd find something, see something, make sense of the nonsensical.

Edward's case was pending in front of Moge — and he couldn't figure it out either. "Look, Dave, it's why we have trials," he told me during one of our many conferences about the case. And after a few more months of confusion, I was inclined to agree.

With nothing left to do, it was time to pick a jury.

"When can you be ready?" Moge wanted to know.

"Let's do it next week," I said.

"Fine," said Moge, and then, turning to Edward, "This is pretty much your last chance to take a plea, sir."

Edward, whose stoic reserve was almost unfathomable, looked up at Mogulescu and said, with utter calm: "Okay. What do I get?"

I couldn't have been more stunned. Edward was a dignified, quiet man who addressed me with incredible respect and calm reserve. He'd never said anything other than that he was innocent. Simple, direct questioning and thoughtful nodding marked our conversations as he processed whatever I told him. Edward was clearly smart — always reading serious books and chatting amiably with me about them in the client interview room in the jail. His guilt seemed so out of the question that I hadn't even really engaged in any plea-bargaining.

"Ahhhh, can I have a few minutes with my client?" I asked the judge, not sure I'd heard right.

"Of course," said Moge as they led Edward back upstairs to the cells.

Upstairs it was clear to me I'd heard wrong.

"I want to go to trial," Edward told me quietly and firmly as we sat down together in the client interview room. "I know you believe in me," he said, "and I trust you."

"You got it," I told him. "We'll start picking a jury next week."

"Okay!" he said, smiling. "I'll see you then."

I couldn't sleep that night. All my public defender instincts were telling me that something was dreadfully wrong — an innocent guy that calm doesn't just panic and offer to take whatever the judge is going to give him. Something was wrong, but I couldn't figure out what.

It was exactly the kind of situation that Robin is good for.

"Rob, I want you to come talk to Edward with me," I said the next morning. "I need your read on this."

"Sure, babe," she said. "Let's go."

As we threaded our way through the lower mezzanine of criminal court, I filled Robin in on what had happened the day before. "It was like, just for a second there, he wanted to fold — it was like this little glimmer of total capitulation, but by the time we got upstairs, he was back to trial only. I just don't get it."

"Weird," Robin said as we walked into the interview room. "Let me talk to him — alone, please."

I introduced them and left.

"He needs to take a plea, sweetie," Robin said when she came to get me ten minutes later. "He's guilty, and he wants to get out of the case."

I couldn't have been more stunned.

"It took me about thirty seconds to figure it out," she said. "He was old and depressed; he'd been cut off from disability and was afraid he'd be evicted. I don't know whether he was thinking about robbing the guy or what, but when he pulled out the gun, he was so nervous and shaking the thing just went off. He was so freaked out, he just sat down in the street and waited for the cops to come. What I couldn't figure out was why he'd been hanging in there so long, and then I realized it had to be you. As soon as I said to him that I'd known you a long time and that you'd love him no matter what he did, he just started crying. He was too embarrassed by what he'd done — he felt like you'd been fighting so hard you'd be disillusioned if he turned around and told you. He kind of thinks his life is over anyway, and he didn't want to go die in prison having let you down too."

I was speechless. We were two days from a trial. I had been so convinced of his innocence that I hadn't tried to work out a plea deal for months. And now it might be too late — and all because I liked Edward so much that I utterly failed to understand the potential pathology of what was going on between us; it was the dark side of my self-important crusading and tough-guy posturing. Having him believe in me that much had fulfilled something I'd set out to be as a public defender, but it had also had disastrous consequences for the very person I was hoping to help, shelter, and protect.

With no plea bargain in the offing and Edward newly determined to get out of the case, he was forced to plead guilty to the entire indictment. After a sentencing hearing, Moge gave him eight and a half years, five more than I could have gotten him at the beginning — the price of my own vanity.

I learned a painful lesson from Edward about trying to hear

clients clearly without the distortive clamor of my own ego. Unlike TV shows in which criminal defendants are constantly looking to get over by using a difficult childhood as an excuse for barbaric behavior, most clients just won't talk about their lives much. The reality is that clients don't really want you to know that they were in sixteen group homes in seven years, or left in a freezer to die at age two, or that they were hiding in a closet when their older brother got murdered. How, they wonder, could such information ever help? Why would anyone care — especially since no one seems to have cared before? Sadly, in almost every case, they're right — in the criminal justice system, almost no one really does.

⇥⇤

I try to buzz Robin through the intercom, but she's on the phone. I wander back around the corner, and gesturing at my wrist (I don't wear a watch; there are enough clocks within view at court that I am always acutely aware of how late I'm running), I indicate that I need to head back to court soon. Catching my eye, Robin nods and flashes me five fingers.

Back to my office: the phone is ringing again as I walk in. Max is calling from a jail in Manhattan on a TDD — a telecommunications device for the deaf. He types his part of the conversation, and the phone operator reads it to me.

"Please, please, you are the only hope," the operator reads with no affect whatsoever.

Though born in the Dominican Republic, Deaf Max has lived in the United States nearly his entire life. Just over a year ago, Max pled guilty in Manhattan to a misdemeanor assault. He was sentenced to a year in jail. The problem is that Max's lawyer didn't realize that while the assault conviction is classified as a misdemeanor in New York, because the sentence was a year or more, federal authorities considered it an aggravated felony requiring deportation. Perversely, even though Max has already completed his sentence, the DA won't agree to retrospectively resentence him to 364 days — even though doing so would avoid having him deported to a country he's never known. It would be a simple change in the paperwork, with no practical effect other than to give him a chance to stay here with his family and young son. In the DA's mind, though, "a deal is a deal." The fact that Max's lawyer screwed up seems of no consequence, and unless I figure something out soon, Max will be deported.

"I'll try, Max, I'll try."

I can hear the operator's fingers typing my reassurance.

"Thanks," she reads blankly, and then, in the same monotone: "The caller has disconnected."

I look through my new messages. One is from a Supreme Court judge. He's called to ask if I'll represent a defendant in a domestic rape case. "I didn't rape her, I just finger-fucked her" is the statement and presumably the very bad defense.

Jason sticks his head into my office.

"Got a second?" he asks as he perches his avian frame on the arm of my black faux-leather couch. Today he's in a memorable getup — a thick, elegant shirt with thin blue and gold stripes that make the material warm and luminous. I'm frightened to think that it also has French cuffs — but a quick glance confirms that it does. To go with the shirt, he is sporting a peach-colored tie that, if I was a bit more fashion forward, I would appreciate more than I do.

"C'mon in," I tell him.

Jason hasn't been with the office that long. Then again, it doesn't take long to be exposed to the absurdities of criminal court. Judge Raymond Bruce, who once furiously declared, "When someone gives you a horse as a present, you don't look at its teeth!" (his way of chastising Jason and one of his clients for not taking a plea), presided over one of Jason's first trials — a blind man accused of assault. The prosecution's theory: "he's not blind." Indeed, that's what Assistant District Attorney Dan Kraft claimed throughout the trial as the man's seeing-eye dog lay lazily by the defense table. "He's faking," Kraft insisted as the defense introduced medical records indicating the client had been blind since birth. "I will prove that this man is a liar and can see!" Kraft swore, hinting that he had some secret evidence with which he'd prove this increasingly bizarre contention. An official certificate of legal blindness issued by New York State didn't dissuade him, nor did the testimony of the client's girl-friend (who was also legally blind).

And so, when Kraft's moment finally came, when he rose to cross-examine the client (who had been guided to the witness chair by the seeing-eye dog), everyone was rather interested to see what this secret proof might actually be.

"You say you're blind, sir!" Kraft said, sarcasm dripping from his voice.

"Yes, I am blind," said the blind man calmly.

"But you check out girls on the street, don't you?"

"Excuse me?"

"Sir, I'mmmmm told that you check women out. Isn't that a fact?"

"Um, I can't see anything — also, I have a girlfriend."

This line of questioning didn't seem to be getting Kraft where he wanted to go, so he deftly changed tacks.

"Well, you read, don't you?"

"Braille."

"Oh, nooooo sir, you read *magazines! Normally printed magazines!*"

"Um, no."

"Well, what's this then?" Kraft demanded, holding up a glossy magazine addressed to the client. This was his gotcha! moment.

"I don't know," said the client. "I can't see." The seeing-eye dog let out a tiny, almost inaudible sigh and licked the court reporter's leg. The court reporter burst out laughing. Kraft was deadly serious.

"It's a magazine addressed to YOU!" he nearly shouted.

"Well, I get magazines," Jason's client said simply. "I have them read to me."

This apparently was something ADA Kraft had never consid-ered. For nearly a year Kraft had insisted that the blind man could in fact see, and it seemed that, all of a sudden, he was the one left in the dark.

Quickly ending his cross-examination, Kraft rose to deliver his summation: "He may be blind," Kraft conceded, "but I still think he can see more than he's letting on."

Jason won that one.

Today being a normal day, Jason is probably carrying about eighty cases (though the load can occasionally reach one hundred). Partially because my cases tend to be the most serious in the office, and partially thanks to the privilege of rank, I have fewer — usually between forty-five and sixty. Of course, part of my job as the trial chief is helping the other lawyers figure out their cases, so when I'm not working on my own cases, or on the phone or in court, there is almost always someone in my office with a question, sometimes legal, sometimes tactical. Even walking in and out of the office, I'm regularly stopped with a "what is this case worth?" kind of question, a request for my sense of the numbers — representing years of someone's life — answered while barely breaking stride.

Sitting at the lunchroom table his first week, Jason had overheard another lawyer telling me she'd picked up a bad case — assault in the first degree.

"What's the weapon?" I asked.

"Machete," she said.

"What's the injury?"

"Hand."

"How's the hand?"

"Off."

"All the way off?"

"Yeah, straight through."

"That's a bad fact."

"They surgically reattached it."

"Well," I said, nodding, "that's something. Guy gotta record?"

"Nothin'."

"Both drunk?"

"Looks like it — fight between two Salvadoran guys."

"Just one whack?"

"Yeah, one swing, and then the hand's on the ground from the wrist down."

"I'll bet you can get two, maybe even less."

"They're offering three and a half preindictment."

"Hold out — you'll do better."

"Okay. Thanks, Feige."

Today, Jason has his own sentencing question.

Over the years, New York, like almost every other state, has reformed and rereformed its criminal sentencing laws. The adjustments, announced during every election cycle or after any particularly horrific crime, are always bad for my clients. In the time I've been practicing, the minimum sentence for a first-time offender convicted of a class B violent felony like armed robbery has gone from an indeterminate sentence of two to six years, to an indeterminate sentence of three to six years, and finally to a determinate — that is, fixed — sentence of five years. Learning the sentencing rules — and learning them thoroughly — is one of the best ways to gain power in the system. Because change is so common and ignorance so widespread, actually knowing the correct answer to every sentencing question leads everyone else in the courtroom to trust and then rely on your assertions — a fact that can become quite useful when trying to work out a plea deal.

Jason's question had to do with merger: what happens when someone is sentenced to two different terms of incarceration, one for a misdemeanor and one for a felony? The answer hinges on how the New York City Department of Corrections calculates jail time and, oddly, whether the client is locked up in a jail at Rikers that inmates call the "six building" and DOC describes as a "sentence facility."

As I'm explaining this to Jason, Emma Ketteringham pokes her head in. Emma is the office über-WASP. Tall and slender, with long blond hair and sparkling blue eyes, she is one of the only lawyers we ever hired directly out of a fancy law firm. Big-firm lawyers usually can't handle the transition to state-level public defender work — they're too used to focusing on just a few cases, too used to cozy offices and large paychecks, too used to the reverence with which others react to the invocation of the law firm name. Fancy résumés from Paul, Weiss; Shearman & Sterling; and Fried, Frank had come in many times over the years, and though the associates looking to make the switch were sometimes bright and always unusually confident, we'd never been convinced that any of them would last. The firm folks normally exhibited an intellectual attachment to the *idea* of the work, rather than a passionate commitment to the clients themselves. You can usually see it in their eyes during an interview — a vague fear of the comparatively shabby offices or the under-resourced and overworked conditions.

Emma, though, was different. In the six or seven years that I was involved in hiring public defenders, she did one of the best interviews I've ever seen. In a room full of grizzled public defenders firing skeptical, even derisive questions at her, Emma was astonishingly poised, tempered, and articulate as we took her to task for not doing more pro bono work, grilled her about her commitment to clients, and even suggested that she was a sell-out for having worked at the firm at all. Through it all, she was utterly composed, her long, elegant fingers gesturing gently, her stylish but understated suit suggesting competence without asserting privilege. She left convinced we hated her. In fact we loved her. We figured that if she could take what we had just dished out she'd have no trouble at all dealing with angry clients and intemperate judges.

I glance up at Emma. "I gotta grab some lunch — can we do this tonight or tomorrow?" I ask her.

"Oh, sure," she says, turning gently toward her cubicle, lighter on her feet than physics should have dictated. "It's no big deal."

Jason follows her out.

"Thanks, Feige," he says.

Grabbing my keys from the desktop, just in case we're driving, I head back around the corner to pick up Robin. Together, we trot through our library / lunchroom, toward the reception area.

"Alvin's on the phone," Lorraine calls after me, with a smile that says she understands. Waving my hands like a football ref calling an incomplete pass, I shake my head.

"Sorry, sweetie," I hear her say as I push through the door. "He's at lunch, but you can call him again later."

Aboard Robin's well-worn Volvo, we head for the gas station, just a few blocks from a halal slaughterhouse advertising live animals and bearing a bright sign with the memorable slogan

"We roast goats." We park past the pumps and walk in — the cooler and food counter are on the left; wiper fluid, oil, and candy on the right.

Unlike Jason and Emma, who always seem perfectly put together, I am a mess. My suit is already rumpled from the morning's sprinting around, my tie is a bit askew, and my hair could use a trim. I have, as we sometimes joke, the appearance of impropriety.

Unfortunately, in our world of quick decisions, appearances can often become reality — a sweet kid decked out in a blood-red do-rag can find himself in jail for looking like a menace, while a badass con man in a creaseless suit can strut out the front door. Though I initially resisted this idea (for years I sported a long mane of unkempt hair and wore the same pajama-like suit nearly every day), I have reluctantly come to accept it.

"You know," a client will sometimes say when I'm in a particularly nice suit or have just made a particularly strong argument, "you could be a private lawyer." They always say this in a conspiratorial fashion, as if they want to share a really important secret just with me. At first I'd get offended when they'd say it, as if their limited ambitions for me were dismissive, but over the years I've come to see the remark as the compliment it is. Their lives are filled with angry caseworkers, suspicious child welfare agents, distrustful probation officers, and, occasionally, uncaring public defenders. When someone breaks that mold, whether it be at probation, welfare, or the criminal courthouse, the natural reaction is "You're so good — why are you here helping me?"

"But I like you," I'll say.

"Yeah, but you could be making money, brother."

"But I like you — and I want to be your lawyer."

This almost always provokes a perplexed but somehow satisfied silence.

⟶⋅⟵

It's a few minutes before 2:00 when we get back from the gas station. In the Bronx, most courts don't get going in the afternoon until 2:15 or 2:30, so I have some breathing room. Back in my office, I settle into my chair to bang out another lunchtime project: a quick letter to Fred, an old client who is incarcerated in Arizona.

Generally, I'm not much for inmate correspondence. Given how much time inmates have on their hands and how little I've got, writing is usually a losing proposition for me. Anyone who is incarcerated has extraordinary needs that can be a full-time job to fulfill, and short of trying, the nicest thing I can do is send a thirty-dollar money order here and there to help with commissary.

Before starting on the letter, I call the judge back. "Yes," I say, "I'll take the finger-fucking case." Next, I buzz Emma on the intercom and answer her question, and in the succeeding ten minutes I manage four more "yes everything is fine with your case" calls before banging out a quick ten-line "hope you're well" letter to Fred. It's almost 2:20 as I wearily grab my suit jacket and head back to criminal court.

Weaving my way out of the office, I dart through the alcove that passes as our library — mostly several long shelves of anno-tated New York State statutes, set off against titles like *Practical Homicide Investigation, Criminal Interrogation and Confessions,* and *Forensic Evidence: Science and the Criminal Law.* There's hip-hop coming from one of the rooms where the Bronx Defen-ders runs programs for neighborhood kids, and over the din I can hear one of the participants taking another to task. "Yo, that argument is totally wrong — you need to work on your facts, B."

Just across the hall from the kids is the trial suit closet — the site of one of my most memorable breakdowns. Nearly everyone I've ever worked with has been reduced to tears by the job at some point or another. I'm no exception.

I am not quite sure how I wound up in the trial suit closet. I remember storming out of Robin's office. I remember heading for the door. I also remember thinking that no matter how pissed off I was, I couldn't really leave my boss and friend alone in the South Bronx at 2:00 A.M.

The closet was small, filled with musty suits, worn shoes that no longer fit, and boxes of blouses. Most of the clothes, all of which are donated by staff and friends, had been hanging there for months or years. They were "trial suits" — shirts and shoes waiting to dress up a poor person about to face trial.

Climbing in, feeling the womblike comfort of the small space, I pulled my knees up to my chin, wrapped my arms around my shins, and put my head down to muffle the sobs. *There has got to be a better way,* I thought to myself over and over, rocking gently back and forth in the cramped alcove. "I can't do this another day," I muttered to my thighs, glancing up at a decade of donated suits, several of which bore witness to my own ever-expanding girth.

It takes a strange mix of isolation and immersion for me to get over those moments when I actually want to hang it up. Part of me wants to climb into bed and never come out, and often, after a really rough few days, I'll do that — just pull the covers over my head and vow to change my life. I'll promise to never go back to those hellish courtrooms, never again risk as much, never again get kicked around by insulting, idiotic judges. But after a day or two, or sometimes just a night of heavy drinking, the faces and the voices of the clients I love start filtering back — Alvin's endless neediness; Cassandra's empty, expressionless face; Clarence's constant cockamamy theories; and Gary's never-ending bewilderment at being arrested yet again. Besides, every once and again, I do make a difference — sometimes by fighting harder, occasionally by thinking better, but usually just by showing up and being willing to care. Often, at least for my clients, that's more than they expect and all it takes. Do they need me? They do. Do I need them? I suppose I do too.

Of course, the trial suit closet isn't meant to shelter shattered public defenders; it exists to clothe clients who can't afford, or simply don't have, decent court clothing. Left to their own devices, many of my clients will show up for trial in the same jailhouse do-rag they've been sporting for months. Many of them don't have family to take care of them, and the few clothing items they own have been winnowed by jail regulations or frayed by constant wear. Even for those who have nice

154 / DAVID FEIGE

clothing, for some reason it doesn't occur to many of them that looking good might make a difference. They seem to forget that a jury is about to inspect every inch of them, studying their every move for some hint of guilt or innocence. The closet addresses this information gap, making them just that little bit more presentable during the week in which their lives are on the line.

When the closet is bare we generally reserve the clothes for trial situations, but when it's full — as it has been for a while — it's a free-for-all.

Several months ago I got a call from Luther. I've represented Luther for years — ever since he was arrested for carrying a loaded handgun. He called, as he often does, without warning. "Hi, Dad," he said, with his mischievous lilt, "I gotta come see you."

"I'm running out, Lu, I gotta get to court. What do you need?"

"What time you back?" Luther asked.

"Six," I said, hanging up.

When Luther actually showed up at 6:00, I knew something was up.

Though articulate and extremely smart, Luther, like a lot of my clients, has a self-destructive streak. Making appointments is tough, and staying in touch in between appointments almost unheard of. When absent, Luther is usually doing something pretty good — like going to school or looking for work — but whenever anything seems to go too smoothly, or expectations are raised even slightly, Luther will find a way to disappoint.

At ten after six, sitting on a couch in my office, he let it fly: "I need a suit, Dad," he said.

A suit? Luther is usually dressed nicely, and he doesn't have the ghetto obsession with shiny white sneakers that swallows most of my other clients' minimal disposable income. But still . . . a suit? I was trying to imagine what he might need it for.

"That's great, Lu, but, uh, how come? You got a date or something?"

Luther just grinned: "A job, Dad, a job," he said. "And a sweet one too. Victoria's Secret."

"Oy."

Luther loves women, and they, almost invariably, love him, and the thought of him set free to ogle and coo to his heart's content in a store full of women browsing for high-end lingerie was almost comical. I couldn't imagine he'd make it through the first day without sidling up behind a shopper to say something approving but a bit too provocative. But, hey, Luther had a face-to-face interview, and the job required a suit.

"Okay, buddy, let's get moving," I said, heading toward the trial suit closet.

A nice blazer from Saks was too tight in the shoulders; a dark-blue suit was way too short. The camel-colored three-piece was rejected for its color — Victoria's Secret had been very clear, a black suit, or if not black, then very dark. Colleagues drifted out of their offices, offering their help.

By the time we were pawing through the big basket for a pair of shoes, I thought we were set — with a nice navy suit and a bright-red tie.

"So, was this yours?" Luther asked.

"No, buddy, I'm not sure who this one came from," I told him.

"Well, let's see your stuff, Dad."

"It won't fit you, Lu. Let's go with what we've got here."

"Naw, Dad, let me see it. Please."

Luther can be hard to resist. And so, digging deep into the closet, I found a sharp charcoal pinstripe from my summer as a big-firm lawyer — Hugo Boss from the Barney's warehouse sale. Luther slipped it on and almost disappeared. Luther is tall, muscular, and very handsome, but he's narrow, and although the suit fit perfectly in the arms and shoulders, it was clearly meant for someone quite a bit stouter.

"No way, Lu," I said.

But it was too late. Luther was already straightening his tie and preening for the mirror.

"It's perfect, Dad," he said, grinning.

"Luther, it's huge!"

"Naw, Dad, it's sweet," he said, smoothing his lapels.

"I'm telling you, Lu, there is no way Victoria's Secret is going to hire you in that thing."

"Definitely, Dad, definitely," Luther insisted.

"All right," I said. "If you insist. Call me and let me know how it goes."

Luther gave me his megawatt grin. "All right, Dad. Thanks."

I didn't hear from Luther for nearly three weeks. And when I finally saw him again in court, in my old suit, I couldn't help prodding him just a little.

"I guess you didn't get the job, huh?" I asked him.

"Naw, Dad," he said as the clerk called our case.

"Well, at least you learned to dress up for court," I said as we stepped up.

"Good morning, Mr. Feige," the judge said as I reached the defense table.

"Good morning, Your Honor."

"Nice suit," he said to Luther.

<hr />

As I head back through the reception area, Lorraine is juggling calls, and the couches are packed with people waiting to see their lawyers. In a corner, Lillian is still sorting her papers. Lorraine glances up just long enough to give me a smile.

"Gary needs to see you," she reminds me gently as I push through the door, nod to the kid in the gang colors hanging out just outside, and make my way back toward criminal court.

"Gary *always* needs to see me," I call back just before the door slips shut behind me.

Nine

U P THE STREET, just past the welfare building, I spy the line for the courthouse. It is the interminable waiting, as much as anything else, that grinds people down. It's one of the reasons the courthouse is tense, the people volatile — even why innocent people plead guilty. Indeed, once you understand how the system really works, how it wears people down, how high the frictional costs of fighting a criminal case really are, the guilty pleas of the innocent are not only predictable, but also seem a natural product of the way the system is designed. Even without the threat of jail, copping out isn't an irrational choice.

Imagine for a moment being arrested. Assume you'll get special treatment, a speedy arraignment, and a quick release. Your lawyer will assure you that you're free from the most onerous threat in criminal prosecution: jail time.

Let's say you jump a turnstile. The token you put in gets jammed and the turnstile won't rotate, so, late for work and already having paid the fare, you hop over. A cop, just on the other side, pushes you up against the wall and cuffs you. You beg him to just go examine the turnstile, but he tells you to shut up and marches you to the small holding room where you wait while he arrests another half a dozen people.

You go through the system, and at arraignments, the prosecutor offers you a plea: to "trespass as a violation" — more like a traffic ticket than a crime. Pleading guilty won't result in a criminal record, but to get the deal you'll have to do a day of community service. You refuse — after all, you're innocent — you actually *did* pay the fare. Your case is adjourned for several weeks. You are released without bail.

Five weeks later, you take a day off of work to return to court. After waiting on line for an hour or so, you clear the metal detectors and find the courtroom where your case will be heard. It is crowded, and the long wooden benches are filled with people looking nervously at one another or staring downward, scrupulously avoiding eye contact. For the next two hours, you sit and wait as case after case goes before the judge. You have not yet seen your lawyer. You are not allowed to read.

Just around noon, your public defender rushes in, calling your name as he shuffles through a stack of thin yellow legal-sized files. "Hold on for just a second," he says while he heads to the front of the courtroom to write something on a clipboard and chat with some of the prosecutors in the room. Another half hour passes. Next to you an elderly black man with thick glasses is trying to surreptitiously read a newspaper. He keeps it low — well below the lip of the bench, folded tightly into a tiny square — and he gets away with this for nearly an hour before a court officer barks at him, and rather than face expulsion, he abandons the paper. Your lawyer finally calls your name and motions to you to come outside the courtroom.

Apologizing for the delays, he explains the good news: the prosecutors will once again offer you the trespass violation, which will spare you a criminal record. All you have to do is per-form that one day of community service. Once again you explain that because you put the token in, you never intended to defraud the system — it's just that the turnstile was broken. He listens patiently, nodding understandingly. He's a nice guy and doesn't want to pressure you into pleading guilty to anything you didn't do. Still, he explains, it's a tough defense — your word against the cops — and generally, since this is such a minor crime, you won't even get a jury trial, just a cynical judge who usually be-lieves the police. Also, you need to know that if you lose, you'll be saddled with a criminal record. You won't go to jail or anything — most likely it'd just be a fine or a few days of community service — but that criminal conviction will be on your permanent record forever.

It's late, and the courtroom is still packed. Your lawyer tells you to think about what you want to do. Also, he warns, the system is slow. If you want to fight the case, you'll have to be patient. It looks as if your case isn't going to be heard until after lunch, so he advises you to come back around 2:15, about an hour and a half from now.

Since it's the Bronx, you don't really want to wander too far from the courthouse, so your food options are pretty much confined to the food court in the grimy shopping center across the street. Everything available is fried.

Another half hour in line just to get back in through the metal detectors, a little more weaving through the crowds, and at 2:15 you're back in the courtroom. Around 2:30 your lawyer appears, and after you explain that you did nothing wrong and want to fight the case, he tells you that the next stage is to file a motion to dismiss the charges. It won't be successful, he explains, but he'll do it anyway.

It's been six hours since you first got in the line to come into the courthouse, and finally, your case is called.

"Number eighty-seven on the calendar, 2004BX100001," says the court officer standing in the front of the room. "*People versus*" — and here you hear your own name — "charged with 165.15."

Your lawyer strides confidently up to the well of the courtroom, motioning you to follow. As you tentatively walk up to stand beside him, you hear your lawyer and the assistant district attorney say their names. The court reporter's hands are moving, taking down every word.

"Ahhh. 140.05 and two days' community service," says the assistant DA.

"No disposition. Motion schedule, please," your lawyer replies.

"Okay. File them in three weeks. Come back May sixteenth," says the judge.

And that's it. The whole proceeding took about twenty seconds.

"Wait for me," your lawyer tells you as they call the next case. You watch as he stands up there and does this same type of thing for four or five more people. Six or seven minutes later, he again calls you outside, handing you a little blue slip of paper with the next court date scribbled on it.

"I'll see you on the sixteenth," he says, "when we get the decision denying our motions." And then, handing you another card, just in case, he asks if you have any other questions, shakes your hand warmly, and together the two of you join the steady stream of people leaving the courthouse.

Six weeks later, your new court date arrives. You take another day off work, brave the commute to the Bronx, and once again go through the ritual of a court appearance — the hour in line, three more in the courtroom unable to read, work, or talk, sitting silently as the litany of cases blurs into the monotonous thrum of anonymous criminality. This time, you're done by lunch. The prosecutor didn't file the response to your lawyer's motion on time, so the case is adjourned for decision. Another court date, another blue slip, three more weeks of worry.

Three weeks later, another day off of work, another six hours, and this time you can't find your lawyer. Someone from his office comes in around 3:00 P.M. and explains that he's in the middle of a murder trial. The new guy asks if you want to plead to the trespass violation, which would spare you a criminal record — it'd only be one day of community service, and you could arrange to do it on the weekend. You explain that you didn't commit the crime, and you really want to fight the case — couldn't he just get you a trial? "That's a long way off," he says, smiling.

Around 3:30, your case is called. The judge hands both lawyers a decision denying the defense motions but granting a hearing on a statement you allegedly made: "I jumped over it because it was broken."

Outside, you explain to the substitute lawyer that the statement is true but not complete — "I actually said, 'because it ate
my token,'" you insist.

"Well, the cop says that this is what you said. Most judges
will probably see it as a confession, which is why they want to
introduce it into evidence," the lawyer explains. "The good news
is that we'll have a chance to try to suppress it at a hearing — we
won't win, but we'll get some good discovery. If you have any
other questions, give your lawyer a call." He smiles.

A month later, as you sit in court again, you start to get frustrated. You've burned another day of vacation, wasted a ton of
time, and here you are waiting — again. This time, your lawyer
arrives early.

"Sorry about last time. I was on trial over in Supreme Court,"
he explains, looking a little harried.

"Look," you say, "I really want to get this over with."

"I know," he says kindly, "but I told you, the system is slow
and you have to be patient. Let's see what happens today." He
sounds encouraging. "C'mon, I'll be sure to get you out by lunch
today."

Slightly reassured, you go back into the courtroom to wait.
And sitting there, forbidden to do anything useful with your
time, you realize you have begun to recognize people — the
prosecutors, all young, digging through their cardboard boxes
of files; the court reporter typing silently on her strange little
square of a machine; the court officers roughly leading prisoners
into and out of court from the steel side door; and, of course, the
judge, beleaguered, impatient, and brusque.

It's your turn again.

At least this time when you see the judge, it's more than
forty-five seconds — maybe a whole minute and a half.

"Why can't we get rid of this?" the judge asks. "How about
a straight CD?" Your lawyer leans over to you, explaining that
what the judge means is that if you'll plead guilty to the trespass,
he'll persuade the DA's office to drop the community service
requirement. You'll just promise the judge that you'll stay out of

trouble for a year; it'll be no fine, no jail — just like unsupervised probation.

Standing there, before the judge, you find yourself actually considering it. You're tired. It's been too long, too much for a stupid case like this. "It won't be a criminal conviction?" you ask.

"No," your lawyer says, "just like I explained it to you. It's more like a traffic ticket."

"But I'm still pleading guilty, right?"

"Yes," he says, "to the violation of trespass. It's not a crime, and technically the record is sealed, but there will be a record of it as a noncriminal conviction accessible by the police, prosecutors, and others." (It used to be that these records were considered sealed, but in the past few years, with the advent of ever-better computers, whenever a high-profile case hits the papers, these sorts of noncriminal convictions always seem to pop up, suggesting that the police department doesn't really see "sealed" in the same way you or I might.)

This is right about the time that most people just go ahead and plead. Guilty or not, they're exhausted and frustrated, and want the whole thing over with. And so innocent people — people just like you — wind up pleading to a trespass violation, or to disorderly conduct. But somehow, standing there before the judge, you summon up an uncharacteristic well of resolve.

"I'm not pleading guilty. I'm fighting this case," you tell your lawyer.

"No thanks, Judge," is all he says to the court.

"Fine. Get him the discovery, People."

"Yes, Judge," the bored-looking ADA says.

Outside the courtroom, you get another blue slip and another court date.

Next time you get another.

And the next time, another. You've used a third of your vacation time for the year, and there is no trial date in sight. Downstairs in the trial assignment part, you're discouraged to find that most of the people have been waiting for trials far longer than you have — many of them two years or more. For all of them, and for you, the same excuses: the district attorney isn't ready, your lawyer is on vacation. So again and again it's the trip to the courthouse, the scanning and searching, the halls full of crying, angry people, a day of waiting, a minute or maybe two with the judge, and another blue slip with still another court date.

Sometime in August, your child is sick, your boss needs you at work, or your court date falls during a vacation you scheduled six months ago. You call your lawyer, leaving a message explaining that you can't make it to court. When you get home there's a message from your lawyer: "Because you failed to appear in court, the judge has issued a warrant for your arrest. Please call me as soon as possible."

You call your lawyer. "I left you a message," you explain angrily.

"Yeah, I know," he says. "I explained the situation to the judge, and he says that if you voluntarily surrender in the next day or two, he'll expunge the warrant."

"Yeah, okay, but doesn't that mean they can come and arrest me again?"

"Technically, yes." Your lawyer's voice is oozing with patience. "But there's not much of a risk in the next few days. The warrant will have to be sent over to the police department's Warrant Squad, and that usually takes a few days, so if you just come in tomorrow or the day after . . . really it's not a problem."

A warrant for your arrest.

And finally, more than before, more than that time in front of the judge, you just want this over; you don't want to talk to your lawyer anymore — you don't even want to *have* a lawyer. You never want to go back to that courthouse again, never stand in the lines, never deal with the searching, the scanning, the tears, and the crowds.

"I want to get this over with," you tell your lawyer. "I can't take this anymore."

"I'll see what I can do," your lawyer promises as you make plans to surrender yourself on the warrant early the next morning.

In the morning heat, the line seems unusually long. Maybe it's the sticky summer air, or the additional apprehension of knowing that somewhere there is a warrant out for your arrest, or because having finally decided to plead, to capitulate, you've become like everyone else in the line: ground down by the system, beaten by it. And now, having joined them, everything feels different. You shuffle along with the same distracted gait that everyone around you sports. The building seems grayer somehow, the chatter darker. The constant barrage of barked orders from the dozen uniformed court officers manning the magnetometers seems more ominous, more controlling, the inevitable argument or ejection, or the occasional arrest, seems profoundly part of a vast regime of calculated brutality.

Inside the courtroom, the court officer looks at you with raised, impatient eyebrows.

"I h-have a warrant," you stammer, "and, uh, my lawyer told me to tell you and give you the docket number so I can get it taken care of."

Scribbling the docket number on a scrap of paper, the court officer looks at you with utter indifference.

"Take a seat" is all he says.

The day drags on with the usual rhythm. One after another, the people surrounding you on the benches get up for their forty-five seconds with the judge. Your lawyer checks in once, late in the morning, and explains that because you're a warrant, the DA's office doesn't have the file — you can try to see the judge and then come back another day, or wait until the afternoon, when, if you're lucky, the DA's office will be able to have someone find your file in the warrant room and bring it down to the courtroom.

"Let's just get it over with," you hear yourself murmur, agreeing to come back at 2:15.

You skip the fast-food offerings of the food court across the street. Hungry or not, it's better to just spend a few hours quietly reading in the hallway rather than deal with coming back into the courthouse after lunch, and so you sit, waiting as the building empties out, recently released inmates bounding down the stairs, their orange jail-issue slippers flashing in the midday light, lawyers by twos and threes chatting animatedly to one another, dejected girls with tear-streaked cheeks muttering, "No, Mommy, he ain't comin' home today" into their cell phones.

The doors swing open around 2:20, and you are swept into the courtroom with the tide of lawyers and defendants eager to have their cases called first thing after lunch. There's no judge on the bench; she doesn't arrive until about ten minutes after the floating sea of humanity has settled down, and in the meantime lawyers and cops fill in the front row, a kid with an oversized Pelle Pelle jacket and dreads slumps defiantly in the last, and everyone else spreads out evenly in the six rows in between.

Your lawyer strolls in, sees you, and waves. "Hold on," he tells you, "I need to make sure the DA's office got your file. You still wanna just get this over with, right?" You've rarely wanted anything so much in your life.

"Please" is all you say.

Your lawyer and the ADA slip outside through a back door, the one the judge just came in. You get a quick glimpse of a ratty, unembellished hallway beyond, and then the door closes and the first cases of the afternoon are called. Finally, the ADA and your lawyer reappear, and your lawyer strides purposefully out through the swinging gates, hitching a finger at you, beckoning you out into the public hallway.

"There's good news and bad news," he says, starting abruptly. "The good news is that if you want this over today, we can still do that, and do it without pleading you guilty to a crime." He looks at you soberly and then, plowing forward, explains: "The bad news is that we can't get the conditional discharge back — the ADA is being all stupid about the warrant and about why it took you so long to take the plea, and so she's back to a day of community service."

You feel your face start to flush as the futility of trying to fight begins to sink in. You're already imagining yourself in one of those jumpsuits, cleaning a park with one of those weird, pointy sticks designed to skewer garbage, a nasty woman with a Queens accent pestering you to hurry up; you can almost feel the shame and humiliation, the damp, cool air on your skin, the depressing view of the tumbledown urban park, the idling minivan waiting to take you back to the pick-up point, and you're back to thinking, *To hell with this — let's go to trial,* when your lawyer continues: "But she's agreed to a fifty-dollar fine instead." The building knot between your shoulder blades starts to subside; all of a sudden, paying the money seems like a relief — the fine like some kind of oasis, a link to a familiar world far from the lunacy of this building. A fine you can do. A fine's fine. You almost feel grateful.

"Oh, one other thing," the lawyer explains as he makes an undecipherable notation on his file. "With the mandatory court costs and victim services fees, that'll actually come to almost one hundred fifty dollars — I just thought I should let you know so you're not surprised."

Well, you are surprised, but you're also kind of limp, exhausted from the process, feeling as though if you could just be done with this, just get it over with, you can go back to your life, put the whole thing behind you, forget that the Bronx Criminal Courthouse even exists.

"I don't have that much on me today," you explain.

"Oh, no problem." He shrugs. "You'll have three months to pay it."

You agree and return to the courtroom; now that it's 3:30 or so, the audience has gotten thin. Without much ado, your case is called.

The judge starts in on you before you have a chance to say anything.

"Where were you the other day?" she demands.

You weren't ready for this — it's one of the only times the judge has ever addressed you directly — and you notice that just behind you, a court officer slides into place, blocking your exit, gently unsnapping the little black leather belt pouch that holds his handcuffs.

"Ah, Y-Your H-Honor," you stammer, explaining the situation, the words tumbling out, "I called my lawyer in advance and tried to explain. I can show you proof." The judge obviously couldn't care less about any of it, and it feels as if things are getting out of control, when your lawyer interrupts.

"Judge," he says calmly but firmly, "we have a disposition of this case." This seems to back the judge off, and she turns to the ADA.

"People?"

"The People's offer is a 140.05 and a fifty-dollar fine," says the ADA.

The court officer seems to relax slightly.

"Your Honor," your lawyer says, a practiced staccato rhythm taking over, "after consultation with my client, I have been authorized to withdraw all previously entered pleas of not guilty and to enter a plea of guilty to a violation of penal law section 140.05 — that's trespass as a violation, not a crime — in full satisfaction of the docket. We'll waive allocution and stand ready for sentence with the understanding that it'll be a fifty-dollar fine."

The judge listens impassively, scribbling a seemingly more complicated note on the file. "People?" is all she says.

"That's correct, Your Honor," says the ADA, with barely a nod in your direction.

"Fine," snaps the judge. "Is that what you want to do?" she asks you. "Plead guilty in this case?" Her voice comes to you from far away. It's hard to believe you are doing what you're doing, and as you stand before the judge pleading guilty, agreeing to pay a fine for a crime you didn't commit, there is a strange disjunction, a disconnect between your brain and your mouth.

"Yes, Your Honor," you manage to croak.

"Now, did anyone force you or threaten you to make you plead guilty to this charge?" the judge asks. Once again, flashes of the mountain of blue slips, the interminable delays, the stress, the warrant, the lines. Your lawyer glances over at you, sensing your momentary hesitation.

"No, Your Honor," you murmur quietly.

"And are you pleading guilty because you are in fact guilty?"

And there it is: the ultimate question. The judge hasn't even looked up. In some crazy way you want your lawyer to stop this train, to pipe up and insist here and now that you take back this horrible plea, that you, an innocent person, demand your trial; you want him to protect you from what's happening. Just like the judge and the ADA, he is simply waiting for your answer, for the moment when, under oath and in a court of law, you admit to a crime you didn't commit.

Another moment of hesitation, and it's just then that the judge looks up and raises her eyebrows. The air is heavy; the court officer behind you seems alert again; the prospect of coming back is too much to bear. You've come this far; you're on the spot and seconds from having the whole thing over. *Just do what you have to do,* you tell yourself, swallowing hard.

Your lawyer turns to you, whispering, "I thought you wanted to get this thing over with?"

And then, taking a lungful of air, you grit your teeth, square your shoulders, and say it: "Yes, Your Honor."

You barely hear the judge as she pronounces, in the same monotone you've heard her use a thousand times over the past year: "I accept your plea and sentence you to a fine of fifty dollars — mandatory surcharges are imposed. So, that's one hundred forty-five dollars payable at the cashier on or before October twenty-first. Next case, please."

And that's it. The judge tosses — literally tosses — the stapled sheaf of papers that represents your criminal justice nightmare into a wire basket on the side of the bench, next to where the clerk of the court sits. You're mesmerized by the slowly spinning, airborne file. The court officer melts back, allowing you to walk out, following your lawyer, who, smiling kindly, hands you a slip of paper with the amount and payment instructions, shakes your hand, wishes you good luck, and, in a single, smooth gesture, turns smiling toward yet another waiting client.

⇒•⇐

And that's how it goes. Day in and day out, the rage and frustration, the volume and delay, grinding people down until the only plausible option for most is to opt out of the system entirely. That's the goal, of course: realistically, the system can only try one of every hundred cases, which means there has to be a way to make the other ninety-nine cop out. When arrest rates for minor infractions are as high as they are (in the Bronx alone, there are more than fifty thousand misdemeanor arrests a year, and citywide that figure has been as high as a quarter of a million — almost all of them tiny infractions like trespassing, train hopping, disorderly conduct, or possession of marijuana), the system *must* be rigged to coerce pleas. Judges know this. Everyone knows this. When the NYPD makes 62,691 marijuana arrests in a single year, there can't possibly be enough judges, public defenders, and courtrooms to create a just hearing-and-trial system. The only alternative is to make exercising your rights functionally impossible.

Of course, the people like you — those pleading guilty to the noncriminal offenses — have it easy. As frustrating as the waiting is, it does not begin to compare with the experiences of those who are actually in jail — the more than fifteen thousand New York City residents (many of whom are incarcerated on misdemeanor charges) who on any given day are not perched on the benches where you sat, but are instead sitting in the steel cages just behind the scarred metal door at the other end of every courtroom, waiting, in jail, for their turn in court.

⇒⇐

I have four things left to do — four courtrooms left to visit before the day shift is done. And so, after jumping the line, passing through the metal detectors, and loping down the escalator, I'm once again juggling the probabilities and wait times, hoping that I can see everyone who needs to be seen and do everything each of them needs me to do. Cassandra's case is to my right, Najid is to the left, Hector waits in AP-10 on the third floor, and just below that is Jaron and his drug felony.

Time to get to work.

Ten

2:37 P.M.

TAP-1 IS ALWAYS PACKED, so I figure I'll go there first, sign in Najid's case, and then try to sneak over to either the arraignment part to get Cassandra out or up to AP-10. As I approach TAP-1 it's easy to spot Najid. He's outside the courtroom in a huge, puffy lime-green down jacket. With his shaved head and expressive face, he looks like Gandhi at a fruit-themed costume party.

A charming, impish man, Najid holds an advanced degree and an enthusiasm more befitting someone about half his age. A tiny, wiry Persian with dancing eyes and a perpetual grin, he is well known as a green-space activist in the South Bronx, where he transubstantiates weedy abandoned lots into green oases of community commitment. Along with a ragtag crew mostly composed of recent college graduates, Najid runs the More Gardens! Coalition.

Najid doesn't actually live in the Bronx — he has a small apartment in the East Village, which is often used by some of the vaguely itinerant activists who pass through his organization. Older than the bulk of his group, Najid is a kindly leader whose calm and purpose seem to animate the younger tattooed or pierced kids who come to keep the Bronx green.

The former headquarters of the More Gardens! Coalition was less than a block from our office, in a beautiful flowering garden presided over by a huge bright-yellow sunflower sculpture and a small cinder-block casita where Najid led classes for local elementary school kids, teaching them about seeds and vegetables and gardening. One rainy fall morning, the city bulldozed the casita and plowed under the garden. Najid had known that this might be happening. Though he'd helped to negotiate a large citywide agreement on the preservation of certain community gardens, he'd lost several battles over specific gardens near our office. For weeks there had been rumors about the destruction of the garden with the casita in it, but as the days passed without a bulldozer in sight, it seemed less and less likely that the city would actually destroy one of the more charming green spaces in the South Bronx.

But they did. Looking to make room for some housing they'd long been planning — two family homes that would sell for several hundred thousand dollars — the city had quietly decided that the garden had to go. The fact that there were seven large vacant lots within a block of the casita seemed to have no impact on the decision.

With negotiations at a delicate stage, and a creeping sense that the city and the developer might not be playing completely straight about their plans for the little garden, Najid often slept in the casita, hoping he wouldn't wake to the sounds of the police or heavy machinery. But when he did, he was ready. Quickly climbing to the roof, he managed to send out a cell phone distress call just before chaining himself into a specially prepared cinderblock cylinder, in what is known in civil disobedience circles as a "sleeping dragon."

A sleeping dragon is a length of steel pipe with a rod welded into the center. A spring clip attaches the protester's hands to the rod in the center, making it nearly impossible to remove his or her arms without breaking them. Usually the police are forced to carefully cut through the steel pipe at the point of the weld in order to unclip the hands and remove the arms. In Najid's case, the sleeping dragon was actually built into a cement portion of the roof of the casita, so that the police would have to cut away the concrete flute as well.

Unfortunately, when I pulled up that morning — just after 9:00 A.M. — that was exactly what they were doing. A huge crowd stood across the street, held back by fifteen or twenty policemen.

"Save our gardens!" the crowd chanted in the rain.

"Fuck your gardens," one of the patrol cops muttered, pissed off at being stuck doing crowd control in the cold rain.

I walked up to the nearest captain, introduced myself, and explained that they had my client up on the roof — I'd done some work for the coalition in the past and had agreed to be Najid's lawyer if anything like this ever happened.

"Well, Counselor," said the captain, his voice making it clear that in his view Najid might as well have been a serial killer, "your *client* is about to get himself arrested."

"Right," I said. "That's exactly why I'd like to talk to him."

From the captain's face it seemed that the only life-form lower than that of a protester was that of a protester's lawyer.

"Not 'til we get him to the station," the captain said curtly.

"Actually, I'd like to talk to him now, please," I said. "He's unarmed and alone up there, surrounded by a dozen armed men. I won't be interfering; I'd just like to go speak to my client as I have a right to do."

The captain seemed to consider this for a moment, and then, waving over a nearby patrolman, he hitched a thumb at me. "Make sure the counselor here stays across the street, would ya? I don't want him around here."

"Sure, Cap," the patrolman — a thick guy with an Irish name — said with evident satisfaction, and then to me: "Let's go, Counselor."

Right or wrong on the law, they had the guns. I went.

For nearly six hours Najid held off the combined forces of the New York City Police Department. Police choppers hovered overhead, dozens of officers cordoned off the area, and two television stations shot footage of the tiny lone man chained to the roof of the little casita. All the while, community members continued chanting. "Save our gardens! Keep the Bronx green!" I found out later that the officers up on the roof were doing everything they could to break Najid. They'd crowd around him, pushing and shoving, threatening to break his arms and discussing at length all the things they were going to charge him with and the many years he could spend in jail. Several of them heaped insult and obscenity on him. Throughout it all, as they shouted into his face, Najid would smile gently and say to them, "Officers, I respect you greatly, and I know that you are good people. Be professional. Do your job. I am not going to let go, and I'm not going to come out. So do what you have to do, as professionals, and what happens to me will happen to me."

Watching the drama unfold, I was surprised at my own reaction. There was little question in my mind that Najid was engaged in one of the most heroic acts I'd ever seen. He had a quiet dignity that was almost incomprehensible to me. And with the drizzle, the thrumming of the choppers, and the militaristic block-long lockdown, the whole scene felt strangely cinematic. I was deeply moved by Najid and his conviction — and at the ability of one person to slow down the massive machine of the state.

Yet I was almost equally moved by the fact that the police didn't break his arms. There are few things that more clearly reveal the knife edge of oppression lurking behind our everyday life than what happens to someone who really resists the steamroller. Somehow, the fact that our society would spend the time, material, and money on a guy who was flamboyantly breaking the law made me love this country profoundly. And the more I watched, as for six hours they pounded and hacksawed away at little Najid and his sleeping dragon, the more impressed I was with our collective tolerance for dissent.

When they finally freed him, when Najid finally stood up, placing his hands demurely behind his back as they cuffed him and marched him down off the roof, a faint smile discernible through the tired lines etched on his face, a little cheer went up from the damp crowd across the street — an acknowledgment that even though, in the final analysis, none of us may be able to stop the colossus, we can all do a lot more than we imagine ourselves capable of.

The Bronx DA saw no romance whatsoever in resistance to authority. Najid was charged with resisting arrest, disorderly conduct, and obstructing governmental administration. Given the flagrant violation of the law, I'd have agreed to a plea if they'd allowed him to do some community service for More Gardens! or for another progressive not-for-profit, but they wouldn't consider such a proposal. As a result, we'd been fighting his case for well over a year.

Giving Najid a little hug, I apologize for being late and poke my head inside the courtroom to gauge the line.

The place is a zoo.

I sign up the case, scrawling my name and his on the worn clipboard dangling from the courtroom wall. A quick scan of the sign-in sheet makes clear that there are already more than a dozen cases waiting to be called, and that means that I have at least thirty-five minutes to trek to another courtroom and try to get something else done. I apologize to Najid again and tell him to wait — probably for the hundredth time during the pendency of his case.

"Of course," he says, smiling gently, "don't worry about it."

I do worry, though — in fact I often wonder whether fighting the court case is more trying for him than staging the protest was. For him, a day spent in court is a day diverted from the Bronx community, and we're going on fifteen days wasted.

Ducking across the hall, I peek into AR-2, thinking that if it is empty, I can spring Cassandra right away. It's packed as well. Judging from the box of court papers, it looks as if Judge Birnbaum will be working until late in the afternoon. I've got a half hour, two impossible courtrooms, and two more left to try, the narcotics part and AP-10 — the domestic violence part.

The main elevators in criminal court are constantly overcrowded and so astonishingly slow that it can take fifteen minutes to go ten vertical feet. The stairways are for fire use only and don't open onto the proper floors anyway, and so, as I often do, I cut through the back of an empty courtroom to stow away on the judge's elevator.

Upstairs, AP-10 handles exclusively low-level domestic violence and sex cases. It is one of my least-favorite places in criminal court. Measured on an hourly basis, more injustice is perpetuated in AP-10 than in any other place in the criminal courthouse. AP-10 showcases what pissed-off people do to one another after having had the misfortune of having sex: slapping, punching, phone breaking, and decorating the neighborhood with posters such as

WANTED:

For Child Support

Kareem Williams.

Last seen fucking some whore bitch he pick up.

Like all deadbeat he think he some kind of pimp daddy. He lives off people. And when he get a dollar, he act like he is God. That's how you can tell he a asshole, not use to shit.

Because it is accessible only by those vaguely functioning elevators, AP-10 is inconvenient for most lawyers and clients — but it is even worse for incarcerated clients (and there are many of them in that part). Because there are no jail cells on the third floor, jailed defendants almost never get to see their lawyers until they are marched, manacled, into court.

If there is a lesson to AP-10, it is that the absurdly blunt instrument of criminal prosecution is just not up to the task of unraveling the complicated motives and pathological interpersonal dynamics of vindictive people and screwed-up relationships. Every day, AP-10 hosts a parade of people using protective orders as weapons in child custody battles or property disputes, making false allegations against ex-lovers or their new partners, or blackmailing a current lover into being faithful or forking over money. And though there are plenty of real victims and legitimate cases, overall AP-10 is a viper pit of spurious allegations and twisted motivations. In such an environment, calm, reasonable prosecutors and insightful, deliberate judges might be able to competently sift through twisted facts and outrageous allegations. Unfortunately, though, both the assistant district attorneys who populate the part and most of the judges who sit in judgment of the cases see themselves as the saviors of battered

176 / David Feige

women and abused children. While understandable, this savior complex makes an already bad situation far worse, particularly in cases with reluctant complainants or sparse facts. Just as politics makes it nearly impossible for all but the bravest judges to grant reasonable bail, the politics of domestic violence make AP-10 a supercharged and dangerous place to be for victims (particularly those who may want to patch up their relationships) and defendants who are often actually innocent.

This was something Ron learned the hard way.

On his way to a job interview one summer morning, Ron was arrested and charged with groping a girl. The girl had been grabbed from behind and dragged toward the front door of a building — one of about a dozen in a massive housing project in the middle of the Bronx. Ron, who lived in a small, overcrowded apartment jammed into the huge complex, had been walking down the street on his way to the train station when the police picked him up.

Almost everything in the case suggested that a mistake had been made. The girl explained that she never got much of a look at her attacker, and she couldn't provide a description much beyond a black guy in a do-rag, hardly uncommon in the projects of the Bronx. When the police grabbed Ron about a block from the attack (even though the man who assaulted the victim appeared to flee into — not away from — the projects), they didn't even bother to bring him over to her for a proper identification. Instead, from a distance of one hundred feet, the girl indicated that Ron looked like the guy, and that was that.

Identification cases plague the criminal justice system. In fact, the single greatest cause of wrongful prosecution and unjust imprisonment is misidentification. But even among ID cases, the case against Ron was a joke. There was no other evidence in the case and nothing to connect Ron to the attack; indeed, he had an alibi — his mother was able to testify that Ron had left the apartment just a few minutes before his arrest and hadn't even been outside before that. Someone had done something horrible, but it sure wasn't Ron.

Given all that, Ron might have had a good shot at finding some justice in the Bronx criminal court system. That is until he drew the perfect storm of prosecutorial and judicial perversion: Sarah Schall and Judge Diane Kiesel.

Prosecutors' offices usually define success not by the justice of the result, but by the number of convictions. This creates a perverse incentive structure that rewards aggressive prosecutors looking for scalps rather than those searching for fairness. And though there are certainly bad guys who need locking up (I've represented several), when the enormous power of the state is arrayed against some poor kid from the projects, having a zealous prosecutor who is just looking to win will often result in a miscarriage of justice.

Even among domestic violence prosecutors, Sarah Schall is one of the worst — so sleazy that defense lawyers just laugh when she routinely claims to have "just found" paperwork she should have long ago turned over. Schall is small and mean and twitchy, and she tends to march rather than walk. Though she has pretty shoulder-length hair, between her edgy affect and a wardrobe that always seems slightly misassembled, her overall look is far more dowdy than cute. For Schall, every case is the crime of the century, often much to the detriment of her own complaining witnesses, who find their cases to be less about them and their protection than about Schall and her ego.

Domestic violence is a serious problem, and no one condones it. Women often call the police because they are terrified, helpless, or being seriously hurt. But they also call to remove angry, drunk, and often dangerous lovers and spouses, to report threatening phone calls, or even to tattle on loudly arguing neighbors. And once the police are called and mandatory arrest policies enforced, women lose control of their own destinies. Forgivable transgressions quickly become stuck in the court system as prosecutors supplant women as the arbiters of intimate relationships. Unfortunately for many victims, prosecutors often have an agenda quite different from their own. Sarah Schall is one of them — the kind of ADA that can make a woman believe that despite her abuse, her real mistake was calling the police or involving the prosecutors, because from the moment Schall is on the case, the interests of a victim and her family are likely to play second fiddle to Schall's personal prosecutorial crusade.

Facing Schall at a trial is an unpleasant enough prospect, but if a defense attorney is trying a case against Schall with Judge Diane Kiesel on the bench, he might as well just hang it up.

There are judges who are gentle and judges who are tough, judges who are cruel and judges who are impatient; there are judges who berate defendants — pushing them to plead guilty while their lawyers stand there mutely — and there are judges who kindly respect whatever a defendant chooses to do in a case. And then there are judges like Kiesel, a former Manhattan prosecutor whose icy pucker and utter detachment perfectly reflect her complete heartlessness.

Kiesel is tall and very thin, with an angular, bony face framed by a severe chin-length haircut. Her hair is processed to the color of curb cement, and she has long, spindly fingers that move impatiently while she presides, sitting imperiously straight in her high-backed chair. There is a pinched intensity to Kiesel; she seems to listen to the proceedings before her with an emotional palate that ranges from disagreeable to sour, the nervous twitching of her Grim Reaper fingers tapping out a constant rhythm of disapproval.

When forced to interact with a defendant — to ask a question during a plea allocution, for example — Kiesel will hardly glance at him or her, preferring to stare down at the bench, over at the prosecutor, or even at defense counsel, anything to avoid acknowledging the humanity of the person standing helplessly before her.

I've often wondered why judges like Kiesel do this — does it come from the recognition that sending someone to jail or prison is a difficult thing and that avoiding eye contact makes it easier? Is it because they don't want to appear too human or accessible to a criminal defendant? Is it that, somehow, being aloof makes them more powerful? Or is it that they're actually just cruel people who despise those who appear before them? With almost all of the judges I appear before, I sense a combination of these factors: painful empathy, self-importance, and abject cruelty. In Kiesel, though, I see only cruelty.

Kiesel will often refuse to accept pleas that an assistant district attorney recommends, her narrow face twisted into a scowl of disapproval — *not harsh enough,* she'll telegraph. She'll also remand defendants after another judge has released them — and do so on the flimsiest of excuses. It seems crazy that a judge and her politics should have as much of an impact as they do. But judges are like the jokers of the criminal case outcome deck.

As a general rule, when a person is accused of a crime, he or she has the right to a jury trial. What most people don't know, though, is that when you are charged with certain misdemeanor offenses, you lose that right. If you don't have a right to a jury trial, what you get is a bench trial — one presided over by a judge who is the sole finder of both the law and the facts. And when that judge is Diane Kiesel, the outcome is a foregone conclusion. The mere threat of being forced to trial in front of her is enough to transform baseless prosecutions into strong cases, terrible plea offers into enticing deals, and it's enough to make utterly innocent people plead guilty.

Kiesel is so openly pro prosecution, so astonishingly biased, and so relentlessly nasty that even assistant district attorneys quietly acknowledge it — and they use it, steering almost all of their cases before her toward bench rather than jury trials. When confronted by a tough case, or a recalcitrant witness, they simply "reduce the case." That is, they cleanly and tactically lower the charges from class A misdemeanors to class B misdemeanors, depriving a defendant of a jury trial but not the possibility of a jail sentence.

And in Ron's case, that's exactly what they did. Between Sarah Schall and Judge Diane Kiesel, Ron hardly knew what hit him.

Ron's lawyer, Ululy Martinez, saw it coming a mile away. Ululy was one of the most enthusiastic people we'd ever met, and but for the strength of his interview, we probably never would have hired him. Raised in the Bronx, he was a striver from an early age — one of those kids who miraculously avoided the pitfalls that snared most of his friends. Ululy deeply understood that making it out of the world he grew up in was as much about chance as it was about skill or drive or even ability. Deeply committed to his community, Ululy insisted, between his invocations of Maya Angelou and his former professors, that his goal in life was to help his people and his community by being a public defender.

At the trial, the prosecution's case against Ron unraveled completely and quickly. The complaining witness and the police contradicted each other. The description of the perpetrator was meager and inconsistent, and the flimsy evidence was rendered transparent nonsense in the crucible of Ululy's cross-examination. The only thing anyone seemed to agree on was that whoever had grabbed the girl had fled in the opposite direction from where Ron was arrested. Through it all, Kiesel tapped and twitched and scowled impatiently.

And after both sides rested and summations were delivered, she didn't even hesitate. There was no real deliberation at all, just an instant, awful pronouncement: "Guilty."

And then, with a sadistic scowl, she ordered Ron to jail and watched unflinchingly as the court officers fitted the cuffs around the terrified kid's wrists and led him away. Ron had never been to jail before. Because a class B misdemeanor is the least-serious kind of criminal offense in the penal law, it is virtually unheard of for a first-time offender convicted of a B to be sentenced to jail. Kiesel, though, gave Ron as much jail time as she could manage. Then she imposed a term of probation to be served after his release.

And she still wasn't done.

Despite the fact that the statute didn't cover Ron's offense, she bent the rules in order to have him branded a sex offender.

Had a jury heard his case, Ron would have been acquitted in an hour. But by gaming the system, Sarah Schall and the Bronx DA's office had ensured he'd never have that benefit. Instead, his promising young life was ruined because Ululy got stuck in front of the wrong judge.

The only advantage to Kiesel is that she is so predictable that no one wants to hang around her courtroom. As a result, the line in AP-10 is usually much shorter than the ones downstairs, where Najid and Jaron and Cassandra are waiting.

Walking into the part, I feel my usual revulsion. Unlike the courtrooms below, which are all designed to process cases rather than try them, AP-10 is shiny and newly refurbished. It actually has a jury box, though so far as I know, it's never been used for a jury; rather, waiting lawyers populate its padded reclining chairs. Scanning the box, it's clear that there are only a few cases ahead of me. I should be in and out in ten minutes or so.

Spying my client, I nod a quick hello.

Hector is an older Hispanic man charged, like so many others in AP-10, with hitting his wife. They've been together for twenty-five years, and neither of them wants anything to do with the case. Hector takes a day off from work every month to come to court, while his wife makes phone calls to the assistant district attorney trying to drop the charges.

Unfortunately, once an arrest has been made it can be very, very difficult to get an assistant district attorney to let go. Many domestic violence prosecutors simply won't dismiss cases even when the complainant wants to, and they will often resort to threats in an attempt to force the alleged victim to go forward. One of their favorite tactics is threatening to take the kids away if a woman doesn't agree to cooperate with the prosecution. Mercifully, my client's children are all grown up and out of the house, so neither he nor his wife have to worry — at least about that.

I give the bridge officer Hector's name and calendar number, and settle into the seat that would, in other circumstances, be occupied by juror number seven. Leaning back in the comfortable chair, I dig out my files and settle in once more to watch Judge Diane Kiesel in action.

Eleven

2:52 P.M.

I'VE BARELY TAKEN MY SEAT in the jury box when two court officers march in a heavyset man of indeterminate nationality. He's wearing a blue mechanic's jumpsuit with a name that I can't quite read sewn on the lapel. Mr. Blue Jumpsuit has been arrested for violating an order of protection. His hands are cuffed, and he's shuffling toward the defense table from the back of the courtroom where the pens are. In the dozen steps it takes him to get before the judge, I can see him looking out into the courtroom at a little, round well-coiffed woman who's seated in the fourth row and who returns his gaze with something like a smile.

Known elsewhere as "stay-away orders," orders of protection are granted to alleged victims and witnesses almost automatically. Those charged, as Blue is, with having violated a stay-away order are subject to a jail term of up to a year — more if there are aggravating circumstances. Though a fine idea in principle, orders of protection are constantly abused. It is not at all uncommon for vindictive, angry partners to use orders of protection to wreak havoc on each other — using them as substitutes for eviction orders or citing them to justify ignoring child custody agreements. Almost everyone in the Bronx knows that the easiest way to gain control of a disputed property is to get a judge to issue a stay-away. One little allegation and within twenty-four hours the enjoined party can be barred from the house, allowed only a few hours to collect his things while accompanied by a police officer.

Just as Blue is taking his place at the defense table next to his legal aid lawyer, his little wife jumps up in the fourth row.

"He been good!" she says emphatically in heavily accented English. "Everything going great. Please, Judge, I am this man's wife, and I'm asking you to please let him come home."

From what I can gather, Blue has been in jail for a week or more. His lawyer, a lanky, clean-shaven man, is trying to explain to Kiesel why it is time to let him out of jail.

This, of course, is a futile endeavor.

"This whole case is a mistake, Judge," the legal aid lawyer says, his voice calm and persuasive. "My client's wife has called the DA's office repeatedly trying to get them to modify the order of protection so that my client can live in the home."

"Yes! Yes! I call! I call!" yells the wife from the back.

"Quiet, ma'am, or you'll have to clear the courtroom!" an officer barks.

Legal Aid continues: "There have been no incidents of violence or aggression or anything — and, most important, no one called the police here. My client was arrested based on a routine check of the house. The complainant in this matter tried to explain to the police that she wanted him in the house, and she's here in court to tell you the same thing."

Blue's wife is nodding — and she's about to speak again when Kiesel spies her.

"Sit down," the judge says sharply. Apparently she's not interested in what the supposed victim wants.

"Down, ma'am!" says a court officer. "Sit DOWN!"

Blue's wife sits.

"Is there an offer here?" Kiesel wants to know.

"The People's offer is a B and thirty," says a young assistant DA from the domestic violence unit, conveying the standard offer. She's wearing tired pumps and a beige Ann Taylor dress.

"Does your client want it?" Kiesel asks dryly. She couldn't be less interested in Legal Aid's explanation.

"Judge," Legal Aid replies, "my client wants to go home to his family — where his wife and children want him. I'm asking you to at least listen to this woman — this is what she wants too."

Glancing over at Blue's wife, I realize that her husband is almost certainly in jail because the original assistant DA didn't bother to return the woman's calls requesting a modification of the order of protection to allow Blue to live at home.

"Does he want it?" Kiesel asks sharply.

"Judge," Legal Aid tries again valiantly, "she tried to get the order of protection limited."

But Kiesel doesn't care. She's heard enough. "It's MY order," she says. "Theyyyy" — she stretches out the word so the condescension is lost on no one — "don't get to make those decisions."

There is silence in the courtroom. Several people in the audience are shaking their heads and lowering their eyes, evidently astonished. They don't know Kiesel like I do.

"So I take it your client doesn't want the offer?" Kiesel sneers. "Defense motions are due . . ."

"I'll waive motions!" Legal Aid declares — averting a disaster that a less-alert lawyer might have fallen for. Motions — for discovery, suppression of evidence, or for almost any other relief in a case — are the bread and butter of most lawyers. At big law firms many so-called litigators never set foot in a courtroom; they're considered litigators mostly because they negotiate with opposing counsel and file a bunch of motions. But motions practice in the Bronx is usually a futile endeavor, and strange as it may seem, in many cases involving incarcerated clients charged with misdemeanors, just chucking the entire exercise is actually the smart move — not just because it's futile, but because it's time consuming, and time is something that indigent, incarcerated clients can ill-afford. Like so much else in Bronx criminal practice, the decision about when to give up motions is about poverty and power.

Blue is in jail because he doesn't have $750 — the bail amount set by the arraigning judge. And because he doesn't, he'll sit in jail until he pleads guilty or manages to get a trial. Right now, the DA's office is offering Blue thirty days at Rikers, of which, thanks to the good-time rules of the Department of Corrections, he'll serve twenty. He's been in jail for about a week already. If the judge or the DA can stall the case for just two more weeks, Blue will be in the position of staying in jail even longer than he would if he just pled guilty and ate the twenty days right now. Every single lawyer in the courtroom knows this — and so does Kiesel. It is the dirty little secret of the adjournment game. Legal Aid is willing to waive motions precisely because he knows this too. The motions schedule is a Kiesel power play designed to punish Blue for not playing along with the plea-bargain game.

"Judge, the complainant is here in court." Legal Aid is really giving it a go. "Would you consider reducing the bail?" If Kiesel were to reduce the bail, Blue could get out, and then, with time no longer of the essence, the case would inch toward a trial at which, when his wife didn't show up, the charges would almost certainly be dismissed.

Fat chance.

"Do you want a motions schedule or not?" Kiesel asks, ignoring the request altogether.

Blue's eyes are darting between Kiesel and his lawyer, trying to follow the action, but as with so much of the rapid back-and-forth in criminal court, the lawyers and judges are talking in a code larded with implications that aren't obvious to the casual listener and certainly not to an incarcerated client who hasn't even had a chance to talk to his lawyer before getting marched in.

"I'm waiving motions — I want an immediate trial," Legal Aid says, defiantly holding his ground.

"Judge," says the ADA, affecting an almost bored tone, "the People aren't ready today." She too is looking to delay the case, to force the plea.

"Their witness is right here in court!" Legal Aid protests.

"We want time to investigate," the ADA says utterly mendaciously.

"Fine," says Kiesel, announcing a date three weeks away.

"Judge," groans an exasperated Legal Aid, "that's too long. I'm waiving motions so I can get an early trial date."

"The trial parts are very busy," replies Kiesel dryly.

"Can I get an earlier date?"

I have to hand it to Legal Aid — he's doing everything right; it's just that he's in Judge Kiesel's courtroom.

Perversely, she offers a date two days earlier than the one she previously announced, a worthless concession.

"Judge," Legal Aid implores, "adjourning the case even that long will be penalizing my client for going to trial."

"Which date, Counselor?"

Kiesel's eyes are cold, and she has the fingers going now. It's abundantly clear that things are about to get much worse for Blue if Legal Aid keeps fighting. There is a pause, just for a heartbeat, as Legal Aid considers his options. This is too long for Kiesel.

"Case is adjourned," she says flatly, giving the latter of the two options as the date to reconvene.

Legal Aid looks stricken — he's just been whupped. He leans over to his client and starts whispering. Sensing what is happening, the wife in the audience begins to cry.

"Step outside, ma'am," a court officer tells her.

I can't hear exactly what is transpiring, but I've been in this position hundreds of times and know by heart the horrible explanation. I've delivered it myself dozens and dozens of times:

"I've been trying to get you out of jail. The judge knows that your wife wants you home. She knows your wife is here, and she knows that you tried to get the order of protection changed. She doesn't care. The DA is offering you thirty days in jail if you plead guilty — that means you'll be out in twenty days including the time you've already been in. I've already asked for a trial, but the problem is, the judge won't give us a trial date until the seventeenth — and that's more than two weeks away. I'm not defending this, but the reality is that if the case were to go to trial that day, which is unlikely, you will already have been in for more time than if you just plead guilty right now. I'm not defending it; I'm just telling you that unless you think you can find someone to put up the bail money, you're gonna be in here for at least another few weeks, and longer if we keep pushing for a trial."

There are few things I hate more than giving this speech. It confirms everything my clients think about the system — that it's coercive and unfair, and that within it the deck is stacked against them because they're poor. They're right, of course, and it galls me to have to admit that I am complicit in this abuse and worse, that despite my fancy law degree and my big vocabulary and my tough-guy posturing, I'm a weak little pawn in a very ugly system and there is not a goddamn thing I can do to stop them from getting fucked.

Worse still, of course, is that Blue, like so many of my clients, is about to wind up with a permanent criminal record, which will, in turn, almost certainly mean that he'll lose his job and have a very hard time getting a new one unless he lies about the conviction. Still, almost anything is better than more time in jail.

Blue shrugs the kind of defeated shrug I've seen a thousand times over the years, his head shaking just a little bit, amazed at his predicament.

"Fine" is all he says.

Kiesel has been staring off into space during the forty-five seconds it takes to have the brutal talk with Blue, her fingers thrumming an impatient rhythm on the bench as she waits for what we all know is coming.

"Your Honor," says Legal Aid, using a term clearly inapplicable to the situation at hand, "we have a disposition."

Kiesel barely reacts, and Legal Aid continues: "After consultation with my client he's authorized me to enter a plea of guilty on his behalf to attempted criminal contempt in the second degree. He does that with the understanding that he'll be sentenced to thirty days in jail."

Kiesel is still staring out over everyone, her eyes focused on an imaginary spot somewhere on the back wall. "And abide by a full, permanent order of protection," she adds distractedly.

Blue winces, and I'm briefly glad that the wife is outside — she came to court to try to explain that she wanted her husband home and that she didn't want or need an order of protection. Now, not only is her husband going to jail, the judge is reissuing an order barring him from his home, his wife, and his children for another year.

"J-Judge," Legal Aid stammers, "the *complainant* doesn't

want the full order of protection. She's come to court to explain that — she's made it clear to me and to the DA's office and tried to make it clear to you that she wants him home. Please, just limit it so that he can live at home."

"Do the people want a *limited* order of protection?" Kiesel says, glancing over at the young ADA who has remained impassive throughout the proceedings.

"No, Judge," says the ADA, "my file says full."

"Well, then," says Kiesel, looking back at Legal Aid with a contemptuous look, "would your client like to withdraw his plea?"

Blue looks as if he's going to cry. From the side I can see his shoulders start to heave, jerking his hands, cuffed behind his back, up and down. His head is bowed, and it's clear he's breathing deeply just trying to keep control of himself.

"Just get me out of here," he mutters audibly to Legal Aid, though whether that means he wants the plea or just wants to go back to his cell is unclear. Legal Aid leans in close, and I can see Blue shaking his head. "Just do it," he says. "Get it over with."

"No, Judge," Legal Aid says flatly, "my client wants to plead."

"Sir," Kiesel says to Blue — she's doing that amazing trick of talking to a defendant without really looking at him — "your lawyer tells me that you want to plead guilty to this criminal offense; is that what you wish to do?"

Blue just shakes his head in disbelief.

"You have to say yes," Legal Aid instructs.

"Yes," says Blue, his shoulders shaking, his breathing quick and shallow.

"Has anybody forced you or threatened you to plead guilty?" Kiesel asks in the same flat tone.

"No," mutters Legal Aid under his breath.

"No," murmurs Blue, though everyone in the courtroom knows it's not true, and I know that only 750 bucks would have made the difference — the essential divide not race but cash. Had Blue made bail this whole thing would have gone away, or at worst he would have been offered a plea to a noncriminal offense with no jail time and a limited order of protection.

"Fine," says Kiesel, "I accept your guilty plea and sentence you to thirty days in jail and a conditional discharge, the special condition of which is that you abide by a full, permanent order of protection — that means you can have no contact with your wife, none whatsoever. It doesn't matter whether she wants to see you or not. I'm ordering you to stay away from her. Is that clear?" I could swear there is a sadistic sparkle in Kiesel's eyes.

Blue just nods, but Kiesel wants an answer.

"Clear?" she asks again.

"Yes!" hisses Legal Aid.

"Yes," says Blue.

"Good," says Kiesel. "Next case, please."

I'm getting nervous. Cassandra and Najid are waiting downstairs, and I still have Jaron on the main floor. The clock is edging past 3:00, and that leaves less than an hour to get everything done since most judges like to be off the bench by 3:45 or so. Unfortunately, there's still one more case before mine.

I decide to hang tight.

Glancing back at Hector, still sitting in the second row, I give him the "just be patient" sign — palms down, fingers spread, gesturing gently toward the floor as if to say, *Don't worry, be calm, it won't be long now.* Hector rolls his eyes just a little and shakes his head incredulously — every time he comes to court, he can't believe what he sees.

Neither can I sometimes.

I swivel my head back toward Kiesel just as a thick dark-skinned man with long, twisted dreadlocks comes shuffling out.

"Add-on to the calendar," announces the bridge officer calling the case.

Being an add-on almost certainly means that Dreads has been in jail for a short time. Adding a case onto the calendar means that it wasn't normally adjourned last time, so he's either coming straight from a different courtroom or his adjournment was so short that the case didn't make it onto the daily lists compiled by the central clerk's office. As it turns out, this is Dreads's third courtroom for the day. Dreads had been out on bail the last time he came to court a few weeks ago. Like many others, he'd spent much of the day in AP-10 waiting for his case to be called. When the time finally came, Dreads had explained that he needed to run to pick up his kids from school.

"Can you just send me the order of protection?" he'd asked his lawyer. His wife had already called the DA and the lawyer explaining that she didn't want the order anyway.

"Actually, I can't," the lawyer had told him. "You'll have to wait."

So Dreads waited.

And he waited, and after waiting for forty minutes, he couldn't wait any longer — it was 3:10, and he had to pick up the kids at 3:30.

"I can't wait anymore, mon — I gotta be gettin' the kids," Dreads explained to the court officer. "I can come back tomorrow and pick it up." The court officer just shrugged.

As any prosecutor will happily tell you, orders of protection are enforceable even when someone hasn't signed them — so long as they are duly served so that the recipient has notice of the order. Technically, since Dreads was notified during the court proceeding that he was still subject to an order of protection, his signature was just a formality.

But Judge Salvatore Modica thought that Dreads's leaving was disrespectful. Dreads's lawyer had long since decamped for another courtroom when they finally called his name. The court officer Dreads had spoken with had never mentioned the situation to Modica, so Modica, on his own, had Dreads's case recalled — without the lawyer or the client or anyone except the ADA present — and because Dreads didn't sign the order of protection, Modica issued a bench warrant. "Set bail," he scribbled on the court papers — which is exactly what Judy Lieb, the duty day judge, did on the day that Dreads showed up again for court.

Having set bail as instructed, Judge Lieb then sent the case back to Judge Modica, who increased the bail from the $500 that Judge Lieb set to $2,500. Then he sent the case back to AP-10.

By the time I see Dreads come into AP-10, he's been tossed into jail, had his bail raised, and is completely freaked out. "*Please,*" he begs his lawyer, "you gotta call someone — I got to pick up dem kids again. I'm tillin' you, my girl been down here to drop dem charges — been down to tem office tree times. She sign dere papers! *Please,* call her! She'll tell you, mon."

"I know," says Dreads's lawyer — as it turns out, Dreads's girl has called him several times too, conveying the same message.

Kiesel is drumming away, the ADAs are shuffling their files, and Dreds's lawyer is whispering to one of the ADAs in a plaintive tone that's barely audible when I make out one of the few magic words in AP-10: "Andy."

Andy Liu is one of the few really decent ADAs in the DV unit. Born in Michigan of Chinese immigrants, Andy was raised in Santa Barbara and got a philosophy degree from UCLA before coming east for law school. If you are lucky enough to get him on the phone or corner him in court, Andy, unlike most of the rest, will listen carefully and respond reasonably. He has a stellar reputation with the defense bar and (perhaps surprisingly) within his own office, which has promoted him steadily into the supervisory ranks. Andy is unfailingly personable and so principled that even when he refuses to do what I think of as the right thing — either because it's beyond his jurisdiction or because we have a disagreement about what the right thing is — he's almost impossible to resent. What sets him apart is that he's never punitive. So far as I can tell, Andy has never kept someone in jail on an untenable case just because he can — and that alone, in the world of ADAs, is enough to make him almost saintly.

"Can I have a second to make a phone call?" the ADA asks Kiesel.

"Sure," says Kiesel, standing up and striding off the bench.

"Court will take a five-minute recess!" the court officer declares as Kiesel walks stiff-legged toward her chambers. As soon as she gets up, Dreads is marched away. I glance back at Hector again and shrug. Nothing to do but ride this one out.

Five minutes later, Kiesel returns, Dreads is brought back out before the court, and the ADA asks that the case be dismissed. Kiesel seems momentarily perturbed, but there is nothing she can do. The court officers remove the handcuffs, Dreads stretches his shoulders, and after a day of useless incarceration, he walks out of the courtroom.

If Andy hadn't picked up the phone, Dreads would have stayed in jail and his kids would have been left stranded in front of their school. If Dreads hadn't been in front of Judge Modica, there never would have been a bench warrant issued. And if Ron, the innocent kid Ululy tried so hard to save, had gone to trial in front of almost any other judge, his life wouldn't have been ruined.

The capriciousness of the system is often overwhelming.

It's not just the prosecutor and the judge, of course. The defense lawyer makes some difference. Certainly, a client unlucky enough to get a lawyer who just churns cases by taking pleas is going to have a hard time finding justice. But even with a good lawyer, a client who draws a nightmare prosecutor has basically been handed a one-way ticket to jail or prison. This is especially true when litigating against an awful prosecutor who has an ally like Kiesel on the bench. Then the frustration and powerlessness can become almost too much to bear. It's those times that we do everything right on behalf of a deserving client and still wind up getting crushed that can drive defense lawyers completely over the edge. That's certainly what happened to a lawyer I once knew.

Standing in front of a gallery of waiting clients and enervated witnesses, she is rumored to have done what I've wanted to do many, many times after a horrible, unconscionable ruling: she looked up at the judge and reportedly said, plain and simple, "Fuck you, you nasty bitch." It wasn't under her breath, and it wasn't the whisper that a lawyer can often get away with. It was loud and proud and impossible to ignore.

"Fuck you, you nasty bitch."

I don't know whether the judge tried to hold her in contempt right then or whether the courtroom was silent for a second as, perhaps realizing what she'd just done, or perhaps having second thoughts about having done it, she turned away from the judge, away from her client, and away from the defense table and sprinted toward the exit. What I did hear, though, is that she ran. And when the shocked court officers grabbed her, trying to figure out what to do, she struggled, and that — far more than disrupting the court or even calling the judge a bitch — was (at least in the bizarre world of the Bronx) unforgivable. She was arrested and charged with criminal contempt and resisting arrest. Within hours, news of the incident had spread like wildfire throughout the courthouse.

I've often wondered what I'll do when (not if) the time comes that I reach that moment — that day when I've finally been pushed too far. I know how it feels to be there. It's what I felt the morning I turned my back on Blog — the moment when I was willing to feel the steel, willing to surrender my law license, willing to face any consequence and every imaginable sanction rather than one more second of the horror of criminal practice. I'd like to think my *fuck you* would be only the tiniest taste of the obscenity-laden vitriol I'd empty over the judge, the prosecutors, and the courtroom. I'd like to think that I'd begin a disquisition for the ages — a raging soliloquy, part Martin Luther King, part Mamet, about a foul, disrespectful, unfair system. In my imagination, I'd like to think that while being marched out of the courtroom, hands cuffed behind my back, I'd be walking proudly, still emphasizing the judge's moronic heartlessness, astonishing callousness, pathetic jurisprudential shortcomings, amoeba-like intelligence, and so on.

I never faulted this woman for saying what she said. Like most defense lawyers, I looked at her and thought, *there but for the grace of God go I.* What I fault her for is running.

The case against her never even made it to court. Instead she was reassigned to a different borough, a traditional solution for lawyers who have, even briefly, gone a little nuts. Still, hardly a week goes by that I don't sit in AP-10 and wonder about her story.

I wonder whether doing what she did made her feel better, whether even a briefly tarnished reputation justified the outburst, whether in the dark night of her soul she holds up that crystalline moment in time and thinks: *There — the one time I finally said what I believed.*

Dreads has hardly made it to the door when the bridge officer looks my way. "Mr. Feige," she murmurs, her way of letting me know that Hector's case is up next.

Hector's case is done with in thirty seconds. "Are the people ready for trial?" Kiesel asks.

"No, Judge," some random assistant district attorney says. "No complaining witness contact."

"Fine," says the judge. "What date, please?"

I provide a date another six weeks in the future — a day when I'm already scheduled to be in the part.

"Fine," Kiesel says again, adjourning the case.

"See you then," I mutter to the prosecutor as I scribble the new date on a little blue slip of paper so that Hector won't forget. I'm turning toward the door when I hear Kiesel: "Are we ready on that other case?" she asks one of the court officers.

"Yes, Judge, he's in the back now," the burly officer says.

Glancing back, I can see that Kiesel has that sour look again. "Let's bring him out," she says.

"Okay, Judge," says the officer, and then, turning to the audience, he declares, "Everyone take seats please." Turning to me, he clarifies, "That means you, Counselor."

"I'm just leaving," I tell him, heading for the back of the courtroom, where another officer has blocked the door. Realizing I won't be leaving just yet, I sit down on a bench toward the back to watch what happens next.

A little man is brought in wearing handcuffs and leg irons. He is surrounded by five buff court officers. They are wearing blue riot helmets, with plastic face guards, thick leather gloves, vests, and jackets marked "New York Court Officer."

"What the hell?" I ask, turning to the officer in the back whom I know vaguely.

"Tried to bite a CO," he tells me, sternly using a shorthand that could suggest either a court officer or corrections officer.

The man is small, and he winces every time an officer moves his arm. It's clear he has been beaten. His lawyer speaks briefly, and the case is adjourned. The court officers — one in front, three at the side, and one at the rear — march him quickly back into corrections.

Finally free to leave, I head around the corner to use the judge's elevator. Behind a nearby steel door, the little man is being beaten. I distinctly hear the thudding noise his body makes as it is kicked. His cries are horrible and plaintive. The door rumbles with the impact. A kid in a black hoodie sitting on the bench just outside the courtroom catches my eye as I pass and shakes his head knowingly. "Take my advice, brother," he says somberly, "stay single, pay for pussy."

With all the pounding going on, I'm glad when the elevator finally arrives. I step in with an ADA named Anna Almarante right behind me.

Even in a massive court system like New York, prosecutors and public defenders inevitably get to know one another pretty well. Eventually everyone will face the same adversaries, so reputation becomes critically important. Under these conditions, it's good to know how to charm the opposition. Eric, a young lawyer frustrated with not managing to "connect" with a few of the assistant district attorneys, once pioneered "the elbow touch" to see whether physical intimacy might get his clients better offers.

It did.

I don't much go for physical intimacy with prosecutors. It's against my religion to sleep with them. But the fact that I despise them and what they stand for doesn't mean I'm not occasionally tempted. Anna Almarante is one of the few that tempts me. Big, swaggering, and busty, Anna has a way of standing in the courtroom that always does me in — her weight on one leg, opposite hip jutted out defiantly, her head sliding around like a bobble-head doll. No one else makes quite the same production out of a simple court appearance. "Ya Honor!" she declares, one hand up in the air, palm out, like a diva stopping traffic. "The People's offer is thirty days' jail! He beat huh!" Although there might be fifty identical cases on the calendar that day, Anna always acts as if the facts of her case are somehow terrifyingly new or unusually alarming. Her antics make even fellow prosecutors smile with amusement.

"Hi, Feige," she says, pressing the button for the main floor.

She has an unusually pouty look today, the thick waves of her black hair obscuring part of her profile.

"What's the matter, Anna?" I ask, shifting my weight slightly and leaning toward her just a bit.

"I don't know . . . ," she trails off. "I was just thinking."

"What about, babe?" I ask. I can't take my eyes off of her.

"I was thinking about hell," she says.

The elevator doors open, and a court officer gets out. It is just the two of us now.

"Huh? Why were you thinking about hell?" I ask her.

She isn't smiling. She is serious. I find the whole idea utterly titillating.

"I think about hell all the time," she tells me earnestly. "Don't you?"

"Ah, no. I don't ever really think about hell at all, Anna," I say.

"You don't?" This is veering quickly from the flirtatious to the bizarre.

"Anna," I say, smiling, "I'm a Jew."

There is a sharp intake of breath.

"You're a Jew?" she asks, incredulous.

"Yeah," I say, a bit taken aback, "couldn't you tell? Big nose . . . loud . . . Feige. I'm very much a Jew, Anna."

She is still looking perplexed. There is a momentary silence.

"You're a Jew?" she repeats. "So does that mean, like, that you don't take Jesus Christ as your personal savior?" she asks, seeming more genuine in her curiosity than I think possible.

"Yeah, Anna, that's the whole Jew thing right there: Jesus, definitely not my personal savior."

Another gasp.

Her coal-black eyes are locked with mine; her breasts are inches from my chest. I can smell her hair as she shakes her head and bites her bottom lip in consternation. The elevator lurches to a stop on the main floor. The doors slide open.

"You're going to hell," she says. The People's offer: eternity.

That, I think, is the kind of sentence Kiesel might like.

Twelve

3:12 P.M.

AS I STEP AWAY FROM ANNA and the elevator, my brain still reeling from the potent combination of her voluptuousness and condemnation, I realize that I have been so preoccupied with Reginald, Clarence, and Cassandra that I have given exactly no thought to Jaron all day.

Jaron is charged with stabbing his cousin. The prosecutors believe that they have an airtight case, but what they don't know is that tucked in my thin little case file is a packet of papers that makes it pretty clear that Jaron may not be guilty. And while "pretty clear" and "may not" may prove insufficient to get a dismissal, they could, depending on the judge, be enough to get him out of jail today.

When DAs go to court in New York City, more than thirty thousand cops, with their dogs, guns, surveillance technology, and remote-controlled robots, back them up. When ADAs need something from the streets, they can call upon that well-paid army of armed men to knock on doors, serve their subpoenas, and track down their witnesses. Public defenders, on the other hand, are lucky if they have a college intern or an overworked recent university graduate to help. Yet despite this disparity in resources, I've won more cases over the years through good investigation than through motions and trials combined.

Investigators are the eyes and ears of overworked defense lawyers. Generally speaking, they're the ones who find the witnesses, who persuade them to talk, and who know, before anyone else, whether a case is rock solid or utterly flimsy. Good investigators can find anyone and talk their way into any place, and really good investigators unfailingly know when to get a written statement, locking an otherwise hostile witness into a particular version of events, and when to lie low, build trust, and come back another day. A good investigation, more than anything else in a criminal case, can be the difference between prison and dismissal.

One of the benefits of being the trial chief is that I have some latitude in choosing who works on my cases, and though I've had some very good investigators over the years, Ben Wolf, whom I rely on more than anyone else, has been by far the best. Tall and awkward, with a goofy smile and a stuttering, lugubrious Missouri manner, Ben was the kind of white kid that I hesitated to turn loose in the South Bronx. When he showed up for his first day at the Bronx Defenders, wide-eyed and fresh from college (in a hand-me-down suit of his father's), he'd spent a total of three days in the Bronx and just a few weeks in New York City.

"Knock, knock."

We were doing simulations as part of an investigator training I had patterned on Eddie Mayr's Friday-afternoon abuse sessions. I played a reluctant witness. Ben was behind the door, taking his very first crack at getting inside.

"Whatcho want?" I said, opening the door just a bit and channeling a witness I once met.

"Ahhh, um, I'm h-here to talk to you about a shooting?" Ben, stuttering, didn't sound too sure of himself.

"I ain't talkin' to you about no shooting!" I said, starting to close the door on him.

"Wait," Ben said urgently, putting his foot in the door. He didn't want to be humiliated in front of the other new investigators looking on.

"I ain't talkin' to nobody about nothing!" I exclaimed through the sliver that remained.

"But . . ." Ben put just the slightest pressure on the door, trying to keep it open.

"What choo doing?" I said loudly, pushing back on the door. "Don't you try to come pushin' in MY HOUSE! I know my rights! Get the hell out of my house! GIT OUT! NOW!" I slammed the door in his face.

The other investigators looked on horrified as Ben sheepishly poked his head back into the room.

"I guess that didn't go too well, huh?"

"Ah, no," I chided. "Never, never block the door. It'll always get you in trouble."

With the awful timing, terrible judgment, and utter lack of convincing confidence, I feared that Ben was heading straight for uselessness. But within a year, Ben was wowing almost everyone he worked for, once turning in a handwritten witness statement that ran to an incredible forty-two pages, as opposed to the usual six to eight. The case involved terrible allegations — child sex abuse and assault — and our client, the victims' father (who was in jail), insisted that the kids' mother put them up to fabricating the charges. "She's crazy, and she only made this up when I tried to get the kids away from her," he claimed over and over.

"She made them say it" is the kind of defense we hear all the time in child sex abuse cases, and we rarely put too much stock in it — not because it isn't true (it often is) but because we hear it constantly. Still, a good defense required that we investigate our client's claims, and so Ben tracked down the mother and got her statement.

Mom was very clear: our client was a bad man, an evil man, and a child abuser. It all began, she explained, when he smashed her head against a wall and left her for dead, beginning what she described as her "zombie period." The zombie period consisted of eight months spent lying comatose on a heap of dirty clothes inside a small closet while our client and his new girlfriend lived in the house. The girlfriend (who was, according to the mother, a Satan worshipper and child rapist) forbade the children to tend to their comatose mother. Despite this admonition, she told Ben, her heroic children would fish scraps of food out of the garbage to nourish her as she lay unmoving on the fetid clothes heap in the closet.

One day, at the end of the eight-month coma, Mom had a dream in which God, a white man, came to her and said that it wasn't her time to die. With that she woke up from her coma with no recollection of who she was, where she was, or how to speak English. The children, she explained, gradually helped her to remember who she was, while *Sesame Street* helped her learn English again.

Shortly after waking and while relearning English, Mom was told by one of the kids that while she was in her zombie period, our client had sexually abused the children. The abuse occurred in a "haunted house," where our client and his Satanist girlfriend injected all three children with a yellow liquid called "get sexy" and a blue liquid called "be cool" and then sexually assaulted them.

Mom took the children to the police.

The police took the children away.

Shortly after getting the statement from zombie mom, Ben talked to the kids.

"Did you remember what your daddy did to you the day after it happened?" Ben asked one of them gently.

"No," said one of the kids.

"How about the day after that?" Ben tried again.

"No."

"The week after that?"

"No."

"Well, when did you first remember what happened?"

"Oh," said the child brightly, "after I talked to Mommy."

The jury acquitted. Our client had spent nearly eighteen months in jail waiting for his trial. As it turns out, the client was right. But without Ben, we might not have known any of it and certainly wouldn't have had the statement to use at trial.

Not everyone was pleased with the verdict, of course. Back in her small South Bronx apartment, zombie mom still tells people our client is guilty, and she still has the withered rose she says our client (using voodoo) made with her head.

⇒•⇐

Child sex abuse cases are some of the scariest to defend. Many of the cases allege acts that leave no physical evidence. As a result they are often swearing contests between kids and grown-ups, who seldom have a compelling explanation for why a child would make up a story like the one he or she is telling. Between malleable child witnesses and terrified adults, it often feels as if the facts in a child sex case have been reflected in a funhouse mirror of psychic distortion and familial weirdness.

Between zealous prosecutors, lengthy sentences, horrific conditions of confinement, and costly collateral consequences, a child sex abuse charge is pretty much a life-ending proposition. Moreover, given the overwhelming stigma attached to child sex abuse allegations, even the clients who should take pleas that might mitigate the damage will often utterly refuse to do so.

Fearlessness and relentlessness are probably the two most important skills an investigator can bring to the job. No matter how good investigators are, they are going to be spending almost all of their time finding people who don't want to be found and talking to people who don't want to talk. This takes more than a good smile, and it takes more than dedication. It requires a willingness to walk into crack houses and crime scenes and knock on every door in sight, day after day, until you have found and spoken to every single person in the building.

After Ben's stellar work on the sex abuse case, I pretty much use him for everything — gang shootings, one-witness robberies, and almost every murder I have. He's matured into the kind of investigator who can find almost anyone and get them to talk. Sometimes he is ushered inside by people who are terrified that if this goofy-looking white kid spends another minute in the projects he'll be shot. Other times, people invite Ben in because he's charming. Still others talk because he is utterly relentless — showing up at their jobs, tailing them when they leave for work, knocking on the door after supper, or waiting for them by the bus stop when it is time to pick up the kids.

It was Ben who got the dirt on the kid who was probably guilty of the crime Clarence was being charged with, and it was Ben who routinely tracked down cool forensic experts for me.

Ben rejuvenated my stagnant subpoena practice (he thought of places to subpoena I'd never even heard of), and in Reginald's case, Ben was the one who actually found a guy's shoe size so that we could determine whether or not our guy was the one who left the bloody shoe print in a crime scene photo. My faith in Ben's abilities was such that when I got a case that needed investigation, I'd pretty much just shoot him an e-mail, leave the file on my desk, and sit back for a week while he worked his magic.

Sadly, Ben was out of town when Jaron needed help.

There were three people in the room when Jaron stabbed his cousin. One had a knife, one a stab wound, and the third had a clear view of exactly what happened.

Aunt Gloria was having a nice family gathering when the stabbing started. With eyes aged by drink and a smile burnished by a bright gold tooth right in the front of her mouth, Gloria played den mother to Jaron's extended family. She had equal affection for Jaron and his cousin, and no reason to cover for either.

So did Gloria watch as Jaron tried to murder his cousin, as the state claimed, or did Jaron mistakenly stab his cousin while trying to disarm him? Someone had to talk to Gloria, and with Ben out of town and the office short on backup, that someone was going to be me.

It was around 7:30 in the evening when I got to the projects where Gloria lived. The sun had long since set, and though it wasn't my usual practice, I'd decided to go poke around alone. Generally, an attorney who takes a statement can't also be defending the case, since if the authenticity of the statement is challenged, the attorney also becomes a witness. But with no one around, I did what needed to be done. What the hell, I figured — if something great happened, I'd grab a colleague for the trial.

It was a cold night outside, and the lobby of the brick building in the McKinley housing projects smelled like the big blunt two teenagers were smoking in the corner. One — a big kid with wide, dark eyes and a menacing smile — looked up as I walked in. I nodded to him as I crossed the graffiti-covered lobby toward the elevators.

"Yo," I heard behind me. And as I turned, "You know me."

There was a quizzical tone to the statement, and as I tried to decide whether it was a threat or a question, I realized it was Sharief, one of my former clients.

"Wassup, Feige?" he said, nodding, remarkably nonchalant given the fat blunt smoking lazily between his fingers.

Gold Tooth Gloria was on the second floor, playing some strange hybrid of blackjack and five-card stud with three other women. Miller Lite was doled out into Dixie cups, most of which were almost empty. The game was nearly over, or not very interesting, because everyone seemed perfectly happy to stop playing when I explained why I was there and why I wanted Gloria to talk about the stabbing. Gloria was forthcoming and clear. The other women quickly departed, and I sat on the plastic-wrapped sofa in her tiny living room while she talked, slurring her words just a little.

Most criminal defense investigators are former cops or guys who would be in law enforcement if they could. Most believe investigatory work depends on being a tough guy, relying on heavy footfalls and vague intimidation. Most are not great listeners.

This is not to suggest that cops don't often get what they want — they do. But because they so often hear what they want to hear, what they get is a processed and stilted form of the truth. Often, especially when they're talking to a younger generation reared on the aggressive policing of the last twenty years, it's not the truth at all, but nonsense designed to avoid any further discussion.

At the Bronx Defenders we never hire former lawmen for just this reason; college kids, though, set out in the wilds of the Bronx without guns or badges or anything else, quickly learn to master a totally different set of investigative techniques than those that the police depend on — persistence, patience, and kindness. These are, in fact, the qualities on which a good investigation depends. It's something I learned way back, during that formative summer on the streets of Washington, DC, when I was sent out to talk to a woman named Lavonda.

It was 1985, and Lavonda was an eyewitness to a shooting in northeast DC, just off East Capitol, where a little series of tumbledown houses used to sit in the shadow of the city's majestic marble monuments.

Lavonda, a critical witness, wouldn't speak to the previous investigator who swung by her house looking to talk about the case. "I ain't talkin' to nobody about nothin'," she had reputedly declared (repeating the well-worn chorus of investigative work) before slamming the door in the investigator's face.

It was 1:03 in the afternoon when I arrived. Trial was looming, and knowing what Lavonda was going to say could make the difference between taking a plea and picking a jury. The screen door to her building was little more than a hollow frame, and the door behind it swung listlessly open to reveal a dirty, barely carpeted hallway. Lavonda's place was the first one on the left.

I checked my watch (I still wore one in those days) to make sure I had my timing just right. Behind the door I could hear the noises of apartment life — the hum of a fan, the all-important murmur of the television.

"What?" Lavonda's voice was deep, and the door was open just a crack. Inside, true to form, was a small, cluttered living room, with a TV in the corner and two fans parked on the floor, aiming the dead air at a pair of fraying chairs and a sofa arrayed around the TV.

Lavonda was as big as advertised, and she didn't seem happy to see a long-haired white kid with darting eyes staring back at her from the hallway.

"Hi, uh, Lavonda?" I said, glancing over at the TV set. My timing was perfect — an ad for soap or some other household product winked back at me.

"Whatchuwant?" Lavonda demanded.

"Oh," I said, smiling, "I'm an investigator for the Public Defender Service, and I wanted to talk to you about . . . OH MY GOD, is that *All My Children*?"

"Yeah," she said suspiciously. I was already halfway home.

"Okay, oh, I'm so sorry to bother you, then," I said, just starting to lean back from the door, my eyes fixed on the TV inside. "But I missed it yesterday. Did Adam figure it out yet? I'm totally sorry to interrupt — I didn't realize you watched."

"She STILL ain't told him," she said, shaking her head in full-on disapproval of Adam's serial deception.

"Oh my god . . . when he does . . . that is going to be soooo ugly!"

"Ummm-hmmm," Lavonda said as she opened the door a little wider so I could see the TV.

"And Erica, she didn't actually sleep with that guy, did she?" I had wasted an entire semester of college hours watching this dreck, and I'd found a way to make it pay.

"Nope," Lavonda said. "He just thought she did."

"Ooooooh, man." I shook my head at the brilliance of the soap-opera plotters.

"Why'nt'cho come on in?" Lavonda said. "I ain't got no one home; we can watch it together."

"I'd be delighted," I said, stepping gingerly into her living room and settling into one of the chairs, "if you're sure you don't mind."

"Lemonade?" she asked.

"Next commercial break," I replied, smiling as we settled in together.

Investing an hour of TV time in order to get a statement isn't something that comes naturally to cops — they tend to do things on their schedule, expecting people to do what they say and what they want. Instead, I found some common ground with Lavonda — and as a result, I genuinely enjoyed my time with her. She was hilarious, and she had an encyclopedic knowledge of *All My Children*. And so we laughed and gossiped and sipped our lemonade through the whole show. And when it was over, as we sat back while the credits rolled, Lavonda turned and looked at me. "Now, what choo want me fo' again?" she asked.

Once again I explained who I was, what I wanted, who I was working for, and why. And this time, Lavonda sat in her chair and told me everything — not because I had a gun or a badge or any legal authority, but because once she was convinced that I would listen to her and respect her, she was actually happy to talk.

Everyone will talk: you just have to know how to listen.

I spent nearly three hours with Gloria. As it turned out, she saw the whole fight, and she wanted to help. Ninety minutes later, shifting uncomfortably on the sofa, my hand cramping from all of the writing, I had a twenty-page statement.

"It was self-defense," Gloria declared. "Jaron only cut his cousin because he was getting beat senseless. He had no choice. That cousin was a troublemaker and a bully, and Jaron did the only thing he could do."

Halfway down the last page, I scribbled down the final paragraph. "I have made this statement freely and voluntarily to David Feige, a lawyer from the Bronx Defenders. I know that Mr. Feige is Jaron's lawyer, and I have had the opportunity to make any changes, additions, and corrections I desire. This statement is true, accurate, and complete, and signed freely by me." After we read the statement over together, I had Gloria initial every page and sign and date the last page just under the certification.

Statements are valuable for one reason only: they lock a witness in. After a statement is taken, any deviation from it allows a lawyer to confront the witness with his or her prior statement. As a result, they function pretty much like testimony — convincing judges and DAs that a defense lawyer's claims are substantive. After all, if you can produce a written statement made by the witness, the DAs and the judge know that a skilled defense lawyer will be able to keep the witness pretty much on that script.

Witnesses, of course, rarely believe themselves bound by prior statements, and being confronted with one at trial often produces hilarious (and occasionally convincing) explanations ranging from "I didn't know he was an investigator" to "he made me sign it" to "that's not my signature — I've never seen that piece of paper before in my life." (It's why in that last paragraph every investigator is trained to include his or her name, the client's name, and the fact that we are representing the client. It helps later when people claim that they thought they were talking to the prosecutors.)

"I hope you can get that boy out of there," she said, shaking her head. "He only did what he hadta do."

"I sure will try," I told her.

I've had Gloria's statement in my file for almost a week. I doubt it will be enough to get the DA to drop the charges, but I'm hoping it'll be enough to get Jaron out of jail while we fight the case.

I've done my homework. Now it's up to fate — to the luck of judicial assignment and mood. And so, as I walk through the doors to part F, I'm praying that I'll see a friendly face looking down from the dais at the front of the courtroom.

It's Adler. And that means anything can happen.

Judge Harold Adler is one of the completely unpredictable judges. With almost anyone else, I'd know exactly whether or not Jaron was walking out. With Adler it is a complete crapshoot. Gnomish and wild-eyed, with a scraggly salt-and-pepper beard and crazy, unkempt hair, Adler has moments of intense decency that are regularly followed by bouts of ferocious irrationality and utter implacability that can make him one of the least-pleasant judges to appear before. With some erratic judges, a patient student of judicial temperament can predict problem spots — Judge Birnbaum after supper is a good example — but with Adler, even though I've watched him for years, I still don't have a clue as to what sets him off. Adler has done egregious things: denying motions without reading them, sending unprepared lawyers out to trial on other lawyers' cases, or relieving lawyers from cases completely. But he's also done things that are so thoughtful and decent that I sometimes wonder whether he has a split personality. Walking up toward the well of the courtroom, I watch him, carefully looking for some sign of which Adler is up there.

The first case tells me nothing. Adler barely looks up as he adjourns the case. Fishing in my dirty Eddie Bauer soft briefcase for Jaron's file, I pull out Gloria's statement and hand a copy to the ADA, fingering it nervously, hoping it will be the key to Jaron's freedom.

A few minutes later, as the ADA assigned to prosecute Jaron takes his place at the table, Jaron is led out from the pens in the back. I make my application for release as calmly and quickly as possible, and holding my breath, I hand up the statement to Adler, searching his face for some signal about where he is.

As Adler reviews Gloria's statement, I reiterate that the only other person in the room at the time of the stabbing says that Jaron acted in self-defense. Adler's eyes dart around the room. This, I think, is a bad sign. I'm afraid he's getting agitated.

"People?" he barks.

"Your Honor," the assistant DA says, "the people are not dismissing this case."

"Of course you're not!" Adler snaps. "But have you seen the statement and do you have a position on bail?"

Now this is a *good* sign: Adler is asking the right questions and in a tone that is perfectly consistent with what I'm asking for.

"The People oppose any reduction in bail," says the ADA blandly.

"Have you seen the statement?"

"Yes, Judge."

"And you still oppose a bail reduction?"

"Yes, Judge."

"And do the People have any indication that there is any other witness to this crime other than the one Mr. Feige is talking about?"

"No, Judge," says the ADA.

And that does it.

"ROR," says Adler, using the courthouse slang for "released on recognizance."

Jaron sighs, my shoulders slump, and I offer up a silent prayer of thanks to the gods of investigation as the court officer slips the key into the tiny hole in Jaron's handcuffs and, with a delicate twist, sets him free.

It is twenty minutes after 3:00, the day slowly slipping away. "Go home, get some decent food, call me in the office tomorrow," I tell Jaron as I hand him the blue court appearance form, pat him reassuringly on the shoulder, and bolt for the door.

Thirteen

3:23 P.M.

GARISHLY LIT BY LONG FLUORESCENT TUBES, part N (across the hall from where Jaron was just released) was originally designed to allow some natural light to filter in through a narrow recessed window placed just above the dais from which the judge presides. Sadly, not much seems to work out in criminal court — not even the architecture. In front of the weirdly located window, the architect inexplicably placed a series of vertical wooden beams that block out much of the light. The net effect is almost unnoticeable unless a pigeon lands on the ledge outside the window. Then instead of just an example of clumsy design, the construct becomes a perverse tableau. With the birds roosting outside, the window resembles a cell — a tiny pigeon jail atop the courtroom.

Like part F, part N processes felony cases until they are dismissed, pled out, reduced to misdemeanors, or indicted and sent across the street to Supreme Court. And just like part F, part N has no jury box — it's just a big plea-bargaining locale, one of the large sorting machines of the criminal justice system. But unlike part F, part N deals with one very specific subject: drugs. Drug cases are the engine that drives the criminal justice system. In the Bronx, as in much of America, drug prosecutions are so pervasive that they get their own special courtrooms. And in a certain strange way, everyone in the system relies on these cases. But for the continued criminalization of smoking, sniffing, or injecting a lengthy list of compounds codified in the federal Uniform Controlled Substances Act, the entire prison industrial complex might well come tumbling down, leaving tens of thousands of unemployed prosecutors, corrections officers, court clerks, public defenders, and judges.

Given the hallowed place of drug crimes in the machinery of prosecution, it makes sense that part N is one of the largest courtrooms in the criminal court building — and one that is almost always crowded. Drug cases have a cookie-cutter uniformity to them, and they arrive in a nice steady stream. And in terms of producing inmates, drug cases are brutally efficient.

With Jaron free, I should really head back downstairs. It's been forty-five minutes since I left Najid, and his case will probably get called any minute. But just as I emerge, racewalking, from part F, it suddenly hits me — I had Malik produced today.

"Produced" is courthouse slang for "brought to a courthouse near me." Very few public defenders ever go to the jails that hold their clients. The Department of Corrections hates having lawyers on Rikers, so they make it hard to visit and easy to avoid: hard to visit because between getting to the island and navigating the series of checkpoints and passes between the front gate and the client, even a routine visit will eat up an entire afternoon; easy to avoid because with a phone call to the legal division, I can have a client brought to a courthouse near me. The net result is a win-win for lawyers and the Department of Corrections, and a big lose for clients who are woken up at 5:00 A.M., shipped out at dawn, and spend an entire day in the bull pens just to get a few minutes with their attorneys.

I'm no different from my colleagues in this; I have clients produced all the time. And because of a calendaring quirk, Malik is almost certainly sitting in a cell behind part N, not sixty feet from where I'm standing. All I really need is two or three minutes with him, and so, even though I know with total clarity that I should run downstairs to try to catch Najid, I decide to try to squeeze in a quick visit.

My second mistake of the day.

⇒⋅⇐

As I head into part N, I glance over at the case list posted on the worn corkboard outside the courtroom door. There are fifty or sixty people on the list. All of them are charged with drug felonies. So too are the people waiting inside — either on the scarred wooden pews lining the courtroom, or in the crowded cells behind the steel door on the right side of the well. Most of them are charged with low-level drug sales, usually less than forty dollars' worth of coke or heroin. Almost all the rest are charged with possession — a crime that can bring years in jail for half a gram of cocaine and a life sentence for a few ounces.

Most jurors on a drug case, particularly in Manhattan, seem to think that the convictions are no big deal, that the defendant might get a few months in jail. Explaining actual penalties to jurors after a conviction regularly provokes a kind of hostile shock and disbelief. "But we only found him guilty of a twenty-dollar sale," they'll say incredulously when I tell them that the absolute statutory minimum for the client is four and a half to nine years in prison and that the judge is probably going to impose a sentence of around seven and a half to fifteen years.

Even well-educated people don't really understand just how pervasive the mandatory minimums are, nor how astonishingly punitive. Many still imagine that mandatory minimums only apply to big drug dealers or federal cases. Nothing could be further from the truth. In New York state, simple possession can draw decades. Such draconian drug laws create a steady stream of bodies that feeds the criminal justice system. But unlike murder cases or arsons, which begin with the crime itself, drug cases are actually generated by the police. In most cases, in order to charge someone narcotics cops have to go out and create a crime, usually by buying drugs from dealers and charging them with the sale. And at times (as in the rash of cases in which cops, posing as strung-out addicts, beg other addicts for a sip of their methadone and then charge them with selling) the line between entrapment and honest policing can become rather blurry.

Although there are a few variations, the vast majority of the drug sales prosecuted in the Bronx are undercover buy-and-busts — rather unimaginatively referred to around the court-house as "B 'n' Bs." There are thousands of these cases every year, and they run pretty much the same way every hour of the day, every day of the year.

In a buy-and-bust, an undercover police officer goes to a corner or building looking to buy drugs. The dealer asks how many, the "buyer" names a number, and money is passed in exchange for the drugs. The "buyer" walks away. Rather than run to the nearest crack house to smoke as a normal addict would, the officer heads for an unmarked car parked two or three blocks away and radios a description of the seller to the backup team — usually eight or ten other cops parked in various spots between two and four blocks away from where the buy went down, a place described in the strange argot of cop-talk as "the set."

Because drug deals usually happen in public places — busy street corners or the darkened hallways of decrepit buildings — the description of the seller becomes critical. So attached to the description is another vital piece of information: the JD name.

JD stands for "John Doe," which in cop lingo means "suspect." Unique JD names are used to describe each seller, and the JD name is supposed to incorporate the most obvious aspect of the suspect's description — "JD Dragon Tattoo" or "JD Ponytail" or, the best JD name I ever heard, "JD Braided Beard." The JD name and the description are the recipe for the arrest when the backup team roars to the set to apprehend the seller — and the accuracy and specificity of those two items have a great deal to do with the strength of the resulting case.

Of course, drug dealers work fast. A buy usually takes about fifteen or twenty seconds. There is rarely, if ever, haggling over price. Everyone knows what is being sold. Street drugs like crack and heroin come in dimes and nicks — ten- and five-dollar bags or vials so that figures are round and easy to work with. Four nicks is twenty dollars. Three dimes is thirty dollars. (Thanks to inflation, the early days of treys, or little three-dollar starter vials of crack, are long gone.) Because of the easy math and the rules of the street, undercover officers often don't have a lot of time to look at the person they are buying from. Compounding this issue is the fact that street etiquette seriously frowns on people staring at other people's faces. The common position during a buy is eyes downcast, staring at the jacket pocket of the seller or maybe the ground. Staring into someone's face is called "raising up." Dealers don't like it. It can provoke a canceled transaction or sometimes worse.

Because the street price of drugs is so stable, what distinguishes dealers in the minds of their customers is the quality and quantity of the drug they get per five- or ten-dollar unit. And with drugs in bountiful supply and crackheads a competitive demographic, dealers regularly borrow the branding lessons of larger corporations, trying to make their product distinctive — but not too distinctive. Packaging varies widely, and the subtle differences in vials and decks denote different gangs, drug spots, or dealers. For example, if dealers on Morris Avenue are selling vials of crack, those vials may have a particular stopper color. A drug user arrested for possession might admit to "copping red tops at 168th and Morris," meaning that the crack for sale on that corner will have a red stopper.

Generally speaking, crack is packaged in vials or small bags, which themselves come in different colors, while consumer-level heroin arrives in glassine envelopes — tiny squares of waxy paper. Often called decks (ten decks to a bundle or pack), the envelopes are stamped with a unique name. The dope names mirror the weird, vaguely dangerous chic of heroin itself: Poison, Double-Trouble, or 3D.

The downside of branding, of course, is that it gives the police a way to match particular drugs to particular sellers. If, for example, an undercover cop buys three green-top vials at the corner of 183rd and Creston Avenue, and the backup team arrests a seller with a bag full of green tops, that's pretty good evidence that they got the right seller. Similarly, a cop who buys two glassines of Triple Threat heroin is going to be pretty pleased when the seller the backup team snatches is holding twenty or thirty more.

In the slang of the buy-and-bust, matching drugs are known as stash. Stash is half of the simple buy-and-bust evidence matrix. The other half is cash. Cash is technically known as "pre-recorded buy money," and though it sounds like a high-tech crime-fighting tool, it's really just a bunch of regular fives, tens, and twenties that are Xeroxed before a buy. The point is to record the serial numbers of the bills that the undercover cop will eventually use to make buys. When the backup team lines up a few of the guys on the corner who vaguely fit the description, the one with the stash or the cash (that bill with the matching serial number) is almost certainly the one who's going to get pinched.

Because the vast majority of drug sale cases don't utilize anything more complicated than cash, almost every buy-and-bust case falls into one of four essential categories, each replete with a trial strategy and pat explanation. Veteran public defenders, judges, and prosecutors tend to know the four options cold: No Stash, No Cash; Stash, No Cash; Cash, No Stash; and the always very scary and very hard to win Stash *and* Cash.

Omar had both stash and cash.

One of my very first drug trials, Omar's case taught me just how complicated even simple cases could be — and showed me a whole new way of thinking about buy-and-busts.

Omar saw them coming. He'd been selling drugs for half his life and could pretty much smell a cop from a block away. It was getting toward dusk, and St. James Park was almost empty — a few dope fiends lying around on the benches, too out of it to notice much; a couple of kids playing ball on the glass-littered blacktop; a young woman pushing a kid in a stroller. And then there were the narcs, and they were heading right toward Omar.

Normally he might have run or ditched his stash, but the thing was, Omar wasn't actually selling. Ever since he'd gotten out of jail he'd been doing things right. He had a little off-the-books job as a maintenance man, a nice wife, and a decent life. He hadn't been out pitching (being a seller in a retail drug operation) in years, and so, unlike so many times in the past, Omar had that strange calm that only comes from living on the right side of the law.

A shitty rented Dodge sedan pulled up, and four burly men jumped out, yelling at Omar to freeze. Behind the Dodge, two police vans came squealing down the street — all told, nearly a dozen cops. Omar stood perfectly still as they searched, upending the nearby garbage can, looking under the fenders of nearby cars, patting him down, going inside all his pockets, turning his jacket inside out, running their hands over his socks, dipping their index fingers inside the elastic of his underwear — searching everywhere for the drugs Omar knew he didn't have.

There are almost as many official names as street names for narcotics cops. Known in the bureaucracy of the police department as TNT, SNEU, or NBB (Tactical Narcotics Teams, Street Narcotics Enforcement Unit, or Narcotics Bureau — Bronx), the drug teams are infamous for their special brand of rough-and-tumble justice. People on the streets have their own names for the narcs. Some prefer Jump-out, for their signature move, and many still love 5-O (pronounced *five-oh*) as in *Hawaii Five-O*.

"Where are they?" the cop patting Omar down kept asking.

"I don't got nothing, sir," Omar said politely, knowing they wouldn't believe him anyway.

"Where the fuck is the stash?" Another officer now, this one bigger, more menacing. "I said, where the FUCK is the stash?"

The cop handcuffed Omar, roughly turning him around to yell in his face.

"Tell me now, you little fuck, where's the stash?"

The other cops slowed down, their search having turned up nothing.

"I told you, sir," Omar said, trying to fight back panic, "I don't got nothing. I didn't do nothing."

"Put him in the van," the bigger cop said, nodding toward the marked police van idling nearby. There were four other people in it already.

By the time Omar got to the precinct, the reality had set in. Packed into a dirty cell with a dozen other arrestees, Omar was focused on just getting through the process. He asked to call his wife, but, not surprisingly, as the hours ticked by no one managed to let him out of the cell for long enough to call. Though it was now well after midnight, Omar, wary of the other men in the cell, tried not to sleep. He was moved four times between midnight and 5:00 A.M. Once, after they took his fingerprints and his rap sheet came back, one of the officers made a special trip across the room to the cell where Omar sat.

"You got no idea what you in for, motherfucker," the cop said. "You're fucked."

⇒⟶⟵

"People, what've you got in this case?"

That's all the judge at arraignments wants to know — the big question in every drug case: "Is there buy money [cash] or additional drugs [stash] recovered?"

Omar couldn't have been more surprised by the answer.

"Both, Judge," said the ADA, shuffling through the file.

Omar almost collapsed.

"What?" he said urgently, tugging on my shoulder.

"Stop it," I hissed.

"But I didn't . . . I didn't," he whispered, eyes wide.

"Quiet!" I snapped, making a bail application that focused on his ties to the community and the fact that he'd been working and basically out of trouble for nearly a decade. "Please release him," I asked the judge, "he'll come back to court."

"I'm setting bail," the judge announced as Omar's shoulders slumped.

Fortunately, unlike many clients, Omar was able to find several thousand dollars and actually post bail. In one sense this was great — it allowed him to fight the case from the outside, coming into the office for meetings and strategy sessions. But on the other hand, since Omar was facing a mandatory prison sentence upon conviction, any plea he took would mean that he'd have to "step in" — that is, go from being free to being an inmate — something that pushes many defendants to risk a trial rather than surrender.

As the case wore on and Omar, insisting on his innocence, rejected even pleas I thought reasonable, I pushed him harder and harder for an explanation of where the buy money and drugs came from.

"Planted," he insisted implausibly. "I was framed."

"You never had them?"

"They're making the whole thing up" is not a defense I was looking forward to asserting in front of a jury, especially in a Stash and Cash case.

A No Stash, No Cash case is a weak one. It means that there is absolutely no forensic or physical evidence linking the defendant to the crime. The entire case will thus rest on a bunch of cops coming into court and insisting that the guy they bought from is the same guy they arrested despite the fact that he didn't have matching drugs or prerecorded buy money. The defense will argue that the cops made a mistake — they mistook Mr. Nice Client for the JD they were looking for. Because they can't prove the identification, they don't deserve a conviction. These trials are essentially cop-credibility cases, and they stand and fall on two factors: how convincing and personable the undercover officer is and how trusting the jury is of cops.

In the Bronx, No Stash, No Cash cases are almost always winners for the defense. Bronx juries have all seen drug sweeps, and most male jurors have seen or heard of cases in which the police throw a bunch of people up against a wall, search them all, and decide later who to arrest. Bronx residents tend to be skeptical of cops and willing to entertain the possibility that the officer might have made a mistake.

Try that same No Stash, No Cash case before a jury full of white folks from downtown, and the chances of getting an acquittal plummet precipitously.

Things get harder when there is stash or cash, or worse, both. In almost every one of these cases, the defense is either what I call "big mistake" or "buyer not seller."

Being a drug buyer is a criminal offense, since by definition the client, at some point, was guilty of simple possession. The trial strategy in buyer-not-seller is to go for an acquittal on the sale counts and accept a conviction on a misdemeanor possession count. This is because seventh-degree possession (the most minor of all six drug offense levels) is a misdemeanor rather than a felony, punishable only by up to a year in jail. Because most clients will have already *been* in jail for more than a year by the time they actually get to trial, a possession verdict is considered a win. Moreover, the buyer-not-seller defense dovetails nicely with the mistaken ID defense used in the No Stash, No Cash cases — the officer may remember the guy he arrested, but only because he was right behind him in line to buy. After a few years, almost every public defender has tried some variant of the buyer-not-seller defense.

On the other hand, Cash, No Stash cases have to explain the presence of the money. These cases go two ways — one of which requires admitting contact with the seller. In the first, the defendant bought right after a police officer and got the pre-recorded buy money as change (drug dealers regularly seek to cycle their cash for exactly this reason). The absence of drugs is explained by having either ditched them or (in crack cases) already smoked them.

The second variant of this Cash, No Stash configuration completely denies contact with the actual seller — the "milk and Pampers" defense.

The milk-and-Pampers defense hinges on the deal going down near a retail establishment — usually a bodega. Most people in the Bronx understand (and police will often admit) that drug dealers often churn their cash via local businesses. Given that fact, it's not so far-fetched to believe that the client got the money as change when he innocently wandered into the bodega to buy milk or Pampers for his child's mother right after the drug dealer was inside. The real seller, it turns out, had just churned the cash by buying something else in the store.

But of all the predictable defenses and all the possible con-figurations, Omar had the worst. He had a Stash and Cash case, and he had a defense I could barely understand.

They're making the whole thing up.

This was Omar's mantra, and for seven months I'd been utterly unsuccessful in my attempts to move beyond it. Taken alone, it was an impossible defense, yet Omar was resolutely sticking to it despite my pounding away at him. And so, sitting in my little office behind my battered desk overflowing with papers and case files and arrest photos, I fixed Omar with an exhausted look and delivered my ultimatum.

"Omar," I said, "I've been your lawyer for seven months now, and I feel like our relationship is deteriorating. The case has been transferred to Judge Rivera, who is going to be the one try-ing it — and not so far in the future, either." Omar held my gaze — he knew exactly what I was getting at: Rivera could be trouble.

From what I could tell, Reinaldo Rivera had lifted his judi-cial vocabulary from *Star Trek*. He spoke in a gravelly voice, shaking his head as if the routine pronouncements he made from the bench had the gravitas of Delphic prediction. "Make it so" was one of his favorite phrases, as was "I declare it." He favored verbal trilogies, and where most normal judges would just ask a client, "Do you give up your right to a trial?" the Rivera version would be "Now, sir, I will now ask, and I query you: do you renounce, give up, and forfeit your right to a trial?" It was hard not to laugh sometimes, but Rivera could be prickly, and clients had to be carefully prepared to appear in front of him.

Rivera was all about appearances — bring in a client in a good suit, you got a break; forget to tell your kid with the drug case to dress up, or worse, have him defy you and show up in baggy sweats, an NBA jersey, and a hoodie, and you'd be lucky if Rivera didn't find a reason to put your kid in jail that very day. There were dozens of occasions on which I intercepted clients outside the courtroom, calling their parents or sending them home to change lest Rivera decide based on the clothing alone that the kid was guilty or menacing.

Well beyond fashion, stage management was the most important factor when trying a case in front of Rivera. This was especially true in his plea allocutions — the series of questions a defendant has to answer in order to enter a guilty plea. Rivera's allocutions were famous, not only because they were insanely wordy, but because he deliberately made them difficult. In every plea bargain there is a delicate moment in which a client admits guilt to certain specified offenses. It's the scariest moment of the plea process — the place where clients balk or judges renege — and most judges try to soft-pedal it, asking the prosecutor to read the specific legal offenses and asking the client whether he or she admits the offense. Generally a simple yes will do, and getting a yes is relatively easy.

Rivera, though, had his own notions of what a plea should sound like. And so, after the long-winded waivers of every imaginable constitutional right, when he got to the most important part of the plea, Rivera would lean back, a taunting smile on his face, and looking down at the client from the bench, he'd say: "Now, sir, tell me in your own words, *WHAT* did you do to make yourself guilty of this crime and *WHY*?"

This was an all but impossible curveball for an unprepared client. Most could get the first part. "Ah, I robbed a kid?" they'd say quizzically, or "Ummm, I sold drugs to a undercover?" But even when they got the *what* part of the question, the *why* completely flummoxed them. And Rivera rarely let a plea proceed without his beloved explanation.

What made *why* so difficult is that my clients rarely had any idea *why* they did things. With some therapy perhaps they'd conclude that they were drunk, or pissed off after a lifetime of abuse, or desperate for some cash, or in love with the sexiness of the gangster lifestyle, but none of these explanations trips off their tongues when confronted by Rivera's expansive curiosity. As a consequence, their answers are often amusing stabs at elusive self-knowledge.

"I was hungry?" one client asked, trying to explain a theft.

"He looked rich?" mused a robber.

"I thought I could get away with it?" muttered another.

"I didn't know he was a cop," said a drug peddler.

Since Rivera never seemed to reject a plea for an insufficiently insightful answer, the transcripts of his cases were monuments to the stupidity of his insistent need for explanation.

With Rivera being the trial judge and Omar insisting on a trial, it was critical that I get more from Omar than "they're making the whole thing up."

"So, Omar," I continued, "I'm feeling like you don't trust me, and I'm thinking that maybe you'd be better off with a different lawyer. I want to defend you. I believe in you, and I believe what you're telling me. But I cannot go to trial in a drug case where there is buy money and stash and just claim that there wasn't. This has to be specific to you, not just some general 'cops are assholes' bullshit. I need to understand — why would any cop risk his pension just to frame your sorry ass?"

Omar looked at me closely, his handsome face framed by a silver goatee: he had one eye half closed, and he was squinting as if trying to size me up. Seconds ticked by in silence, and then, pursing his lips slightly, he looked across the desk at me and uttered a single word: "Negro."

"Huh?"

"They wanted Negro."

"Who the fuck is that?"

"Negro — guy I used to sell for — moved like half a kilo a week in Sunset Park. Just got out again."

"Who wanted him?"

"Narcs. They come to me over and over: 'We know you selling for him again.' No, I tell them, I'm working now, I got nothing to do with him no more. 'Yeah,' they say, 'we know you selling.' No, I tell them, but they want me to snitch for them, to work for him again, but I refused so they planting all this shit on me 'cause I wouldn't go back into the business. They know I'm innocent."

"Omar, you're telling me they're framing you because you refused to cooperate with them?"

"That's what I'm telling you, Mr. Feige."

"Why did they want you?"

"I used to be a snitch."

"What?"

"I used to be a snitch for them. I had a CI number and everything, and I was making cases for them and everything — big cases, and then one time someone come to my house and starts shooting through the door, so I think maybe someone found out. So I call my handler, and I say, you gotta get me outta here, move me, like into witness protection, 'cause it seem like someone know I'm snitching. And he says sure he gonna help, but then no one does shit, and I'm scared for my family and everything and I think they gonna send someone to come kill us, so I jet — I go to Texas for like four years, and that was it."

"You went to Texas?" I'm incredulous. In seven months I've never heard any of this.

"Right. So then, when I finally come back a few years ago and get a job and everything, I'm out of the game totally, but then Negro, who they busted, gets out of jail — he been down for like ten years or so — and he go back into business, and first they think I'm working for him, but then they realize I'm straight, so then they trying to get me to work for him, and I tell them they fucked me once and I ain't dealing with them no more. So then this old DT rolls up on me one day — a guy from back in the day, and he still on Brooklyn South."

"Brooklyn South Narcotics Unit?" I'm scribbling notes now.

"Yeah. He still working out of there, and he roll up on me and tell me to get in the car, and he take me for a ride and be threatening me — saying everybody know I'm a snitch, and if I don't go set up Negro, he gonna put the word on the street that I'm snitching again, and then I'm dead. So I tell him everybody know I'm outta the game, nobody gonna believe I'm snitching 'cause everybody know I gone straight."

"Okay."

"So he driving me around in the undercover car — all around the neighborhood — and he got me in the front seat where the windows is clear, and so everyone can see that I'm talking to the cops, and then he tell me to call him when I decide to do the right thing, and I tell him I ain't gonna call him, 'cause I'm done with that, and then he look at me and says: 'Omar, I know who you are; I know where you live. You know we got a history. Don't fuck with me.' And I get out of the car, and I'm shaking and nervous and shit, and I just go home and tell my wife what's up.

"So then, like a week later, I see the same cop riding around, and he's axing me am I gonna roll with him, and I say, no, I'm clean now, you guys already fucked me once and I ain't messing with you no more. So he just says, 'Watch your ass, Omar.' And rolls off. And then like four days later, I'm just chilling in the park, and they roll up on me and this other dude and charge me with selling, and I ain't even sold."

This was *interesting.*

"Omar," I said, "can we prove that you were a snitch before?"

"Of course. I got my snitch papers."

"Official snitch papers with your agreement and your confidential informant number and everything?"

"Yeah, but we can't use it."

"Of course we can. That's called a defense."

"Mr. Feige," Omar says, fixing me with a level stare, "my codefendant, he's still in the game, and if he finds out I was a snitch, if he sees my papers, it's over — they'll kill my family. We can't say anything about it or my kids are dead."

"I need those papers, Omar, and as far as your codefendant . . . well, that's a risk we're going to have to take."

Omar just stared at me, shaking his head.

"I'll blow trial before I give that shit up," he said. And he meant it. Finally I had a defense — one I couldn't use.

It was two weeks later that I appeared again in front of Judge (or as he preferred to be addressed, "Mr. Justice") Rivera.

"I need to make an ex parte motion," I told his law secretary, Patricia DiMango. Pat DiMango was an ambitious woman who wanted very much to become a judge (she later succeeded). Thin, with a shock of wildly streaked, vaguely blond hair, DiMango was a parody of a wisecracking Brooklyn gal — tough and smart but washed out somehow after too much time feigning attentiveness to Rivera's buffoonery.

"For what?" She didn't seem particularly receptive.

Ex parte motions — those argued directly to the judge without the presence of the opposing side — are extremely rare and only allowed under extreme circumstances.

"I'll explain it to the judge — in chambers and on a sealed record."

"I can't just let you talk directly to the judge," she said.

"Well, that's what I need to do," I insisted. "This is a matter of life and death."

That got her attention.

"Why don't you outline it for me informally, and I'll take it to the judge," she suggested, not unreasonably.

"Fine," I told her.

Two minutes later, reclining in Rivera's office, I explained to DiMango that I needed to split Omar's case from his codefendant's. Pulling out a copy of his old snitch agreement, I outlined the defense that I'd be unable to present if the case went to trial with the codefendant present. Not only did I want a separate trial — I wanted the courtroom sealed during opening arguments, closing statements, and my client's testimony. DiMango seemed to mull this over for a few minutes. "I'll get the judge," she said.

Rivera came in a few minutes later, and after a minute or two of chitchat, the three of us got down to business.

"So, Feige," Judge Rivera said as he fixed me with his appraising grin, "Patty tells me you want an ex parte severance."

"Yes, Your Honor."

"Tell me something, and I'm serious now." Rivera paused to size me up. "Is this for real, or is this bullshit?"

"Totally real, Your Honor," I said, handing him the confidential informant agreement. "This is the defense right here, but my client won't let me present it if the codefendant is present."

Rivera looked over the agreement and thought for a beat. "So I guess you won't object to sealing the courtroom for the undercover's testimony, eh?" he said slyly.

I knew immediately that this was a trap. Prosecutors love to seal the courtroom when an undercover officer testifies — it cloaks the officer in the mystique of cool and dangerous police work, as if the very fact of showing up for trial and facing the defendant is somehow a feat of unprecedented derring-do. Obviously, there are times when undercover work is dangerous and secrecy is reasonable, but prosecutors regularly make the motion to seal the courtroom for tactical rather than security reasons. Not surprisingly, the defense often objects to sealing the courtroom for the undercover's testimony and insists on what's known as a *Hinton* hearing (so named for the case — *People v. Hinton* — that created the procedure) to determine whether sealing is really necessary. Rivera figured that if I was really going to cross-examine the undercover about my client's status as a confidential informant, I would also want the court-room closed. Sometimes all you can do is double your bet. "Judge," I said levelly, "not only won't I object to sealing the courtroom for the undercover's testimony, I'll agree to have the entire trial proceed under seal." Now *that's* the kind of thing Rivera might think was cool.

Sure enough, Judge Rivera looked intrigued. He paused for a moment to process this rather novel idea, and then, having made up his mind, he nodded sharply at DiMango.

"I will make it so!" he declared.

The case dragged on for weeks, with the prosecutors nearly apoplectic at the idea that we were alleging a cop conspiracy designed to punish Omar for his refusal to snitch. It was a bright May Tuesday when the jury went out, and it was still Tuesday when they returned, after only a few hours of deliberation. As Omar and I stood to face the verdict, my heart was pounding and I was trying hard not to hyperventilate. Omar looked cool as a cucumber. On every count they said the same thing: "Not guilty." In the rest of my career, I'd only win one other buy-and-bust where there was both stash and cash.

⟶⋅⟵

I open the door to corrections and step into the well. Because of the late hour, the well is far more crowded than the courtroom. Most of the people at liberty have already been seen, those who are incarcerated more likely left for last.

"Yo, Yo, Yo, it's the white Johnnie Cochran," Malik yells through the bars of his cell as I step through the second locked wire-mesh door. The other inmates crack up.

"You a private lawyer?" one of them asks me.

Before I can answer, Malik pipes up. "Naw, man, he a Bronx Defender. What's up with my case, B?"

Unfortunately I dragged Malik in to give him an answer I'm sure he'd rather not hear. What's up is that Malik is getting screwed. The DA's office won't split his case from that of a codefendant; they'll only let him go to the drug treatment center he desperately needs if both he and his codefendant plead guilty together. The problem is that Malik's codefendant had fifteen hundred dollars for bail and Malik didn't. That means Malik will spend the next two years of pretrial delay eating bologna sandwiches at Rikers while his codefendant will be home having dinner with his mom. It also means that Malik has a reason to plead guilty. Malik may end up spending two years in jail waiting for his codefendant to plead guilty or go to trial just to get a treatment bed that is available now. And there is almost nothing I can do about it.

Sitting there in that little booth, already half spent from a day running around yet somehow running in place, looking helplessly through the wire mesh at Malik, I get a jolt of the dislocating despair that sometimes takes over my work life. I can't help Malik; I can't seem to get Clarence's case dismissed; I helped put Cassandra in jail. My entire day has been delaying inevitable injustices, trying to hold a line that continues to crumble around me. And as much as I know deep down that I'm fighting the good fight, I can't help getting that creeping feeling that I may never win, that in some sick way, the joke's on me. It makes me furious.

⇒―⇐

Anger works. Anger is rejuvenating. It is anger — that smoldering fury — that allows a public defender to survive. Without it, the never-ending flood of cases can leave even the thickest-skinned lawyer jaded, cynical, and burned out. Of course, being pissed off all the time can also lead to heartbreak, heartburn, and probably even the occasional heart attack. But without that fury, and without the human connection it depends on, even veterans start to tune out the defenses and the explanations, and succumb to the routine of processing cases rather than touching lives.

"It's bullshit, brother — I know it's bullshit," I say. "But there's nothing I can do right now. I promise you, though" — my voice is urgent — "I will try again; I'll go to the head of the bureau if I have to. I will."

Malik is looking at me beneficently, his hands quietly folded on the steel shelf behind the slot through which we sometimes slide legal papers. His lips are pursed, and he's nodding slowly.

"Just get me outta here, Dave," he says evenly, and then making a fist with his right hand, he places it heel-side out against the mesh.

Clenching my fist and holding his gaze, I raise my hand, the heels of our fists barely touching through the metal — a jail-house handshake. "You got it, brother," I tell him, promising something I fear I can't deliver. I stand up to leave.

→•←

"You know, Feige . . ."

Jason's owlish glasses were set high on his nose, and his face was twisted into a toothy, goofy Jason Miller grin. We were in arraignments one night just after Jason had started taking felony cases. He was holding a file, having just come back from interviewing another client in another drug case, when he popped the question.

"I've noticed that people seem to use the same defense a lot. It's almost like there's a drug defense school or something."

"Milk or Pampers?" I asked.

"Weird," Jason said, shaking his head. "How'd you know? It was Pampers."

"Of course it was." I grinned. When you've heard every defense a thousand times, true or not, they can all start to sound like bullshit.

"Jason, the most dangerous thing there is to do in the Bronx is go out at night to buy milk or Pampers for your baby mother. This is a good thing for you to learn. The cops don't bother you if you happen to need some Rice-A-Roni or coffee-flavored Häagen Dazs — they're looking for the milk-and-Pampers guys."

The unsettling thing is that many of the guys with the milk or Pampers defenses actually *are* innocent. What I never understood was why they were telling me a story that sounded so stupid. But just a few weeks after my encounter with Jason, I finally figured it out. I was talking to a long-term client of mine who'd been rearrested on a drug sale and was now looking at a potential prison sentence.

"Dave," Jonathan had said to me urgently, "I didn't do this one — I'm serious, brother, I ain't do this one. You know me, you know I fuck up sometimes, but I didn't do this."

"Okay, so how did you wind up arrested?" I asked him, knowing the answer.

"Okay, check it," he said. "I was just going to the store, looking to get some stuff for my baby mother. . . ."

"Milk, right?" I say. I'm taunting. I shouldn't be.

"Exactly!" he exclaimed. "How'd you know?"

"Jonathan," I said firmly, "how long have I represented you?"

"Long time, Dave." He was nodding as if it meant something to him.

"I ever fuck you over?"

"Naw, man."

"You think I care if you did this?"

"I dunno."

"The last one — the one you *did* do — did I represent you then?"

"Yeah . . ."

"I do right by you on that one?"

"Yeah."

"So you think I give a fuck if you're guilty or not?"

"Naw, I guess not."

"I don't," I said firmly, looking into his eyes. "But giving me some bullshit story don't make it any easier for me to do what I gotta do, which is bust you out of this."

Jonathan stared, his lips pursed just a little bit. He seemed to be thinking this over, just a bit embarrassed.

"But, Dave, I'm telling you I *didn't* do this."

"I believe you, brother," I said, staring across the table, "but you gotta tell me what the fuck was really going on out there."

Jonathan took a breath and leaned back in his chair, fixing me with an appraising glance. "Okay," he said.

"I'm in an alley shooting dice with some guys from the building. There's a few guys hustling down the street, and sometime they shootin' and sometime they pitchin'.

"So, you know, I ain't payin' it no mind, 'cause that's their business, you know, and so we just drinkin' and playin', and all of a sudden the cops roll up from like everywhere, and they grabbin' up everybody and searchin' everybody, and I just won some so I had like forty, fifty dollars on me, and they be lookin' everybody over and they just grab me — but I didn't do nothin'."

"You know the guys selling?" I asked.

"Yeah — by face. They from my building. But I ain't sayin' that — you know."

"I understand," I said, looking at him hard. "But, Jon, why'd you tell me that bullshit about the milk?"

"Dave," he said gravely, "you a good man. You already done me solid on the last one; I don't wanna come in here sayin' I'm chillin' with a bunch a gangsters and shootin' dice and drinkin', you know."

"Okay," I said. And all of a sudden it hit me: my clients, scared of the system and the lawyers who represent them, don't want to look like lowlifes — they're desperate, even in handcuffs or behind bars, to appear respectable and responsible, and the easy default way to express that is by claiming they were going to do something wholesome, like buying milk or Pampers. It's why it's never ice cream. Ice cream or beer or cigarettes is frivolous; the trip to the bodega has to be an errand of necessity, engaged by a responsible adult. Much of the nonsense my clients proffer is not an attempt to bamboozle the judges, cops, and lawyers they are already convinced are out to get them, but to protect the thin thread of decency on which they imagine their dignity depends. And that they'd risk truth, or freedom, to insist on that last sliver of dignity speaks volumes about the system and what it can and cannot crush.

As it turns out, people in the criminal justice system lie all the time, for all kinds of reasons (not just to make themselves less culpable). I pled a young kid named Eric in a shooting case even though I knew he was covering for his big brother who had a worse record than him. He went to prison for more than two years. Just a year later, I wandered into criminal court to find the brother Eric had done so much to protect charged with stealing a car. They got out about the same time. I've seen this happen dozens of times.

Turning away from Malik, I head back toward the doors to the courtroom. It's getting late, Najid is wasting another day of his valuable activist life, Cassandra is still sitting in a little smelly jail cell two floors below me, and Malik is going to rot at Rikers for no good reason. Add to that the guy getting his ass kicked upstairs in AP-10, and by the time I've covered the twenty feet to the corrections officer guarding the steel door to the courtroom, I'm really spoiling for a fight.

"You're looking pretty pissed off, Counselor," the corrections officer teases me. He's huge, easily six four and 285 pounds. Huge has the good-natured disposition of men unused to being physically challenged. His hair is pulled up in short twisted braids, and he's smiling as usual.

"You don't know the half of it," I tell him.

"Client an asshole?" Huge opines.

"No, DA's an asshole," I tell him.

He just snorts and bobs his head as if he's heard that one before — which, of course, he probably has.

"Hang in there, Counselor," he tells me, "they're lucky to have you."

"Thanks," I say as he swings open the dark-blue steel door to let me into the crowded space between corrections and court.

Fourteen

A NERVOUS KID WITH CORNROWS is standing in front of the judge when the door from the pens glides open, and I begin to shimmy my way through the handcuffed men, heading out into the courtroom.

The kid is taking a plea. His answers are stilted and halting, and his eyes dart around the room, telegraphing something more akin to confusion than discomfort. It is clear he's taking a simple plea — a plea that will set him free — but it's equally clear that he is so out of it that even the judge is starting to catch on.

"Does your client understand what's going on here?" the judge demands.

"Yes, Judge, he's fine — just a little nervous," his lawyer replies.

It's clear that this is a lie.

The kid's lawyer is a well-intentioned long-haired woman from Legal Aid. She is leaning over toward the kid, trying to soothe him, to coax him through the next forty-five seconds. She knows that if she can just get him to stay calm and say yes about four more times, she'll walk him out the door. I can feel the delicacy of the moment, and so can she. Foolishly, I pause to watch.

As Long Hair leans in, the kid shifts his weight, almost twisting his body around the hands that are cuffed behind his back. I can almost hear her soothing cadences — but they're not having the desired effect. Finally, she slides her hand across the small of Cornrow's back, lowering her head toward his like a mare nuzzling a foal, her hand gliding across to his shoulders, and I can imagine her saying, "It's gonna be okay. I promise. You're almost there." And then it happens: the kid relaxes. I can see his shoulders slump, his head rise slightly, his breathing stabilize.

"We're ready to proceed, Judge," she says quietly. Less than a minute later, with Long Hair's hand still gently rubbing his shoulder, the kid is free.

Nearly half the attorneys in the Bronx Criminal Courthouse would have blown that plea. Unwilling or unable to understand that the kid just needed a calming hand on his shoulder and a gentle voice in his ear, far too many lawyers (men especially) would have answered the judge by turning to their clients and asking them right in the middle of the courtroom "Are you all right?" or "Do you understand what the judge is telling you?" They'd use this strange, exasperated, I've-done-everything-I-can-for-you tone, and then shrug helplessly at the judge, as if to say, "Hey, I can't help it that this kid's an asshole." For that kid, such an act is a one-way ticket back to the island. Equally sad is the fact that not only would the bad lawyers have blown the plea, they'd have scoffed at the idea that all it might take to get the kid out was a gentle touch.

The truth is, many times the difference between good and bad lawyering *is* just that gentle touch. Often, all it takes to solve a client's problem — inside the courtroom or out — is a moment of sensitivity or insight. Arben was the perfect example.

Arben couldn't sleep. Night after night he tried, but the neighbors wouldn't shut up. He spoke to the landlord. The noise continued. He asked the neighbors, gently, to lower the noise level, nodding in his native Albanian and speaking as one Eastern European immigrant to another. That didn't work either. So he tried arson.

"Sleep," he explained to me, his huge, fleshy face alive with the import of the sentiment, "very important." Sleep deprivation and a minor psychiatric history will drive a man to do strange things — in this case, to try repeatedly to light an oozing liquid he had poured under his noisy neighbor's door. As luck would have it, antifreeze is not flammable.

Because there was no real damage to the apartment, and because of a creative social worker at the Bronx Defenders who found an Albanian-speaking therapist, I managed to get Arben out of jail. That was the easy part, and all was well for a time. But just three weeks later he was in the office and very agitated. I asked how he was doing, and he began again to complain about the noise from the neighbors. This was a very bad sign, and as visions of actually flammable liquids and front-page headlines in the *New York Post* began to dance about in my head, I had a moment of insight.

"Look, Arben," I said, "I am sorry you can't sleep, but haven't you ever heard of earplugs?" He looked at me blankly. *"Earplugs,* Arben . . . little foam things that go inside your ears to block out the sound. They help you sleep." This was met with utter incomprehension.

I sat Arben down, then gave an intern five bucks and told him to run to the store. He was back in ten minutes, and then, like an AIDS counselor in an African refugee camp demonstrating the use of a condom, I carefully, theatrically unwrapped a set of earplugs and showed Arben how to use them.

He put them in and slowly turned his head from side to side, his face a mask of wonder and delight.

"Go home and try these," I told him, "and report back to me." Four years and no arson later, Arben is off probation, done with counseling, holding down a good job, and sleeping very, very soundly.

As I head toward the back of the courtroom, I'm thinking about Long Hair's deft save. Of course, even really good lawyers occasionally have carefully crafted pleas go awry. Often it's because clients who are pleading guilty are inclined to minimize their participation when it finally comes time to publicly admit their wrongdoings. Some judges, when they want to see a more severe sentence, will even use this equivocation as an excuse for "bouncing" (refusing to accept) a plea. Yet even when a plea goes down smoothly, a case isn't over until the sentence is imposed, and sometimes not even then.

The more serious the case, the more dramatic the sentencing can be. This is especially true if the client and the victim or their families come face to face. Then the strange polar experiences of the criminal justice system create an almost electric intensity — like a capacitor about to discharge. It is in those moments of confrontation that the human toll of the criminal justice system is most apparent — furious words that fail to bring back dead loved ones; tears that fail to alleviate the harsh sentences that result.

No one wins. No one ever does.

I experienced this most vividly standing next to Roger as he was being sentenced for killing a man named Wale (pronounced like *Wally*) Faust.

We'd been on the verge of trial, at that tricky and subtle point in pretrial negotiations when the defendant most acutely feels the weight of a possible conviction and the People most desperately fear a loss. In the bizarre bazaar of plea-bargaining, there is a price for every crime, a price that takes into account the nature of the case, the strength of the evidence, the record of the offender, and a hundred other little details that lawyers exploit to get the best deal they can for the party they're representing. In this case, the evidence tying Roger to the crime was not as strong as the district attorney might have liked, and though it certainly didn't excuse his murder, Wale had been a fairly successful (and rival) drug dealer who had engaged in some bad acts of his own — something that would come into play in an "I shot him because he was gonna shoot me" kind of case. It's why I was holding the line. Plea-bargaining is about numbers — it always is. That the currency my client is paying in is time only serves to muddy an already opaque moral equation.

For months the prosecutors had been insisting on a fifteen-year sentence, and for months I'd refused to consider anything more than ten. In the end, after a final round of posturing, I got eleven years. Of those eleven years, Roger would actually serve just over nine and a third, and since it took me about two years to work out the deal (during which he'd been in jail) it really meant that he had a little more than seven years left to serve. It was a good deal.

The sentencing took place on a lazy, overcast afternoon in one of the cavernous courtrooms of the Bronx Supreme Court. Roger, a high-security inmate, was led into the courtroom, shuffling the way that people do when they're restrained by leg irons. His hands were jammed into long orange tubes called "enhanced restraints." The tubes are designed to keep handcuffed inmates from being able to use their fingers, and their thick, padded canvas covers everything from the forearm down before being sealed off by special handcuffs that fit over the wrist area and protrude from a little black box (which is in turn attached to a waist chain) that is supposed to enhance the security of the cuffing system itself. There was enough steel on Roger to create a symphony of jangling metal.

He greeted me with a smile.

"You ready for this?" I asked him, putting my hand gently on his shoulder. Roger nodded. "You're going to be sentenced to eleven years in prison today," I reminded him. Another nod.

"Everybody ready for sentence?" the judge asked.

"Yes, Judge," I said.

"Yes, Judge," said the ADA, "but the decedent's family does wish to make a statement."

This is fairly unusual, but the more serious the case, the more likely it is that there will be what is known as a "victim impact statement." The thing is, victim impact statements in cases in which someone has taken a plea bargain are a charade. No matter what the family says, the judge can't increase the sentence without allowing the defendant to withdraw the plea — something that almost never happens. Mostly it is a chance for the family to confront the defendant and feel as though the court is listening to them.

"Do you object, Mr. Feige?"

I could have successfully objected. Without the proper notice, which the DA hadn't bothered to serve, victim impact statements aren't permitted. But as with most notice issues, objecting just means adjourning the case and doing the whole thing after the DA sends the proper form. Looking around the courtroom at the decedent's anxious family, I felt there was no reason to make them come back another day just because the DA was too lazy to send me the notice. It wasn't going to affect the outcome anyway.

"No objection," I said.

"Okay — bring them up."

Wale's sister stepped up to the podium. Tall and thin, with an elegant face and stylish glasses, she placed a large photograph of her dead brother on the table facing my client and me, and then, reading from papers clutched in trembling hands, she began to speak in a clear, piercing voice.

"You took my brother," she said, so quietly I had to strain to hear her. "You gave him the death penalty, and all you'll get is eleven years. Eleven years of commissary and family visits. Eleven years of life. My brother will never eat again, and the only family visits left for me are with his headstone."

Her still, clear voice began to fill up the courtroom.

"You . . . you'll emerge from prison able to know your son. Wale will never know his child. *He will never* feel his father's touch, never know his father's charm and beauty, never even know what you've taken away from him, from me, from my family. I wish you'd gotten life." She looked hard at Roger, her eyes scanning his face for some sign of apology or explanation. Roger was so trussed up he could barely move, and he stood there returning her gaze with a steady, sympathetic look. "I wish you'd have to suffer some small part of the loss I feel every day of my life," she said.

Standing there, feeling the contemptuous, anguished sweep of her eyes, I found myself moved by the capriciousness of her loss, and I was acutely aware of standing next to the man who had slain her brother — a man about to get the benefit of an extremely good deal that I had negotiated for him. I could feel her disdain — for Roger, for me, for a world that had taken her brother.

Yet touched as I was by her evident and heartfelt loss, when she finally turned away, surrounded by the sad comfort of a grieving family, I still understood why despite her very real pain and loss, I was standing right where I should have been. Because as deeply as I felt Wale's sister's anguish, I also felt, as acutely as ever, how desperately Roger and the rest of my clients — even the guilty ones — need protection from the punitive ravages of a vengeful world. Wale's sister had lost a loved one, and for that there was no excuse, but her victimization was hallowed, respected, and validated by the world around her. But without a proxy, there was no one to ameliorate Roger's fate, no ears attuned to his claims for mercy or justice, and no one else to shield him from the life sentence or even the death penalty a justifiably angry sister might (were she able to) have imposed. And ultimately, protecting Roger — from a vindictive system fueled by grief and loss and anguish — ensuring that at least one person was there for him, actually felt good.

And if that seems strange, simply consider this: even after more than a decade in the system, I still fundamentally believe in the possibility of redemption and the value of every individual. I care for my murderous clients much like Wale's sister loved her drug-dealing brother. Their shortcomings don't disqualify them from my caring. But somehow, when I try to explain this in the context of my work, I'm met with blank confusion. Everyone seems to understand and indeed to celebrate the ability of a born-again Christian to see potential in everyone, and to love each individual no matter what they've done — this is, after all, the essential teaching of Christ. But somehow, when I present this same basic belief in the context of a secular humanist thrust into the brutal world of criminal justice, it loses its coherence.

Roger got the eleven years.

⇒⟨⇐

Just outside the doors, I quicken my pace, heading back down the escalators toward TAP-1, where Najid is still waiting.

"They already adjourned my case," he tells me as I approach. "We were one of the last cases, and the judge said he wasn't going to wait for lawyers anymore. There was some guy there, I think from your office, and he did the case. We're supposed to come back in like three weeks."

I'm crestfallen. My visit with Malik meant that at the end of the day, I'd totally missed Najid's case.

"I'm so sorry," I tell him.

Judges wouldn't dream of calling a private lawyer's case without the lawyer present. But they do it all the time to public defenders — going so far as to dispatch their court officers to roam the halls to corral a colleague to "stand on a case." And while rich defendants would never think to allow a judge to proceed without their lawyers, my clients, even the savvy ones, have no such sensibility. Even if they were to balk, a judge would read it as uppity rather than reasonable.

"Really, Najid, I'm so sorry you had to waste another day on this. And I'm sorry I kept you waiting too."

"Don't worry about it, man!" Najid says brightly, giving me a huge hug. I can feel his slight frame through the puffy green coat. I can't figure out how Najid manages to be constantly smiley and enthusiastic: he seems to think that his criminal justice odyssey is perfectly normal.

"So I'll see you next time?" Najid asks as I copy his court date into the little black book I use to track court appearances.

"Don't forget about the dance!" he adds. Two weeks ago, Najid left me an invitation — a handcrafted note with a little packet of flower seeds — and tickets to the More Gardens! dance.

"I'll try to make it," I tell him. And with that, he turns his acrobatic little body away from me and, leprechaun-like, floats down the grimy hall toward the escalators and the fading winter light beyond, his ragamuffin crew of garden do-gooders trailing just behind.

⇒⋅⇐

Across the hall, in arraignments, Judge Birnbaum is still plowing through his stack of misdemeanors.

"I'll give her two days of community service!" I hear him say as I come through the doors. The girl standing before him has a hip jutted out and a scowl on her face. Her disaffected pose seems to have struck Birnbaum the wrong way.

"But, Judge," her lawyer is saying, "her codefendant just got a conditional discharge."

"Well, for her it's two days!" Birnbaum snaps. He doesn't do so well after lunch. Charming in the morning, Birnbaum loses steam in the afternoon as judging takes its toll. It's the same in night court — after dinner he becomes more and more irritable and relies more and more on the snap judgments he seems to form during the first ten seconds of a bail argument.

"Does she want it or not?"

It's clear she doesn't, but it's unwise to decline even a vaguely reasonable offer from Birnbaum late in the afternoon, since along with his irritability comes unpredictability. He's thrown people in jail just to get a case over with, even though three hours earlier he'd never have done so.

The lawyer and the defiant woman huddle for a moment, and Birnbaum's gaze shifts upward.

"Oh, hello, Mr. Feige!" he chimes. For all our occasional friction, I'm one of the lawyers Birnbaum genuinely likes. Over the years we've developed a strange and funny repartee, which seems to work for me and brighten his mood.

"Hi, Judge!" I say, raising my chin slightly as if pointing to the mess in front of him. "I'm just here to take care of that special situation from a few weeks ago."

"Oh, of course!" he says, nodding enthusiastically.

I head toward the door that leads to corrections, quickly piecing together the details of the case Birnbaum is doing. Wagging my index finger toward the still-huddling lawyer and client, I narrow my eyes and nod at Birnbaum as if to say, *This isn't worth the effort.*

Give her the CD, I mouth silently.

Birnbaum looks away, rolling his eyes slightly, ostentatiously ignoring my utterly inappropriate behavior. Squinting my left eye and turning my head slightly, I give Birnbaum an "oh, c'mon already" look, and just as the lawyer and the girl disengage, Birnbaum pipes up.

"I'll give her the CD," he says, shaking his head at me.

"Done," says the lawyer, leaning in again to whisper to his client.

Putting my palms up in a "wasn't that easy?" shrug, I mouth, *You're a good man* to him before disappearing inside the steel doors to the pens.

>—<

"She's yours, right?" Officer Terra knows exactly who Cassandra is waiting for.

Cassandra is sitting on the floor of a small holding cell staring off into space.

"Hi, sweetie," I say as I approach the bars. Cassandra turns and lumbers to her feet.

"Ah, hi, David," she says in her halting way. She's smiling — a good sign. "I'm, um, I'm ready to come out," she tells me, nodding sagely as if she's spent a good deal of time pondering the issue.

"Okay, sweetie, that shouldn't be a problem. Have you been thinking about where you might like to go?"

"A shelter, I think."

"Do you know which one? We had a few ideas for you." I'm trying to be encouraging.

"I think I'll go to Brooklyn. . . ." Cassandra trails off thinking about it, her big round face betraying no emotion. "Yeah, Brooklyn . . . I, I, I like it there. Brooklyn is nice. I'm gonna try not to drink too, David. Maybe just for a few days, just, you know . . . for a few days."

"You know we'll help you if you want to try to go more than a few."

"I know, David, but I'm gonna do it . . . you know . . . for a few days . . . take a few days off. No drinking." She's nodding as she thinks this through.

"That sounds like a really good start," I say. I'm trying to be positive, but all I can see is day three, when crack starts sounding good and she's saved enough money for three or four hip flasks of vodka. I've been through this with her before and know that pushing her doesn't work — she just closes up completely.

"Do you think we could make a date to talk in a few days — just to check in?"

"Okay," she says plainly. "I can come. Talk maybe, it's okay."

"Sure, and we can be sure you're still taking your medication. You got that, right?"

"Yes, David."

"And you have the prescriptions so that we can be sure you get what you need when you get out of here?"

"Yes, David."

"And you know that we'll help you if you have to get them filled, or need to talk to someone at a shelter or something?"

"Yes, David."

"Okay, then, shall we get you out of here?"

"Okay." Cassandra nods again, as if freedom seems at least an acceptable alternative to continued incarceration.

"Promise you're gonna come see me?"

"Yes, David."

Terra is shaking her head gently and smiling at me. She knows as I do that I'm going to lose Cassandra to the streets. Everyone knows. It's been nearly seven years, and I've made minimal progress at best. Still, right now, she's medicated, showered, and relatively stable, so hope springs eternal.

"You can put her in the well if you want," I tell Terra as she lets me out.

"She's going home, right?" Terra asks.

"Something like that," I say, a twinge of sadness creeping over me as I ponder just what constitutes "home" for Cassandra.

⟶⟵

"Feige" — Birnbaum says my name as if it's spelled *Fiegeee* — "what was I supposed to do with this one?"

"Dismiss the tickets and let her out," I tell him firmly. "This is the woman I asked you to put in a few weeks ago — I've been working with her for half a dozen years."

"Oh, riiiight," Birnbaum says, seeming to recall the unusual approach. "What were the tickets for?"

"Nonsense. Open-container stuff mostly. I surrendered her, remember?"

"Riiiight. Ready to do it?"

"Sure am."

"Bring Mr. Feige's client out, please," Birnbaum instructs one of his court officers.

"Sure, Judge."

There are still six or seven cases left, and the pews in the courtroom remain sprinkled with defendants, lawyers, and spectators. Hearing the door to the pens opening, I take up my place before the judge.

"How's an ACD?" Birnbaum asks, referring to what is known as an "adjournment in contemplation of dismissal" — the next best thing to an outright dismissal.

"ACDs are fine," I tell him.

"ACD on this first case," he says. "Her other tickets are dismissed as covered."

"Thanks, Judge. Always nice to see you."

"Good to see you, Mr. Feige. Good luck, Ms. Stallings. You have a fine lawyer there."

"Okay," says Cassandra.

"I'll wait for you outside," I whisper to her.

"Okay, David," she says as she's led away.

Right on cue, ten minutes later, Cassandra comes trudging out of the courtroom. She's in the same worn hiking boots she was wearing when she went in. They're a few sizes too big for her, and I imagine she got them from the trash or from a shelter.

"Hi, David."

"Hi, sweetie. How's freedom feel?"

"It's okay," she says.

⟫⟪

It's well after 4:00 when I finally make my way back in through the office doors, Cassandra in tow. I set her up with one of the available social workers to ensure that she'll get train fare to the shelter in Brooklyn and back.

My mailbox is full again — letters from clients in prisons across the state. There are messages too — a flutter of little pink squares — from impatient judges who insist on leaving word with Lorraine rather than on my voice mail.

Upstairs, a management meeting is in full swing, Robin presiding in her little fishbowl of an office. I should be there, but it's been a long day, the meeting is almost over, and I have less than an hour before I have to go to night court. Walking past the office, I give a little wave, intending to just keep walking. Robin, though, motions me in for a brief appearance.

Back in my office ten minutes later, there are a dozen new voice mail messages. I'm tired, and I just can't deal with voice mail right now. So after dropping the afternoon's files on top of the bulging Redwelds devoted to Clarence and Reginald and Alberto, I turn my attention to the stack of letters. The phone rings.

I've been in my office for less than two minutes.

It's Gerald — I haven't heard from him in months.

"Happy Chanukah!" he says. It's the first time his salutation is even close to appropriate; the calendrical propriety of the greeting never seems to occur to Gerald — there were several times over the summer, after I first met him, that I'd pick up the phone in my sweltering office only to hear Gerald cheerfully announce: "Happy Chanukah!" Gerald is obsessed with Jews, and he often goes out of his way to identify someone as Jewish ("Horowitz," he'll say, "that's a Jewish doctor"). I can almost hear him nodding with satisfaction at the other end of the pay phone.

The pay phone he is calling from is on 20E — the locked psych ward at Bellevue Hospital. I had dropped Gerald off there back in July after he got arrested for allegedly pulling a knife on a security guard at the psych ward at Lincoln Hospital.

Handsome, calm, and in his midforties, Gerald showed no obvious signs of mental distress. He'd gone back to Lincoln to get some of his things. When they'd discharged him (after a short voluntary stay for some auditory hallucinations), the hospital had sent him packing without his belongings. The security guard had given him the runaround and even refused to let him talk to the people who had his stuff. Gerald admitted to a heated argument but said he'd never even pulled out the knife.

Judges, of course, are always afraid to let people out when they're alleged to have a mental illness, and despite Gerald's calm deportment and lack of criminal record, I was worried that a judge might actually hold him.

"Jail is the worst possible outcome here," I declared when Gerald's case was called. "If you think there's a psychiatric issue here, just let him go and he'll go to Bellevue for an evaluation."

"And how do I know that, Mr. Feige?" the judge snapped, a sour look on her face.

"Because I'll take him there myself. Tonight. After court," I told her.

"You will?" She was a bit incredulous.

"Yup. If that's what it takes, I sure will," I said firmly.

And that's why, on a sweltering night at 2:15 in the morning, with Gerald in the passenger seat humming loudly along with the radio, I found myself pulling into a parking spot just off First Avenue and strolling the halls of the hulking hospital, my footfalls echoing on the old granite floors. Bellevue was mostly empty, and as we made our way from triage to the psych ER, past a door marked "Elopement Precaution," accompanied by a Guyanese nurse with darting eyes, I wondered whether they were actually going to admit him and what the hell I'd do with him if they didn't.

Luckily, they did.

"Hi, Gerald! So how's it going?" I ask. Apparently he'd been released but is now back for another short stay.

"I'm good, Dave," he says frankly, "I'm good. The food isn't up to my standards, though. I cook for myself, you know . . . that's how I keep my strength."

"I remember, Gerald."

"Well, I just wanted to say hi." There is a little pause at the other end of the phone, as if Gerald is making sure he's accomplished the purpose of his call. It seems he has. "Okay, Happy Chanukah, thanks for everything, and keep up all the good work," he says cheerfully.

"Okay, Gerald — always a pleasure to hear from you. Feel free to call anytime if you need anything."

"Will do, Dave. Thanks!" he says, hanging up.

And that was it.

—⇒•⇐—

The mentally ill and the mentally retarded are a unique and acute problem in the system generally, and for public defenders in particular. Learning to deal with them takes great care and patience — and a really good social worker. Over the years, I've represented all kinds: lost people like Cassandra and sociopaths like George — who despite being acquitted in two separate trials, just kept on robbing gypsy cabs until a judge sent him away for twenty years. There are clients like José (charged with first-degree murder but so retarded that his IQ measured in the mid-fifties), who look normal, and those who don't, like Luis, a twenty-three-year-old with a big round head, goofy eyes, a crooked smile, and the mental capacity of a five-year-old. Luis was arrested for trying to show a ten-year-old girl "a bunny." In fact there really was a bunny — sitting behind the vegetable stand Luis's father ran. But the little girl, scared at the prospect of being alone with Luis, quickly reported that Luis tried to kiss her (which he might have actually done). The net result: the police came, put Luis in handcuffs, and took him away. His parents were hysterical and terrified, but as it turned out, they had nothing to worry about — Luis was having the time of his life. He had absolutely no clue what was going on. "I rode in the car!" he told me excitedly at arraignments. "A car . . . with the lights! The flashing kind!"

Mercifully, Rikers was never in the cards for Luis. Luis's big, drooling visage revealed a kid so obviously severely retarded that after a few court dates and some mental health records got turned over, his case was dismissed.

Sadly, it's seldom that easy with mentally retarded clients. And it's harder still with those who are mentally ill as opposed to mentally retarded. Most challenging of all are the few who are both mentally ill and violent. Few things scare judges quite as much.

James was one of the most mentally ill clients I've ever seen. A white kid with a shaved head and bulging blue eyes, James would rock back and forth, his eyes scanning the room as if the walls themselves were threats. He was paranoid and sometimes nearly incoherent — so much so that if James were portrayed accurately on TV, most reviewers would savage the actor for overdoing it.

When I first talked to him, late one night, in a special cell that the police department uses for people it senses are security threats, James, like so many of the mentally ill I've represented over the years, was in complete denial about what was going on.

I started with the basics.

"James, my name is David Feige. I'm going to be your lawyer. I'm going to tell you a little about what you are being charged with, and then we can talk about anything you want . . . okay?"

James just sat there for a minute, looking around as if surprised by every unchanging feature of the room.

"What do you mean?" he said eventually. "There ain't no charges against me."

"Well, James," I said, "actually there are. Your mom says you hit her."

"No she doesn't," he said.

I slowed down, deliberately overenunciating my words.

"Yes, James. She does. That's why you're here. Because your mom called the police, and they arrested you, and now you are charged with hitting your mom."

"So I'm going home?"

"I'm not sure yet," I tell him. "I'd like to talk to your mom and see what she thinks . . . okay?"

"Yeah, that's good. She didn't do this . . . she definitely didn't do this," James said.

Outside, sitting in the cavernous courtroom in which arraignments are conducted, I found James's mother. She was small and pretty, with a black eye and a spent look. Animated and loud, she spoke in a heavy Italian accent. We stepped out of the courtroom, and as we crossed the threshold she unleashed a torrent.

"I don't a want him in the house!" she exclaimed. "I had

enough a him already . . . somebody gotta do something with him. I can't stand it; I had enough." She continued in this vein for several minutes before I could interrupt her.

"So you want to go forward with the prosecution, and you don't want your son back at home?"

"I told you already. That kid, he needs help. I can't do it no more. I had enough a him, someone gotta do something."

Back inside, I tried to explain to James that after speaking to his mother I didn't think he would be allowed to go home. I tried to get him to give me an alternative address so I could assure the judge that he'd stay somewhere else, but James had no friends, no other relatives he thought might take him in, and he remained convinced that he could in fact go home. Worse, as I looked over his rap sheet it became clear that this was the third time this sort of thing had happened.

Called out before the judge, James stood blinking in the light, looking confused. His mother was in the audience watching as the assistant district attorney asked that James be held on fifteen hundred dollars' bail. I urged the judge to release him — James, after all, was my client, and even though I was pretty sure his release would be bad for both his mother and him, release was what James wanted. And so, as his lawyer, release was what I asked for. The judge set five hundred dollars' bail. I requested that James get evaluated and medicated while in. I also asked for mental observation.

Five days later, I saw James again. He was in the basement of the criminal court building, in a section usually reserved for high-security inmates. It was instantly clear, though, that James was not a security risk: he was a target. He was covered from head to toe in long dark-blue and purple bruises.

"What the fuck?" I asked a corrections officer.

"A fellow inmate," the officer explained drolly. "Kid kept screaming racial epithets. Didn't make him too popular inside."

I was horrified, and guilty — I should have asked for protective custody immediately. That I didn't, that I focused just on the evaluation and the medication, meant James resembled an albino dragged through a blackberry patch.

Even the judge winced when he saw James, but he didn't wince enough to let him out. Mom wanted him in jail, the prosecutors wanted him to pay for what he'd done, I wanted him in treatment, and James just wanted to go home. As obliged, I championed James's position while also trying to set up the treatment I thought he'd eventually need; the prosecutors did what their victim wanted, advocating for a long jail sentence; and the judge did what judges do, eventually offering James a plea and sentence, after which, to no one's surprise and despite an order of protection, James headed right back to his mother's house — the simple in-or-out polarities of the criminal justice system having solved absolutely nothing.

→>◦<←

After getting off the phone with Gerald I turn my attention to my "immediate action" files. I realize that there are three motions that are already past due. Deadlines are fairly flexible in criminal court, but if I don't get them in by the end of the week, I could be in trouble.

Figuring I'll bang out a motion or two, I fire up the computer and ignore the steady accretion of e-mails in my in-box. Calling up my Supreme Court motion template, I fill in the particulars of the case — indictment number, court part, charge (in this case, attempted murder). The process takes no more than ten minutes, and I'm flipping through my file, deciding what hearings to ask for, when the phone rings again.

It's Alvin — again.

"I can't talk now," I say in the singsongy voice that an exasperated parent uses with a child.

People in the office tease Robin and me about Alvin Hastings. He's like our crazy, impossible, mentally ill adopted son. We have represented him since he was fifteen and got arrested after running away from a group home. Once again he is in jail.

One of the things Alvin is obsessed with is his birth certificate, both because it causes him constant problems and because it is a perfect metaphor for the rest of his existence. When Alvin's drug-addicted mother gave birth to him, she didn't get around to naming him for months, and so his birth certificate only says "Hastings — boy." This made it hard for him to get an ID, which he desperately wants. Combine that with an itinerant childhood, and Alvin has constant trouble just proving that he's himself.

To make that easier, Alvin conscientiously collects letters from his lawyers. For some reason — probably because he lost the original — Alvin decided he needed another copy of a particular letter from his old family court lawyer. So he did what he always does — started calling obsessively and then, when he didn't hear back in time, just showed up and demanded his letter. This wasn't a good strategy, and when a court officer told him he wasn't welcome at family court, Alvin got insistent.

"I have a right to see my lawyer," Alvin protested.

"Get out" was the court officer's simple position, and when Alvin hesitated, the officer grabbed him in an attempt to steer him out of the building.

Alvin reacts badly to anyone touching him. Fifteen years in group homes can do that to a kid, and when the officer took hold of him, Alvin spun around and pushed him down. In seconds, he was tackled, beaten, and arrested — charged with a felony assault on a court officer. Hence his current indictment.

For Alvin, bail was out of the question — he had no money. And even though the injuries to the officer were negligible, a trial would take a long time, and it might be hard to persuade a jury to acquit someone charged with hurting a court officer. As so often happens, a plea was the only answer. And since the judge could give Alvin pretty much anything, including a sentence of time already served, we set about trying to get him a decent deal.

Writing sentencing letters is a miserable task. They seldom work to moderate harsh sentences, and writing them usually ends up feeling like pissing into the wind. But Alvin is before a judge who we think might actually listen, and maybe, just maybe, a sentencing letter will help. It's been a long day, and all I've really done is adjourn a bunch of cases. Maybe this will make a difference, I think, as I start to hammer out an abbreviated list of Alvin's group homes, psychiatric diagnoses, medications, and tragic circumstances. And the more I type, the more I find myself amazed at the resilience of the human character, astonished not that Alvin is in jail, but that he manages to wake up every morning and continue to face the prospect of his life. I'm also shocked not by how horrible his circumstances are, but how typical, and sitting there, behind the green glow of the computer screen, my suit jacket carelessly draped over the back of my chair, I take a moment to consider that behind the faces of the people I pass in the courthouse day after day there are stories of nearly incomprehensible pain and loss. It dawns on me, as it often does, just how much compassion it takes to begin to understand the psychic damage wreaked by an abusive, drug-addled parent, by a procession of alien group homes, by knowing that your own mother lost her rights to you and that somewhere you have siblings you never knew. In a certain way, it is no wonder the system just tunes all of this out. Listening would be deafening.

Satisfied with my little catharsis, I print the letter onto letterhead, sign it, and head around the corner so that Robin can sign as well. Reading it over, she shakes her head, understanding exactly what I'm thinking.

"You know she'll never do it, right?"

I just nod.

Sure enough, the thirty-minute investment in a sentencing letter for Alvin makes no difference whatsoever. Judge White sentences Alvin to nine months in jail, leaving him to rot at Rikers for a few more months.

⇒⇐

It's almost 5:00 when Lisa comes in with a pained expression on her face. Lisa Hoyes is tiny and very pretty, with soft dark eyes and ringlets of long brown hair. Since graduating from NYU Law School she's been a community organizer, an advocate for troubled kids, and, finally, a public defender. Lisa has a sentencing tomorrow before Judge Massaro — one of the most odd and temperamental judges in the Bronx. He has already remanded her client, and she's praying he'll let her out tomorrow.

The crime: assault on a police officer.

Lisa's client is a young girl who had never been arrested before. An orphan, she was trying to get her little fourteen-year-old brother registered for school. Thanks to school bureaucrats, she'd tried and failed to do this three times already, having been turned away for providing insufficient or incorrect paperwork. On their way out of the school, two truancy cops tried to detain her brother, claiming that he had no right to be in the school in which he was trying to register. The cops grabbed the kid, and she tried to snatch him back. They pounced, and one of them hurt his finger. Sis got arrested. And now Judge Massaro may send her to state prison.

"I swear I'll kill myself if he sends her upstate," Lisa says gravely.

Burnout is stealthy. It rarely arrives with the bang of revelation; rather it's the creeping suspicion that maybe everyone around you is right — your clients really are scum, the system really is completely broken, and you can't really touch anyone's life anyway. It is the sneaking sense of futility that undermines your resilience, that makes you unable to wake up the morning after a defeat, ready to fight twice as hard. Burnout sets in when outrage ends. It happens over time, and it hastens with every cataclysmic conviction. My personal theory is that most public defenders can't survive much more than three of these before they start to fry.

The ones we plead guilty don't count. Neither does the incarceration of clients we care about — that stuff happens every day, and if we only had three of those in us, we'd last about a week in the work. By cataclysmic convictions, I mean the unjust conviction of beloved clients at trial.

The first time it's a shock. Watching them drag William away, I was utterly uncomprehending. *There must be something I can do,* I kept thinking to myself. The finality of the judgment hadn't yet set in. But as hard as that was to survive, I came back stronger after William — more determined than ever to be sure that it never happened again.

Then I lost Juan. I sobbed uncontrollably after they took him away. And for a while afterward, I thought I'd never be able to go back to work. Juan was a big, slow goofball of a client who'd been present at a fight between two groups of kids in which one kid took another kid's jacket. All were charged with armed robbery. All of them were convicted. The kid who took the jacket got fourteen years. Juan got the minimum — two to six years — but he should have been acquitted.

I felt it acutely after Juan. It was, at that point, the worst conviction of my life. I began to despair. The system was grinding on, and I was being ground down. Exhausted and overwhelmed by the futility of my struggles, I began to take it out on my clients. I stopped listening, stopped feeling, and lost the ability to muster the wherewithal and compassion that a defender depends upon.

It took me months to get over it, to find my way back. But eventually, after some drinking, some sleeping, some soul-searching, and a little vacation, I picked myself up, dusted myself off, and devised the three rules that I decided could ensure my longevity as a public defender: trust yourself, pace yourself, forgive yourself.

Given the volume of cases, a public defender has to make an almost unfathomable number of snap decisions during the course of the day — take the plea or get a trial date, deal with the DA or go straight to the judge, send a client to the grand jury or just wait for trial. Every one of those decisions has potentially catastrophic consequences for a client, and being an effective decision maker requires a preternatural confidence. That's the first part — *trust yourself,* trust your instincts. Generally they're good.

Second, remember that no matter how hard you work and no matter how efficient you are, no amount of work will ever be enough. There is an inexhaustible supply of clients, and almost every single one of them will need more than you have to give. There is never going to be enough money, enough time, or enough compassion to do much more than triage. Even when you do focus on someone, their needs are usually so beyond your capacities that no good will come of the effort. Accept this as a condition of your life and work as hard as you can for as long as you can every single day, and then when it's finally time to go home, accept that you've done all you can do — *pace yourself.*

The problem is that with all that volume, with all those decisions, you will screw up. It's inevitable. Every public defender is going to make mistakes, and those mistakes are going to take a terrible, inexcusable, and unforgivable toll on the lives of the clients you love. It's just going to happen. You will err, and someone will go to jail because of it. Somehow, to survive in the work, you need to find a way to forgive the unforgivable, to accept and acknowledge that you've screwed up, and to recognize the price of that screwup without becoming so paralyzed that you can no longer do the work. As bad as you may think you are, clients need you — they are desperate for decent lawyers. Don't be your own worst enemy. *Forgive yourself* — or you'll burn out in two years.

For many years, trust, pace, and forgive worked well as coping strategies, though in my heart of hearts I knew that their talismanic power would be unlikely to protect me a third time.

In the ensuing decade, I walked some clients out from under overwhelming evidence — Steve, caught red-handed in the apartment of the man he allegedly kidnapped, bloody duct tape and guns recovered from the scene, a gold identity bracelet with the complainant's name on it allegedly recovered from his pocket: not guilty.

I also lost some I should have won — Jason, convicted of assault for slashing his cousin's face at a kid's birthday party despite the strong evidence of self-defense: he got four years, got out, and a year later, thanks to the conviction, got deported.

But none of them were the third strike — not even Ron, Ululy's client, whose life Judge Kiesel ruined with a fraudulent conviction. That stung, and it made me furious, but it wasn't my case and it wasn't the third strike.

The third strike was Ray.

Interrupting my thoughts, the intercom buzzes: it's Robin. "You know we've got night court tonight?"

"I know," I say, sounding more annoyed than I actually feel.

"Please don't be late again — it's heavy over there."

"I'm on my way," I say wearily as I send Lisa off with a reassuring smile and a promise that Massaro will give her client probation (he does). I grab a pen, pull on my crinkled suit jacket, and head back toward criminal court, toward another stack of court files, another overworked judge, and another cell full of poor, incarcerated wretches living in a long, melancholy night.

Fifteen

5:18 P.M.

I LOVE NIGHT COURT. I love the silence of the courthouse. I love that I can hear my footfalls on the tiles, that there is no line for the magnetometer, that the small complement of court officers greets me with "Hi, Dave" instead of brutish indifference. I love the purity of the empty courthouse, the stability of being in one courtroom for an entire shift, the ability to focus on the cases in front of me without worrying about running somewhere else.

I have done as many as fifty-five misdemeanors in a single night shift.

Somehow, in night court, the regular drone of the system can take on an eerie and sometimes comical cast — as if fighting fatigue, alone together in the building, everyone is finally able to see the tragedy and comedy of things more clearly. It was in night court that I first saw staples in someone's head. They looked just like the staples that are in a stapler: a long row going from the top of the forehead to the base of the skull like a welding job on a robot's head. They were the result of smart-mouthing a cop.

Another night, a forty-six-year-old woman is charged with a gunpoint robbery, her first arrest. The police have no gun, no property, no nothing; it's a one-witness ID case. Still, the assistant district attorney wants her in jail. The judge looks down at the ADA incredulously and asks, "Are you telling me that at forty-six this woman just started doing armed robberies?" The assistant DA has no answer, and the woman is released.

On still another night I'm standing in the small, cramped enclosure between the bars that lead to the cells and the solid steel door that leads to the arraignment courtroom. It is well after midnight, and night court is in full swing and particularly pungent. Eight or nine people are squeezed into an area of less than four by six feet. Everyone has been in the system for at least sixteen hours, and most are sweating and smelly. In the corner, her ass pressed against the bars, a sassy prostitute wearing a skintight flesh-toned halter top is taunting the boys: "Whatch you all looking at my titties for?" she says over and over. "Yeah, you . . . why you looking at my titties?"

The men are nodding approvingly or ostentatiously averting their eyes. Her breasts are, in fact, prominent and spectacular, and her sassy tone and jutting hips add to the effect. And just when it seems as if someone is going to try to grab a handful, her case is called, the steel door opens, and she wiggles her way into the courtroom. In about thirty seconds she pleads guilty, gets time served, and struts out — heading, in all likelihood, back to her stroll. With her gone, the men in the well go back to their dissatisfied, defiant poses.

Night court in the Bronx runs from 5:00 P.M. to 1:00 A.M., 7 days a week, 365 days a year. Although judges are generally assigned to specific courtrooms, every criminal court judge also has to do a short stint in night court every once and again.

Tonight, as I walk in, musing about motions left unwritten and the calls that have gone unanswered, strolling past the magnetometers and the unhurried, friendly court officers, up the stalled escalators to the second floor and into the arraignment part, I'm trying to find the energy to propel me through another eight hours — to forget about Reginald and Clarence, Najid and Malik, Cassandra and Jaron, and focus on the stack of new cases that awaits me.

Two factors are highly predictive of how long and painful a shift in night court is about to be: the judge and the system numbers. Both bits of information reside in the clerk's office, where the rotating schedule of judges is taped to a battered metal file cabinet and the number of arrestees "in the system" can be gleaned from a stack of computer printouts listing in chronological or alphabetical order every arrest in the past forty-eight hours.

If the load is light, it usually means an early night, plenty of time to talk to clients, and maybe even a nice long dinner break. On a heavy night, though, the cases come fast and furious, and there is intense pressure to get the clients interviewed and arraigned as quickly as possible. Then, night court can become extremely unpleasant — a constant battle between an impatient judge and exhausted lawyers who insist on taking the time they need to adequately defend their clients.

Even more important than whether it's a heavy night or not is the judge. If Megan Tallmer or Ruth Sussman or Ralph Fabrizio is on the bench, the best thing you can do for close-call clients is forget about them — let them sit another night and take their chances with the day judge. That's because judges like Tallmer and Sussman and Fabrizio love to coerce pleas and are, therefore, much more likely to set five hundred or one thousand dollars' bail on nonsense cases in which a better judge would just release the defendant.

This radical difference between judges quickly becomes apparent, and I have often seen baby lawyers return shell-shocked from their first awful-judge-arraignment shift. The powerlessness of arraigning case after case before a judge who doesn't listen to a word you're saying and brusquely dispatches almost everyone to Rikers can reduce almost anyone to tears.

Scanning the list, I breathe a sigh of relief — Judge Dawson will preside tonight. Occasionally intemperate, exceedingly smart, and, most important, reasonable, Dawson is a fine draw, and knowing that he'll be up there briefly banishes my fatigue.

The arraignment routine is always the same. In a corner of the courtroom, the Bronx Defenders huddle, waiting for cases to appear. Periodically, someone from the Clerk's Office will emerge carrying a stack of paperwork — one set goes to the court, the other is delivered to us. Each case contains a complaint — the legal document that officially begins a criminal proceeding — a rap sheet and what is known as a CJA sheet, the product of an interview at Central Booking, where clients are asked where they live, who they live with, where they work, and some other questions designed to elucidate their ties to the community.

The complaint is usually just one page — it lists the charges and the specific code sections someone is accused of violating, and provides about a paragraph of detail in odd punctuation and legalese explaining just how someone violated the law.

> *The deponent is informed by informant that At the above TPO [time and place of occurrence] The defendant, aided by another actually present, did forcibly remove property from informant without his permission or authority while displaying what appeared to be a firearm.*

> *The deponent is informed by informant that at the above time and place of occurrence, The defendant did, have sexual intercourse with informant by forcible compulsion.*

> *Deponent observed defendant enter the New York City Subway system without paying the lawful fare by jumping over a turnstile.*

The cases go into a metal basket, and a clerk from our office divides them into a stack of misdemeanors and a stack of felonies. If a bunch of new cases comes in all at once, the lawyers divvy up the spoils.

"I'll give you the rape if I can have the arson. . . ."

"I can't do another DV case. If you take these, I'll do the petty larcenies, the two weed cases, and the car case too."

"Anyone want a drug sale? I've already done two tonight. . . ."

It's just before 6:00 when the first batch of cases comes in. There are about a dozen in the first stack, nothing too unusual — a pile of misdemeanors and a few mostly low-level felonies. Tonight I'm working with a particularly good crew — Robin, Jason, and Aaron, whose steely resolve and clean, elegant thinking make him a powerful courtroom presence. Robin and I divide up the misdemeanors, and I grab a felony or two as well.

"You ready?" I ask Robin as I pick up a pen and a stack of my business cards.

"Let's do it," she says with a smile as we head through the heavy blue doors, into the well, and then back into the cell block beyond.

"Yo! Feige."

I've barely rounded the corner toward the cells, and already I've been made. It's Jermaine, a client I once represented in an assault case. Where I grew up, the "assault" Jermaine was charged with was what we'd call a playground fight. (In the highly policed inner-city school yards of New York City, even a recess dustup can make its way into the criminal justice system.) But now here he is in the cells behind the courtroom, calling my name as if we're out on the streets.

Spotting him, I have that strange mix of feelings — it's always nice to see an old client, but at the same time, seeing Jermaine back here is troubling. Jermaine had been doing well in school and had the kind of positive attitude I really warmed to. I had hoped that his previous escapade might have been his last.

"Feige!" he says, seeming genuinely happy to see me, which I suppose, on some level, he is.

"Jermaine, what the fuck are you doing here?"

"Oh, Dave, man, it's nothin'. Bullshit. For real."

"So what you been up to, my friend? You been staying out of trouble?"

"Yeah, man, I been pretty good — I'm working and everything."

"You been arrested since I saw you last?"

"Nah, not really."

"What do you mean . . . not really?" I ask.

"Well, you know, not like nothin' real or nothin'."

"Jermaine," I say, glowering, "how many times you feel the steel? How many times have the cops actually cuffed you?"

"Oh, like that."

"Yeah, brother, like that."

"Oh, like about six."

"*Six?*"

"Yeah, but not for nothin' serious."

I could smack him.

As it turns out, Jermaine is basically right. As I will find out later in the evening, his current case is for smoking marijuana in public, and the past few were indeed all crap — mostly hanging-out offenses such as having an open container of alcohol or trespassing, which, along with disorderly conduct and resisting arrest, is one of the most abused criminal statutes. When cops do what they call "vertical sweeps" — clearing out a project building from the lobby to the roof — they rarely stop to ascertain who has legitimate friends where. The result is a constant flood of absurd trespass cases, as kids who live in and around the projects are constantly being arrested on their way to visit friends in adjacent buildings.

Of course, the rub is that even without doing much of anything particularly serious, Jermaine is already working up a criminal record significant enough to really damage him in life. Part of it is youthful stupidity, but much more is the omnipresence of policing in his community and the resulting blasé attitude that he and his buddies have toward tickets and arrests.

"You gonna take me, right?" he asks.

"Yeah, brother, I'll do it — soon as it comes in. Until then, sit tight. You're lucky you're in the cell 'cause I'd kick your ass for being so stupid."

"You right, Dave," he says, and smiles his altar-boy smile.

I make a mental note to grab his case when it comes in.

Heading to the second cell, I pause at the bars. The cell is packed, the steel bench that runs around the perimeter crammed with people. A few of the homeless or drug addicted are passed out underneath the bench, behind the feet of the guys sitting shoulder to shoulder. At least a dozen people are standing too, filling up most of the space in the cage. The stale air stinks of urine and sweat, and the thick sticks of incense that the cops burn don't seem to make much of a difference.

"Yo, listen up!" I call out in my loudest tough-guy voice. "I'm gonna call out some names. If you hear your name, you let me know — if you don't, don't ask me. These are the only cases I've got right now, and I'm gonna try to bust as many of you outta here tonight as I can, but I spend the whole night saying 'no, I ain't got your case yet,' then someone's gonna wind up sleeping here tonight who shoulda been going home — everybody understand?"

There is a chorus of "you got it," and I start calling out the names.

My very first client of the evening is a man charged with possession of a crack pipe. His lips are blistered, and much of his body is covered with lesions. He has a massive record — three felonies and three dozen misdemeanors. I ask him if he knows what he is charged with.

"Of course," he tells me quietly but contemptuously. "Look, man, I only got a few months left — my T-cell count is down to nine, and the drugs ain't working for me." He tosses his HIV clinic card at me with a look of quiet resignation. "There's not much joy left for me, and truth is, I like getting high. I just want to be left alone to do that while I'm still here. Just get me out, please."

I do. He gets time served, I hand him subway fare, and by the time I turn around, he is gone.

Next is a sad older man who hasn't been arrested in twenty years but went up to a police officer the other day out of the blue and allegedly tried to grab his gun. It seems it might have been a sad attempt at suicide. The cops certainly saw it this way: they carted him off to Bellevue, where he was given Zoloft for his depression. Then they hauled him to court, where despite my argument and the obviousness of his condition, Dawson sets bail.

I've got a fourteen-year-old who allegedly burgled the apartment next to where his grandmother lives. He and his cousin allegedly broke in, beat the old man, and rummaged through his stuff. The old man restrained them until the cops came.

There's a guy named Rodman (his first name), about six foot six with dark skin, prominent lips, and hair dyed orange. A cop was trying to arrest a woman when Rodman stepped in, saying, "If you arrest her, you'll have to arrest me too." The cops obliged.

On my way back to interview another client, Jason stops me.

"Check it out," he says, pointing out a stinking pile of bloody vomit in the corner.

"Go tell one of the cops," I tell him.

"Yeah, okay," the cop grunts when Jason informs him about the barf. All night long people track it around the cells.

By the time I've arraigned the first five cases, the basket is full of new ones, and grabbing another dozen or so, I head back to the pens to do some interviews. Most of this stack are "disposables," cases that, with Dawson on the bench, are going away tonight: three or four prostitutes who should get time served, three more weed cases that should all be reduced to traffic ticket–like violations, a few trespass cases that should never have been brought in the first place, and a train hop or two. Many of the clients have records already, some are in the system for the first time, and all of them get a sit-down with me that ranges from ninety seconds to about ten minutes.

Finally, just before 9:00, a parolee comes before the judge. He desperately needs a plea to disorderly conduct so as to avoid a parole violation. They offer him one on the condition he perform five days of community service. It has been a long day, and before the plea is entered, he looks over, pained, at the assistant district attorney.

"Five?" he says incredulously. "Five for a bag a weed? How 'bout three?"

The judge and court personnel smile, this being the perfect parody of what defense lawyers do all the time.

The assistant DA looks over and says in a thick Bronx accent, "Eeeh, you wanna make a deal with me?"

"Yeah," the guy says definitively. "I work, how 'bout a fine?"

"How much would you like to pay, sir?" asks the ADA, playing along happily now.

"How 'bout a hundred dollars?" says the guy.

"Done," says the ADA, turning toward the bench where the judge is laughing out loud now.

"Your Honor, we have a disposition of this very important matter."

The parolee gets his fine and his disorderly conduct, and he leaves a happy customer.

It's nearly time for the dinner break. The pens in the back are still stuffed with people hoping to get out. And despite the fact that we've done more than thirty cases, it feels as though we've barely made a dent.

The temperature has dropped considerably, and our breath fogs as we hit the far side of the courthouse's revolving doors. Just about the only culinary options available at this hour are the food court across the way, the *cuchifritos* across the concourse, and even farther, way down by the stadium, two miserable diners. We're feeling a bit rebellious: Jason is fuming about a client who should have been let out (must have happened while I was in back interviewing), Robin hates the food court, and Aaron says he's in the mood for decent food as well. All four of us have been working for nearly twelve hours, and everyone could use a little break. Night court rarely resumes promptly after dinner, we muse, and besides, the system isn't too packed. "What the hell," we say as we pile into Robin's old Volvo and head across to East Harlem for a decent meal.

Sixteen

WE'RE BACK IN THE BRONX less than ninety minutes later, and the parade of cases and clients resumes. I go back to interview some kid charged with jumping a turnstile. At the bars, just about to call out his name, I hear a female cop with a bad attitude saying, "I smell crack, do you smell crack?"

I don't respond.

"Yo! Who the *FUCK* is smoking crack in my cell?"

Sure enough, a client who had just pled guilty is smoking crack back in the cell. He's charged with another misdemeanor.

I sit down across from a handsome, smiling Rasta with thick, snaking dreads that seem to pop out of his head at crazy angles.

"Ja, mon, I know about da case," he says as I introduce myself. "I smoke-a de weed — das wha dis is, right?"

"Right."

"Okay, you tink you gonna get me out, yeah?"

"Well," I say cautiously, "you do have three prior marijuana sales."

"I know dat, mon — but you get me out, right?"

"Well, I certainly think it's possible since this time you were just smoking rather than selling."

"Dat's right, mon — jes smoking da weed, das all."

I make what amounts to the "jes smoking da weed" argument to Dawson, and the guy gets a conditional discharge. Later, just outside the courtroom, he stops me.

"You know, I love the weed, mon. I gotta smoke it, you know. But liar mon, you tink I con clear up my record?"

"Steven," I say, "you have a TERRIBLE record. How 'bout you just try to concentrate on not getting arrested for a few months?"

"Good point, mon," he says, with a vigorous shake of his head. His dreadlocks fly around, and he flashes me his dazzling smile. "I like you. You a good liar, mon. I tink yous a undercover brother."

"Thank you, Steven. Go home. Take care of yourself, okay?"

"You got it, mon."

Another pile.

There's a park piss gone wild, escalating into an alleged assault on a police officer and resisting arrest, and after that, a young Asian woman arrested for supposedly flicking a cigarette in the direction of a cop. Never arrested before, she found herself handcuffed and incarcerated for more than thirty hours. When I find her in the cell she is crying hysterically. All the other women, most with rap sheets, beg me to take her case first and get her out.

I speak to her for a while, trying to calm her down. I explain that we can fight the case and file a complaint against the officer, and that I think she should file a civil suit against the police as well. I burn a favor and get the case called almost immediately. It doesn't even take much argument before Dawson dismisses the obviously fraudulent charges. The woman starts sobbing all over again, and I walk her to the back of the courtroom toward her family, all of whom await her release. But as I console her and urge them to file a lawsuit, I know that they'll never do so. "We don't want to confront the police," they explain. "We're afraid of them."

Another sad truth of the system: no one follows up. No one ever does. It's why police brutality persists. The humiliation and sense of powerlessness that come with that first exposure to the handcuffs are so extreme that all anyone wants to do afterward is make it stop, get it over with, and forget all about it. My clients fear retaliation from the boys in blue if they speak up, and the thought of fighting back, especially by prolonging the case or filing a lawsuit and engaging in protracted litigation, seems so daunting that most of my clients would rather get the case over with — sometimes even pleading guilty to lesser charges just to never have to come back to the courthouse again.

The industrial clock above the worn rail that separates the well of the courtroom from the spectator sections reads 1:06 A.M. when the last case of the night is called. It is quickly disposed of, and the judge makes ready to call it a night. Like Robin and the rest of the Bronx Defender crew, I've been going for fifteen hours, and I could use a break.

There are groans from the audience when the court officer declares, "AR-2 stands adjourned until tomorrow morning at nine. Please exit the courtroom." Dozens of people are still sitting, waiting anxiously for their loved ones to see the judge. They have been tugging on my sleeve for hours.

"Lawyer, lawyer, excuse me, Mr. Lawyer," they implore me, or anyone else who will listen.

"Do you know when my son is going to be seen?"

"Can you tell me if John Franks is coming through?"

"I'm looking for my mother. . . ."

Slaves to the procession of paperwork controlled by the cops and the clerks, we rarely have good answers for them, and so they sit, nights and days, watching the parade of people coming before the judge, waiting, hoping that one of them will be theirs, hoping that everything will be okay, that their friend, lover, son, or mother will come home, or that their lawyer will be able at least to explain what the hell happened.

The anxious spectators are herded out into the hallway. There, in the wee hours of the morning, the confusion and frustration are compounded by the dawning realization that their friends or family members are about to spend another night in a jail cell. There is little I can do or say to make this any better for anyone, but I often try — at least to explain that they shouldn't actually come back at 9:00 A.M., that in reality few people get seen before 10:00 A.M., or that the judge tomorrow morning is even better than the night court judge, and though it means

waiting another night, it also improves the chances that someone will be released.

It's time to go home.

———⟫⟪———

With the area around the criminal courthouse deserted, the drive
back is usually quick and painless, the Harlem streetscapes gliding by in sodium-lit monotony. On the cell phone I fume about
the injustice of the evening to my West Coast friends. It can take
an hour or so to calm down enough to go to sleep, and I often
stop for a drink to nurse the process along.

There is a certain comfort in the regularity of the people who
populate the uncomfortable bars I prefer after night court —
they're whiskey drinkers who have worked a long day rather than
cosmopolitan sippers who've had a good lunch. But even with
the whiskey it is hard to forget the voices of the evening — the
kids desperate for freedom; the women in the throes of heroin
detox; the families waiting and praying outside, confused and
apprehensive, wishing someone, anyone, could explain to them
what was going on, where their loved one is, what's going to
happen.

It's often over a late-night drink that the question of the
struggle pops up. Is it really worth all this? There's not a hell of a
lot of glamour in being a public defender, and God knows it ain't
the money. And being treated like the help day in and day out
can get a bit tiresome. To make matters worse, we spend all day
losing. We public defenders are a strange breed: passionate people
spending ourselves in a Sisyphean struggle for justice in a system rigged to crush us.

It doesn't make a lot of sense. Not when Alton, the sixteen-
year-old kid from the group home who has never been arrested
before in his life, is going to spend the week at Rikers for stealing
some film and a diet soda. Not when Judge Brigantti-Hughes
sets bail on three different drug cases that I know with absolute
certainty will be quickly dismissed on the next court date. Not
when Judge Sussman sends a workingman to jail for spousal

abuse despite the audible pleas from his wife: "Please, he's never done it before. I'm fine. Please, I love him, he'll lose his job. Please!" she cries, until the court officers shout her down and drag her from the courtroom, and Sussman, without batting an eye, sets bail that neither he nor she can make, costing him his job and their only source of income. Two months later they will be evicted for nonpayment of rent and become homeless. When the wife refuses thereafter to cooperate with the prosecution, the assistant district attorney will call the Administration for Child Welfare, and they'll lose their child too — another kid ripped from his parents and placed for six scarring months in the foster care system, which in turn produces, fifteen years later, in all likelihood, another grim-faced client, another kid for whom the system is the enemy, who has never gotten a fair shake and never believes he'll get one, who knows with every fiber of his being that the system is a trap and that the lawyers sent in to help him are really just part of that same monster.

It is because success is so often elusive that the essential challenge in much of public defender work is finding lasting satisfaction amid constant failure. That's what Paula Deutsch was trying to teach me all those years ago at Callahan's: selfishness and selflessness are just two sides of the same coin. "You gotta lawyer for you" means that the narcissistic pleasure of giving doesn't invalidate the gift. It's why, even when we lose all the time, even though our arguments fall on deaf ears and our legal brilliance is regularly thwarted by the politics of the criminal justice system, there is something about the struggle of being a public defender that feels right, and makes it easy to sleep well at night. Because as long as every day we give voice to the voiceless and advance the cause of people who don't believe themselves worth fighting for, it's easy to feel like a righteous outlaw, like the last bulwark between freedom and incarceration, the last hope of a population that no longer believes in hope or help. And for all the grandiosity that such sentiments entail, that is exactly what public defenders are.

Now back to Manhattan, to the Upper West Side, the light

dull orange, the city as close to asleep as it ever gets. It is less than five miles from my office to my home. Five miles: two worlds.

My neighborhood is full of gourmet-food stores and high-end baby clothing shops and, seemingly, a Starbucks on every other block. It is also full of people I could have been: smart lawyers who decided they wanted to spend their time crafting tax loopholes for rich clients worried about their capital gains; smart lawyers who decided they wanted to spend their evenings structuring multibillion-dollar mergers; smart lawyers wearing watches that cost as much as the car they've forgotten how to drive.

I suppose I could have had an apartment that contained more than one room. Someday I might. For now, I have what I have: the small studio that I return home to after my uptown odyssey. There to greet me: a fridge with ham and alcohol; a stereo system that still knows what cassette tapes are; and my bed, which has never looked so appealing. It has been a long day. I argued over thirty cases before six different judges. Nine clients went to jail or stayed in jail, and about twenty-two went back home. Tomorrow I will argue another five cases before three different judges.

Before sleeping, I reach under the bed. There, as it always is — the Ray Hartford file.

Ray was that third strike, the case that nearly sent me to the showers for good. Ray was utterly innocent. Charged with the robbery and attempted murder of a gypsy-cab driver, Ray is in prison because I made the mistake of trusting Judge Massaro when he told me with a grave nod that he was "well acquainted with the problems of eyewitness identification." I believed he was telling me to waive a jury, which is exactly what I insisted on doing. But I erred. Massaro convicted, and he sentenced Ray to fifteen years in prison. Not a night goes by that I don't touch that file and think of him, alone in his prison cell.

There will always be times when I want to hide in the trial suit closet, when I want to chuck it all before my heart breaks for good. I don't want to end my days red-faced in cardiac arrest on the floor of Moge's courtroom. But what I still don't know is when it's acceptable to turn your back, to walk away from an indefensible system, to close your eyes to injustice, to surrender. What I do know, though, is that while I wonder and until I'm sure, I'll be uptown.

Tomorrow, the Bronx.

EPILOGUE

ON THE EVE OF TRIAL, Reginald McFadden pled guilty to manslaughter in the first degree and agreed to serve a ten-year prison sentence. He is currently incarcerated in the Riverview Correctional Facility and is scheduled for release in February of 2010. He'll be sixty-three years old. Edward, too, is still in prison. He will be sixty-six when he's released in 2007. Alberto won't even see the parole board until 2015.

Emma Ketteringham just gave birth to her first child. Though she briefly left the Bronx Defenders to join a small firm specializing in family law, she didn't stay away too long. She's now back at the Bronx Defenders. After three years in the work, encouraged by his wife, Jason Miller left to follow his passion for photography. Ululy Martinez, too, lasted less than three years. He moved on to a job in Bronx politics — far away from Judge Kiesel. Robin, though, remains. After more than twenty-three years in the work, she still runs the Bronx Defenders, fighting the good fight every single day — an inspiration to public defenders everywhere.

Ben Wolf went to a prestigious law school, where he works on behalf of immigrants in asylum cases, and does investigation on capital cases during his vacations and in his spare time. He was recently banned from the San Jose Jail for passing contraband to a client. The contraband? A book by Michel Foucault.

All over the Bronx, the police continue their ticket blitz.

After his release from jail, William Valentine married his girlfriend and, so far as I know, lived as happily ever after as one can after being wrongly convicted of a sex crime.

Ron, though, is still required to register as a sex offender. Over the years he's applied for dozens of jobs. Despite being a great employee he loses each one as soon as his background check comes back. Kiesel should be pleased.

Just last year, the New York State Legislature passed a new law mitigating a few of the worst drug sentences. Now instead of getting a life sentence for possession of four ounces of cocaine, a defendant can get twenty-five years.

Several weeks after making him my promise, I did manage to split Malik's case from that of his codefendant and get him the treatment he wanted.

Deaf Max was deported to a country he'd never known.

The BP gas station still serves salads and motor oil at the corner of 163rd Street and Brook Avenue. Meanwhile, the Feeding Tree restaurant, reopened and remodeled, serves some of the finest Jamaican food in the world. It is located at 892 Gerard Avenue.

Not long after whispering her secrets of survival to me, Paula Deutsch left the Legal Aid Society. She moved to Seattle, where she remains a highly respected federal public defender. Eddie Mayr is still a supervisor at the Criminal Defense Division of the Legal Aid Society. He works in Queens, where he is reputed to be a kinder, gentler Eddie.

Alvin is as wonderful and as difficult as always — he still calls me constantly.

Diane Kiesel, Megan Tallmer, and Ralph Fabrizio are all still on the bench, wreaking havoc on the lives of poor criminal defendants and the lawyers who vigorously represent them. Judge Reinaldo Rivera, on the other hand, apparently recognized for his legal brilliance, was elevated — he might prefer "beamed up" — to the appellate division. Judge Sussman died of cancer on August 28, 2005.

I ran into Judge Cohen on the street recently. He's retired now but seems as kindly and wonderful as ever.

I still see Cassandra too, every once and again. She's still lost, usually homeless, and often medicated by crack or alcohol.

After two years of fighting his case, even Najid got ground down. He eventually pled guilty to disorderly conduct. He nonetheless remains a community activist in the South Bronx, a constant proponent of healthier living and the healing power of green space. He too is an inspiration.

Moge, Dawson, Adler, and Birnbaum still preside in the Bronx. Judge White is still in Manhattan. No one seems to know what happened to Tona.

Andy Liu finally packed up for warmer climes — he now works as an assistant District Attorney in Monterey County, California. Sarah Schall, though, is still uptown, though a recent informal poll of my former colleagues has elevated her from one of the worst ADAs in the Bronx to merely bad. Rumor has it that she recently dismissed a case.

Murray Richman and Mark Brenner are up there too, each still practicing his very different kind of law.

After nearly two years, assistant DA Paul Rosenfeld was replaced on Clarence's case by a straight-shooting ex-military guy named Troy Smith. After reviewing the evidence, Troy decided that he didn't believe Clarence committed the murder, and unlike so many other prosecutors, Smith took a stand, eventually persuading his office to do the right thing and dismiss the case.

Ray Hartford is still serving that fifteen-year sentence and is not scheduled to be released until 2014. The appeal of his case was argued in November of 2005.

After the grand jury refused to indict her, Gillian Sands began a new life without her abusive husband. She moved down south, and last I heard she was doing wonderfully well. Just before she left, she sent me a present: a coffee mug. On it there is a big smiley face and the slogan "I'm so happy I could just shit." It hangs in my kitchen today.

To my utter amazement, Luther eventually got a job at Victoria's Secret.

ACKNOWLEDGMENTS

I NEVER REALLY SET OUT TO BE A WRITER. It was the stories of my clients and the shortcomings of the system that impelled me to write this book. So it is no surprise that my greatest thanks is reserved for the men and women (and you know who you are — Nicole and Gary and Robert and Calvin and J and Anthony — even if I did change your names) who awe me every day with their courage in the face of a capricious system hell-bent on breaking them. To each of them, in their homes, their shelters, and their cells, thank you.

To the lawyers, social workers, and investigators at the Bronx Defenders and to public defenders everywhere, thank you for your work. To those who have fought alongside me over the years, thank you for your companionship and encouragement.

Of all my colleagues over the years, and among all those that have ever stepped up to try a case on behalf of an indigent defendant, Robin Steinberg more than anyone else has my admiration, my respect, and my thanks. The founder and executive director of the Bronx Defenders and a die-hard, true-believing public defender for more than twenty years, Robin is an inspiration to public defenders everywhere and a profound comfort to her clients. She has been my constant companion, my intimate confidante, and my grown-up doppelgänger for nearly a decade. It was Robin who hired me, Robin who promoted me, and Robin who shaped my thinking about indigent defense while allowing me to grow into the trial lawyer I am. She is also the one who let me go — to write and wander and find my own elusive voice. I am eternally grateful to her.

The book would have been a whole lot harder to write without the support of the Open Society Institute. They had the courage to bestow a media fellowship on an untested writer, and thanks to them I was able to devote myself to the book full-time for an entire year.

Kate Black and Joan Nassivera read early drafts of the book; I am grateful for their encouragement. Jan Rostal and Andy Eibel helped me remember the damning details of my early life at Legal Aid; Jason Miller, Ben Wolf, and Florian Miedel did the same for the Bronx. Xana Antuntes, Randy Cohen, Bradley Klein, and Kimberly Stevens provided helpful literary advice. My friends Oren and Paul, Michael and Michael, Peter and Jane, Immy and Danielle, Mitch and Mich, and Til have all been there for me through this process. My agent, Tina Bennett, provided valuable guidance, and my editor, Geoff Shandler, not only moderated my hectoring tone and cured me of my "tommy gun–like" use of the em dash, he also sharpened and focused the book, offering genuine and substantial editorial assistance. In an age of little time and less help, Geoff was both available and very, very helpful. The book is better for his touch.

There would be no book, however, without Susan Lehman. It was Susan who pushed me to "just write a book." It was Susan I called when I needed to know what the hell a book proposal looked like, and it was Susan who read and revised every single chapter of the manuscript. Susan is my sounding board, my shadow editor, my beloved friend, and, in every way, my writing partner. The book is shaped by her insights and inflected with her prose. The months we spent working on our respective books, swapping chapters every week and racing to meet our daily word counts, were some of the happiest and most exciting in my memory. I can't thank her enough.

Finally, my mother, Ruth; my grandmother Trude; and my sisters, Michelle and Lara, have always encouraged me to make better use of my furious but creative impulses.

I hope this book has done that.

ABOUT THE AUTHOR

DAVID FEIGE was the trial chief at the Bronx Defenders. He has written for the *New York Times Magazine, Slate,* and other publications and is a frequent guest expert on Court TV. *Indefensible* is his first book. He lives in New York City.